# No Middle Ground

# No Middle Ground

## Anti-Imperialists and Ethical Witnessing during the Philippine-American War

Erin L. Murphy

LEXINGTON BOOKS

*Lanham • Boulder • New York • London*

Published by Lexington Books
An imprint of The Rowman & Littlefield Publishing Group, Inc.
4501 Forbes Boulevard, Suite 200, Lanham, Maryland 20706
www.rowman.com

6 Tinworth Street, London SE11 5AL, United Kingdom

British Library Cataloguing in Publication Information Available

**Library of Congress Cataloging-in-Publication Data**
Names: Murphy, Erin L., author.
Title: No middle ground : anti-imperialists and ethical witnessing during the Philippine-American War / Erin L. Murphy.
Description: Lanham, Maryland : Lexington Books, [2020] | Includes bibliographical references and index. | Summary: "This book argues the Anti-Imperialist movement, led by the Anti-Imperialist League, followed an evolving path of ethical witnessing where leaders empathically considered the perspective of imperialist violence in the Philippines as expressed by marginalized ant-imperialists"—Provided by publisher.
Identifiers: LCCN 2019043080 (print) | LCCN 2019043081 (ebook) | ISBN 9781498582667 (cloth) | ISBN 9781498582674 (epub)
Subjects: LCSH: American Anti-Imperialist League. | Anti-imperialist movements—United States—History. | Philippines—History—Philippine American War, 1899-1902. | United States—Colonial question. | United States—Foreign relations—1897-1901. | United States—Foreign relations—1901-1909. | Philippines—History—1898-1946. | Philippines—Politics and government—1898-1935. | United States—Foreign relations—Philippines. | Philippines—Foreign relations—United States.
Classification: LCC E713 .M884 2020 (print) | LCC E713 (ebook) | DDC 327.73059909/04—dc23
LC record available at https://lccn.loc.gov/2019043080
LC ebook record available at https://lccn.loc.gov/2019043081

# Contents

# Acknowledgments

In writing and rewriting this project, I have taken a winding road where I have found many supporters whom I would like to thank. First and foremost, I would like to thank my partner in life, Tim, who was there before the beginning and was a steadfast supporter throughout, always believing in me and in the project. He always encouraged me to see it through. This work exists because of his support in all its forms. I would also like to thank my family and friends, who were always interested and supportive, ever patient and proud: Daniel Murphy, Patrick Murphy, Sean Murphy, Anna Murphy, Kristin and Chris McDaniel, Sarah and Joe Gladke, J. R. McHenry and Ziell Zanaill, Carol and Ron Martin, Kathy and Tom Ballard, Patti and Greg McHenry, Marcia Murphy, and Brian and Cherise Murphy. In the past few years, the direction of the manuscript took a different focus thanks in part to my children, Donovan and Cormac. I would like to thank them for their inspiration to focus on the hopefulness of focusing on a future where they have examples of historical figures who were empowered, ethical, responsible, *and* imperfect.

I had the good fortune of some wonderful colleagues who contributed to the birth and growth of this project at the University of Illinois at Champaign-Urbana, offering moral support and encouragement from the beginning. Thank you Yaejoon Kwon, Carolyn Hronis, Heather Downs, Sheri-Lynn Kurisu, Anne McCloskey, Kareem Muhammed, Adrian Cruz, and so many others who discussed and read parts of the project with me as I hashed out the story and refined the focus. They created a supportive and even fun space to work during turbulent political times that echoed the research too loudly. My colleagues at Southern Illinois University at Edwardsville provided a welcoming environment as I further developed the work, believing in its critical edge and the worthiness of its theoretical contributions. Thank you to Dave Kauzlarich, Linda Markowitz, Flo Maatita, Sandra Weissinger, Erin

Heil, and Georgiann Davis for cultivating a unique space of academic support and good humor. I learned so much about teaching and staying grounded in academia from all of you.

My dissertation committee could not have been more supportive. Thank you Winnie Poster, Julian Go, David Roediger, Anna-Maria Marshall, and my generous advisor Moon-Kie Jung. Each one uniquely contributed to the project with their challenging and supportive questions, pushing me to deepen the historical connections and theoretical lessons from the Anti-Imperialist League and anti-imperialisms at the turn of the twentieth century. Moon-Kie's unfailing support, quick-witted, often humorous, comments, searing insights, and questions to which I sometimes had no answers . . . at least at first . . . propelled me forward. He encouraged me not to leave the project and to see it through to today for which I am grateful.

I could not have found the new information on women in this manuscript without the diligent treasure hunting of many collaborative librarians at the University of Michigan's Hatcher Library, Bentley Historical Library, the Library Company of Philadelphia, and the Massachusetts Historical Society. They often helped me track down manuscripts seemingly only tangentially related, but that sometimes yielded new information on women anti-imperialists. The research for this project was supported by multiple grants and fellowships including the Center for Democracy in a Multiracial Society Fellowship at the University of Illinois, the Graduate College Dissertation Travel Grant from the University of Illinois, the Geisert Dissertation Fellowship from the Department of Sociology at the University of Illinois, the Graduate College Dissertation Completion Fellowship at the University of Illinois, and The Library Company of Philadelphia and Historical Society of Pennsylvania Andrew W. Mellon Foundation Short-Term Fellowship. I am happy and grateful that this support allowed me to take on this project and provide my perspective into an all-too forgotten yet pivotal moment in U.S. history. I dedicate this book to Tim, Donovan, Cormac, and to all those walking a path of ethical witnessing as a matter of course, leaving behind them a more connected and more just society for us all.

# Prologue

In February of 2004, the 1544th Transportation Company of the Illinois National Guard shipped out to Iraq. The unit was part of the first military wave sent to Baghdad during the Iraq War, drawing people from around the small town (population 8,900) of Paris, Illinois—including my younger brother, a college freshman.[1] By the time they returned home, the group had lost five people and many more were injured. The transportation unit was on the frontlines, constantly in danger from roadside bombs. A mortar attack killed one of them their first day on base, setting the devastating pattern for their deployment as they experienced attacks daily. When the stories of waterboarding came out, the unit was in Iraq. My brother and his band of brothers and sisters soon realized that they were taking supplies and mail to the Abu Ghraib prison, the site of the infamous, searing images of torture by members of the U.S. military police.[2]

I escaped into the archives at the University of Michigan during that nightmarish beginning of the Iraq War. But on the first day of research, I discovered the debates about the torture method called the "water cure." It was a torture used during the Philippine-American War by U.S. soldiers and their proxies in the Philippines against Filipino nationalists, or "insurrectos," fighting for independence. Each night as I organized my documents I listened to the day's news and learned of the latest revelations of waterboarding, the torture used by U.S. soldiers in Iraq against Iraqi insurgents. The George Santayana quote, "Those who cannot remember the past are condemned to repeat it." took on new meaning for me.

Before I began researching the Anti-Imperialist League I knew little about the Spanish-American War of 1898, save that it made famous "Teddy" Roosevelt and the Rough Riders and the call to "Remember the *Maine*!" However, I had no knowledge of the subsequent, longer, bloodier war in the Philippines, which was omitted from my high school and undergraduate American history courses. Given that the Philippine-American War was a longer war and American history tends to focus on wars, the omissions seemed odd, which piqued my curiosity. Up to that point, only images of the Vietnam War overlaid my mental map of the Iraq War. With my antennae raised by the awkward silence, I found the debates over the "water cure" and the legality of U.S. military violence in the Philippines provided a new point of historical comparison to the so-called War on Terror.

I actively protested the preemptive Iraq War. As I witnessed and participated in the events of the war, for instance, reading the name of fallen soldiers at protests, I was forced to consider how my social position afforded me safety. I vividly imagined the city streets of Baghdad, especially the path my brother took daily: roads strewn with hidden roadside bombs and little Iraqi boys running by and playing soccer. My social position provided me with the economic and cultural privileges of empire, yet class was still a critical element in my position as a military family member. My family had struggled to obtain upward social mobility throughout my childhood but slipped downward once my parents divorced, leaving my younger siblings with few economic resources for college. This situation helped point my brother toward the National Guard—and Iraq. One of the peculiarities of the Iraq War was that the emotional costs of loving someone involved in the war was not something most U.S. citizens experienced or could sympathize with—including the Congresspersons who voted to go to war. For me, the activist maxim "the personal is political" was undeniable and isolating.

I hoped that entering the realm of history would allow me to step out of the day-to-day tensions of living through a war one opposed while loving someone directly involved; I soon realized that it would not be so easy. I had stumbled upon a buried box in the collective shadow of the United States. I only found the "water cure" and waterboarding were each horrific in their own right but more so in their similarities. The broad similarities between the wars sandwiching the twentieth century were just as astonishing to me, such that I was literally disoriented more than once in the archives as I awakened to the mundane realities of empire. However, I gained an unexpected insight out of that disorientation, which grounded me: the significance of the removal of the violent war in the Philippines from the U.S. historical narrative made the current—and indeed any—revelations of violence seem unique, even *exceptional*, to most of the American public. This was a powerful *perception* of reality that influenced support of policy as well as denial of policy implications.

The idea of American exceptionalism often articulated as the belief that the United States is the "leader of the free world" and uniquely superior in its implementation of democracy led to the public's shock over waterboarding.

But, this version of American exceptionalism builds on what American studies scholar Amy Kaplan (1993) has called a long "pattern of denial" of U.S. imperialism, which has essentially become an entire "paradigm of denial" (Kaplan 1993: 13). In other words, fully including the history of the Philippine-American War as American history would allow claiming responsibility for empire and would also allow us to see it as part of a broader pattern and more than an episode of empire. Doing so would mean squarely facing the nation's past—and squarely facing how American exceptionalism actually shapes the continued scholarly and political disavowal of (Jung 2011; Kaplan 1993; Pease 2008) American empire. It would mean owning our imperialist shadow and relating American exceptionalism to renewed celebrations of American empire today (Pease 2010) in grim notions of "Making America Great Again" and "Be Best."

The fact that controversies over torture bookended the "American Century" hardly fit into the democratic "leader of the free world" version of American exceptionalism. Although I was already a critic of American exceptionalism, my new insight into its power as a perception allowed me to grapple with the depth of its power as an unacknowledged, taken-for-granted, and socially constructed reality of America. In other words, American exceptionalism was not just an ideological fantasy that could simply be dismissed as false. The phrase "American exceptionalism" also describes *a shadowed pattern of relations that limits knowledge of U.S. transnational relations* (with real implications that disadvantages the working classes at home) and allocates imperialist cultural, military, economic, and legal resources (material and narrative) at home and abroad. It is more than a way of seeing that can just be reframed. It has far reaching material, mental, and relational consequences— my disorientation in the archives, which was actually a consequence of becoming aware of our imperialist shadow that had been hidden by privilege, was just one example. In the age of Trump advocating to "Make America Great Again," the appeal of this framing has to be considered along with understanding the appeal of the paradigm of denial in his supporters and their refusal of information or perceptions that would undermine their worldview.

Similarities between waterboarding and the "water cure" were just the beginning of the similarities between the beginning and end of the twentieth century. Critics of waterboarding echoed arguments made by anti-imperialist critics of the water cure: both highlighted the inconsistencies between American *ideals* of democracy and American *policies* of colonialism. In the case of the Philippine-American War, imperialists armed with the force of the U.S. military and the racist, exceptional ideology of the white man's burden, pushed through their agenda by arguing the United States needed the Philippines to establish a larger trade presence and fueling station in Asia—an extension of the epic manifest destiny of the United States. It was no surprise, then, that critics and supporters of the Iraq War debated the role of oil in the U.S. invasion, hence the popular anti-Iraq War phrase, "No Blood for Oil." Going back a century to the beginning of the United States' forays with external colonies teaches us how *what we deny about our history drives our current political divisions and affinities*, and just as importantly, how *what we acknowledge has the potential for transformative democratic change*. It's time to bring it out of the shadows and allow our history to be seen in the light. This way we can pursue the radical journey to democracy unencumbered by the invisible baggage of denial weighing us down.

## NOTES

1. Around 50% to 60% of the volunteers were college students. Three of those citizen-soldier-students, who I knew the best, finished their degrees with a major in Psychology, hoping to help veterans with the invisible wounds of war. "From Paris, Illinois to Baghdad: Downstate Guard unit left a small town and paid a steep price in Iraq." Kirsten Scharnberg and Bill Glauber. *Chicago Tribune.* December 19, 2004. http://articles.chicagotribune.com/2004-12-19/news/0412190503_1_unit-mortar-atta ck-paris.

2. "Torture at Abu Ghraib." By Seymour Hersh. *The New Yorker.* May 10, 2004. http://www.newyorker.com/magazine/2004/05/10/torture-at-abu-ghraib

# Introduction

## *Awakening to Empire*

The Battle of Manila Bay effectively ended the Spanish-American War, with only one American casualty, on May 1, 1898. The battle was the final chapter in a series of events, including diplomatic tensions between the United States and Spain over the Spanish colonial government's violent treatment of Cubans. These tensions led to the infamous explosion on the *USS Maine* outside of Havana that precipitated the war the United States fought, allegedly on behalf of the Cubans. Although Cuba was its start and impetus, the Spanish-American War was actually won in the Philippines.

The Philippines were also a Spanish colony, and Filipino nationalists, like Cuban nationalists, had already been fighting for their independence. With Spain as their common adversary, Filipino and U.S. forces formed an alliance. While U.S. forces fought from the water, Filipino forces led by Emilio Aguinaldo surrounded Manila on land, a situation in which Spain could not win. Achieving Spain's surrender, Dewey became the hero of America's "splendid little war," (as John Hay, ambassador to Great Britain, dubbed it, but actually, it would be more accurate to reference it as the Spanish-Cuban-Philippine-American War) while the role of Filipinos went—and still goes—largely unmentioned and unacknowledged in the United States.

Once Spain surrendered, Filipinos/as hoped and expected the United States would leave them to rule themselves. In fact, Dewey had met with Emilio Aguinaldo, which to them suggested that the United States would recognize their independence. He never told Aguinaldo otherwise and even wrote to U.S. officials that Filipinas/os were "fit" for self-government. However, Dewey also met with Spanish leaders. Unbeknownst to the Filipino leaders, Spain agreed to surrender but only to the United States, not to the colonized Filipinos/as. Therefore, when Spain surrendered and U.S. forces took Manila,

The dominant group still
1  persisted — therefore ideas on
race, beauty etc still had opportunity to be pushed.

Filipino forces stayed just outside the city's border. Time drew out and Filipinos/as continued to wait for word of the independence for which they had been fighting for two years. They began to question the intentions of the United States, and tensions between the brief allies began to rise.

Back in the United States, concerned citizens also began to worry about the fate of the Philippines. As the U.S. government dawdled and Filipino/a nationalists waited, the urgency of a political debate over the question of how the United States could possibly maintain its ideals as a democracy and also hold colonies peopled with subjects, not citizens, became clear. Some of these citizens became activists in guarding democracy from imperialism; they marked the beginning of the self-described anti-imperialist movement, the topic of this book.

As public recognition for his accomplishment in Manila, Dewey was appointed U.S. Admiral of the Navy—the only person who ever achieved that rank—with the title made retroactive to the Battle of Manila Bay. Meanwhile, the efforts of the Filipinos who assisted in defeating Spain at Manila on land were actively *de*recognized. Instead, the U.S. annexed the Philippines against the will of Filipino leaders and made it a U.S. "unincorporated" territory (e.g., a colony). For independence, Filipino nationalists would have to continue their fight, only now they would fight their supposed ally, the United States. The layers of betrayal in all of this stung both Filipino nationalists and the now self-identified anti-imperialists. Energized to protect and defend their ideals, anti-imperialists took up the cause at home.

*No Middle Ground* is about the long journey of the U.S. citizens who pursued the fraught path of defending democracy against the tyranny of imperialist racism. The Anti-Imperialist Leagues (AIL) were at the forefront of organizing the anti-imperialist position. For the AIL leadership, anti-imperialism was about politics, but it was also about protecting the dream of democracy as sacred. For many U.S. citizens, the idea that the United States would undermine an anti-colonial revolution in the Philippines in order to position itself as a colonizing power was an unbearable betrayal of these ideals. So when they discovered the extraordinary violence of the U.S. military in the Philippines, they believed the domestic necessity of their cause became even more crucial.

At the beginning, they enjoyed national support by the tens of thousands. But, by the early1920s, the AIL had disbanded, and the Philippines remained a U.S. colony. Steadfast anti-imperialists navigated a path with many ebbs and fewer flows, but they were sustained throughout by the courage of their convictions. Moorfield Storey, President of the AIL, influential attorney (who won *Buchanan v. Warley* in 1917, an important civil rights case that set precedent for fighting segregation), and the first president of the National Association for the Advancement of Colored People, wrote on March 2,

1920, "Between the principle of freedom that all men are entitled to equal political rights and the dogma of tyranny that might makes right, there is no middle ground" (Moorfield Storey Institute 2017).[1] Over the years, this was the AIL's position in a nutshell. This quote inspired the title the book. While it closed the anti-imperialists' journey covered in the following pages, it also represents the principles that inspired anti-imperialist leaders to individually embark upon their next great works after the defeat of anti-imperialism, the larger pursuit of human rights.

Many leaders of the anti-imperialist movement were well-known leaders in their day, and some are still remembered, albeit for different reasons. But, the movement itself has largely been forgotten. This book is an effort to recover that history from the shadows. Looking back at the moment when the United States traded isolationism for imperialism can help us better understand how we arrived at our current age with its commonplace use of *racist exceptions* to justify violence against people of color at home and abroad. At the same time, it provides an example of *ethical witnessing*. Ethical witnessing is a way of practicing citizenship that honors our human connections to one another, allowing us to show up for our own integrity by showing up for one another. It is a self-consciously connected citizenship where one uses his or her structurally privileged position and resources (e.g., access to government recognition and social connections) to bear witness to the grievances of those who are structurally exploited or oppressed. It is a dance bringing that which is in the shadows out into the light. Ethical witnessing tends to the boundaries that generate trust in our social bonds. U.S. citizens, from all strata of society, together chose to face the dilemma of how to oppose imperialism: ethical witnessing was one option and racist exploitation was another. The anti-imperialist story is an example of taking responsibility for citizenship and, perhaps, could give inspiration for reflexive, honoring, and honorable practices of citizenship today.

The stakes were, and still are, high for those of us who wish to honor our connections—not only preventing and fighting racism and injustice but walking the journey to get to a multi-racial democracy. Back then, imperialists rationalized state violence by limiting rights for Filipinos/as through racist legal exceptions. This set a precedent that we continue to see today in the forms of police brutality and government despotism, like family separation of refugees, against blacks and Latinos/as at home, not to mention the secret torture committed against purported terrorists at black sites abroad. Moorfield Storey, president of the AIL based in Boston, a lawyer by trade, and the first president of the NAACP, noted many times: legal precedent does not mean moral precedent. For ethical citizenship, there can be "no middle ground" when faced with the tyranny of racist violence. There can only be the integrity that motivates courage to learn from the past so as not to repeat mistakes and inspiration to tirelessly make the quest toward the principles of freedom and equality.

Initially, I focused on the internal politics of the anti-imperialist movement. I was determined to learn more about the activists who had been overlooked in earlier historical accounts, namely white women, black women, black men, the working classes, and Filipinos/as. Internal divisions contributed to many anti-imperialist failures, and I argue here and elsewhere that this was the movement's undoing (Murphy 2009). However, using the perspectives of the multiple vantage points afforded by their social positions, I was also able to discern different flavors of anti-imperialism within the larger movement, such that it is more accurate to say "anti-imperialisms." With their political resources, anti-imperialists created an environment that helped shape U.S. imperialist policies. Therefore, this project intervenes in socio-historical studies of U.S. empire, citizenship, and racism by reassessing how anti-imperialists' progressive social activism ironically helped fashion U.S. imperialism while also laying the groundwork for a new human rights movement.

My work brings to light two main themes: (a) the anti-imperialists as examples of ethical witnessing that offers lessons for today, and (b) how imperialist policies justified new racist exceptions and codified them through legalizing practices such as the "water cure" (similar to waterboarding) and (re)concentration camps. Furthermore, for the first time this book adds original, compelling evidence of women's anti-imperialist activism to existing historical scholarship. Using a feminist approach that encourages looking to women as valid starting points, I draw a new conclusion about anti-imperialists, which is this: the most influential anti-imperialist activism was a form of ethical witnessing that drew on our interconnections across empire, race, gender, and citizenship and sought to foster empathy and understanding for how imperialist policies inflicted pain and suffering through oppression. In this way, they dreamt of a more fully realized U.S. democracy.

As mentioned earlier, ethical witnessing is a self-consciously connected citizenship where activists, like the anti-imperialists, use their privileged position, such as access to government and social connections, to bear witness to the grievances of those who are oppressed, for example, Filipino/as. In so doing, activists were able to maintain their sense of honor while they honored the experiences of others. This practice of relating to other experiences across social position illustrates their awareness of interconnectedness, fostering their own well-being in honoring the well-being of others. This approach paints a fresh picture of anti-imperialists and asks a new overarching question: How did anti-imperialists' debates over violence in the Philippines influence U.S. imperialist policies? In answering this question, each chapter chronologically details the ways in which leading anti-imperialists worked both within and outside the movement to protect the sacredness of democracy.

Studying the anti-imperialists allows us to reflect on how the ethical witnessing[2] of engaged citizens can be more effective in the present. Through tracing the rise and the fall of the AIL, we not only see repeated inconsistencies between American ideals of democracy and American practices of racist violence, but also see how these inconsistencies came to coexist with little disruption, by denying abuses of power. This denial grew both the American shadow and American exceptionalist fantasy and yielded racist exceptions that actually manifested into state institutions: in "unincorporated territories," in "subjects" rather than citizens, in the lack of protections through the *writ of habeas corpus*, in the forgetting and disavowal of the "water cure." Social historians of the Philippine-American War have paid far more attention to how, like imperialists, many anti-imperialists were often racist, parochial, and privileged white men. I redirect this history to focus on those who were included in the larger perimeters of the movement. In this way, which I believe is in a tradition of ethical witnessing, I contribute to more resources for a public discourse that "fights ignorance" (Stoler 2006: 53) of U.S. history. In this way, I expand on our social map of interconnectedness, reminding readers that like racism, imperialism has always been a constant *and contested* aspect of American history, just as social integrity has been a constant and contested aspect of American history.

## ANTI-IMPERIALISTS AND BENEVOLENT ASSIMILATION

At the turn of the twentieth century, anti-imperialists and imperialists alike were steeped in American nationalism, and many of their conflicts stemmed from historical traditions with competing definitions of what made the United States "exceptional." Anti-imperialists focused on the anti-colonial U.S. history, with its quest for a representative democracy that extended rights to all citizens. Imperialists focused on manifest destiny, the purported moral and political superiority of U.S. institutions, and the mythic duty to extend these institutions to Filipinos/as in the new colonial acquisition of the Philippines.

Imperialists drew on narratives of American exceptionalism, imagining U.S. empire as meaningfully exceptional, infusing policies in the Philippines with rhetoric of benevolence and democratic tutelage. Of course, it is not unique for defenders of empire to claim uniqueness. In *Orientalism*, Edward Said (2003) put it this way, "Every single empire in its official discourse has said that it is not like all the others, that its circumstances are special, that it has a mission to enlighten, civilize, bring order and democracy, and that it uses force only as a last resort" (p. xxi). Indeed, European empires also argued for their unique abilities to "civilize" the "savage" such that exceptionalist arguments turn out to be an unexceptional part of empire (Go 2007; Stoler 2006). True to form, a new narrative of American exceptionalism framed the debates over taking the Philippines and shaped colonial policies (Murphy 2015).

One useful feature of exceptionalist narratives is that they have the ability to suit multiple purposes, a quality of polysemy. For instance, in the United States, exceptionalist narratives have been a popular way of situating the United States in the world and an influential framework for interpreting the history of the United States. As an intoxicating fantasy of white superiority, U.S. exceptionalism, like the white man's burden, has provided powerful rationales for codifying racist laws with dire consequences for marginalized people of color at home and abroad. During Philippine-American War, imperialists used exceptionalism to justify continuing to consolidate power around race and successfully manifested new racist legal relationships. Extending Said's insight into the relationship between exceptionalism and empire, I find with Stoler (2006), "[I]mperial states by definition operate as states *of* exception that vigilantly produce exceptions to their principles and exceptions to their laws" (p. 57). For both imperialists and anti-imperialists, exceptionalist narratives set the agenda. It was a widespread delimiting belief.

Therefore, the terrain over which they dueled was their stance on racist exceptions, the codifying pattern of state racism that has formed U.S. policies from the beginning. When we see rights and protections not legalized, then later legalized but unenforced, all the while coupled with narratives that rationalize violence against people of color, we are seeing racist exceptions in action. By tracing anti-imperialist activities, *No Middle Ground* expands on the theory of exceptions by showing ways to identify and disarm them, in essence providing a mental map with which to navigate them.

With this case, I am able to map how the United States instituted racist exceptions at multiple levels in colonizing the Philippines and how anti-imperialists worked to disarm them. Therefore, using archival sources,[3] I investigate how a varied cast of anti-imperialists debated the racist violence in the Philippines and affected the development of both U.S. imperialism and U.S. human rights activism. This is adamantly not a story about women anti-imperialists or black anti-imperialists alone. At one time, I wanted to tell that story and contribute a clean correction to the historical record, but, to my disappointment, the sources to tell that kind of story alone were not available. Overtime, however, I came to see that regardless of the availability of those archival sources, the most important lesson the anti-imperialists had to teach was about their attempts at ethical witnessing. This can be seen only through the story of how they developed *multiple anti-imperialisms* together and against one another, and that can only be told by accounting for their *varied* social positions. This is a method of messy inclusivity.

Therefore, in the chapters that follow I look at how groups of anti-imperialists approached ethical witnessing—where U.S. citizens saw a connection between imperialist injustices and an ethical responsibility to act together, marshaling their resources to speak out against imperialism. The white leaders shared many of the prejudices of their time. What set them apart was that they were more committed to maintaining the U.S. as a democracy than they were committed to the kind of self-aggrandizing prejudice of white supremacist imperialism. When they showed the tiniest bit of humility through a willingness to listen and consider the views of other anti-imperialists of color, women, and Filipino/as, by practicing ethical witnessing, some were fundamentally changed. Therefore, part I explores how anti-imperialists' social position influenced their perceptions of violence and empire while part II explores how anti-imperialists attempted to undermine colonial violence and the effects these activities had, if any, on (de)limiting the violence justified by benevolent assimilation.

## Going to War

President McKinley asked Congress for permission to go to war with Spain on April 11, 1898. In his message, he claimed that if the United States became involved in war on behalf of the Cubans, Cuba would not become an unwilling U.S. territory. His reasoning was often quoted back to him later. He said, "I speak not of forcible annexation, for that cannot be thought of. that, by our code of morals would be criminal aggression." With those words still ringing in their ears, Congress approved war with Spain and passed the Teller Amendment, which prevented the United States from annexing Cuba.[4] Yet, there was no parallel amendment for Spain's other territories: Puerto Rico, Guam, and the Philippines.

Fearing the potential allures of empire, U.S. anti-imperialists called for similar declarations that would prevent the United States from acquiring any of Spain's territories, especially the Philippines. On June 15, 1898, the AIL was formed to promote the cause.

Then in December 1898, President McKinley kick-started the anti-imperialist impulse across the United States when he declared formal sovereignty over the Philippines in his "Benevolent Assimilation Proclamation" (BAP). Up until then McKinley had left his intentions for the future of the Philippines unclear, but with the BAP, McKinley finally made his intentions plain. The United States would keep the Philippines.

McKinley made the BAP public on January 1, 1899 (Blount 1912). He claimed that the Treaty of Paris, which ended the war (and for which the

U.S. paid $20 million dollars to Spain to take Puerto Rico, Guam, and the Philippines), gave sovereignty of the Philippines to the United States. McKinley pronounced that the occupying forces were not "invaders or conquerors" rather they were "friends, *to protect* the natives." The BAP was exactly what U.S. anti-imperialists had feared, a promise of protection in exchange for submission to U.S. sovereignty and colonialism. As anti-imperialists grew in numbers and became more outspoken across the country, they organized a protest to oppose ratification of the Treaty of Paris. Some of the most passionate anti-imperialists included McKinley's fellow Republicans, like George Boutwell and George Hoar, as well as Democrats, like William Jennings Bryan. However, their reasons for coming to oppose taking the Philippines were motivated by competing political philosophies, which would later threaten the cohesiveness of the AIL and the larger movement.

The progressive Senator George Hoar led the contentious debate for anti-imperialists. But for different groups of anti-imperialists, there were different stakes involved. For progressives, it was the sacred ideals of the Constitution. For white supremacist anti-imperialists, annexing the Philippines meant taking on more race "problems," where it was racial character of the nation-state. For imperialists, it was largely America's strategic global position in the Age of Empire. The debates exposed the competing visions for the future of the United States. This was a division over democratic principles and racism, which were at odds with grasping for global power.

McKinley knew Filipino nationalists had already established a republic in June 1898 when he issued the BAP six months later. They had installed military leader Emilio Aguinaldo as president and Apolinario Mabini, the movement's intellectual leader, as prime minister. In response to the BAP, Filipino leaders advertised the Malalos Constitution, their previously drafted Philippines Constitution, on January 21, 1899, and on January 23, declared the First Philippine Republic. This move inaugurated a discursively legal fight for sovereignty between Filipino nationalists and the U.S. government. It also fueled anti-imperialist debates in the United States, looking to the intentions of leading Filipinos/as.

With soldiers on both sides becoming increasingly agitated as the political situation escalated, Filipinos still outside of Manila and U.S. soldiers in the city, fighting finally erupted on February 4, 1899, just as the debate over the Treaty had reached fever pitch in the Senate. Two days later, the Senate ratified the Treaty of Paris by only one vote. Adding insult, ratification of the Treaty retroactively approved the President's declaration of U.S. sovereignty over the Philippines in the BAP.

This meant the United States never recognized the Malalos Constitution and the First Philippine Republic, officially labeling the arms taken up against the United States as the "Philippine Insurrection." Taking the Philippines broke with the isolationist precedent set by the Founding Fathers and went far beyond the expansionist Monroe Doctrine (McKinley was referring to this precedent when he stated that taking land forcibly "by our code of morals would be criminal aggression"). As a result, the BAP had radicalizing effects in both the Philippines and the United States.

The colonization of the Philippines was a pivotal event in the development of the United States as an empire with global power. As the organization at the vanguard of the anti-imperialist position, the AIL and its leaders ardently believed in the ideals espoused in the Declaration of Independence and the Constitution, and the anti-imperialist arguments centered on defending those ideals. Filipino nationalists fighting against U.S. colonial rule solidified the AIL's conviction of the rightness of anti-imperialism (Schirmer 1972) and fueled their commitment to the cause. For progressive anti-imperialists, Filipinos were the victims of U.S. perpetrations, and they were bound to try to rescue them and the United States from itself.

Historians of the anti-imperialist movement have paid most attention to the activities I just outlined leading up to the presidential election of 1900 than to what happened after the election when the AIL focused on exposing the incredible violence against Filipino/as. Concentrating on this first campaign against the Treaty of Paris and their second campaign to elect William Jennings Bryan has led historians to emphasize the elitism, provincialism, and racist motivations of anti-imperialists' ideologies (Beisner 1968; Lasch 1958, 1972; Welch 1972), rather than anti-imperialist leaders' moral and ethical commitment to democracy and greater racial equality.

I argue that, perhaps ironically, by focusing on the racism of white anti-imperialists, this widely accepted and limited historical interpretation has contributed to the historical erasure of white women, black women, black men, and Filipinos/as in the movement. I correct the historical record by more fully exploring the efforts to conduct an information campaign on U.S. military activities, which culminated in the 1902 Senate Investigation on Affairs in the Philippines (SIAP) but continued even after that investigation's abrupt demise. This third campaign is where I map the development of racist exceptions and the journey of anti-imperialists' ethical witnessing.

Despite their connections and resources, anti-imperialists failed to achieve many of their goals. At a meeting of anti-imperialists in 1903, one of the vice presidents of the AIL, Harvard philosopher, and psychologist William James, put it this way: "I think we have candidly to admit that in the matter of the Philippine conquest we here and our friends outside have failed to produce much immediate effect" (as quoted in Nichols 2011: 105). The Philippines did become a U.S. colony until after World War II after all.

But determining the success of a movement depends on how we define success, and I argue, this is where the anti-imperialists become most interesting. For brevity, it is often expedient for scholars to use the stated goals of a movement as a guide to assessing its successes and failures. However, I choose a more sociological definition of success that includes the unintended consequences of anti-imperialist activism. By looking at the tension between anti-imperialist democratic philosophy and the white supremacy of imperialism, we can see it yielded longstanding, unintended consequences for U.S. society in the form of new normative, legal racist exceptions *as well as* a greater focus on global human rights.

Anti-imperialist activism incited tensions with U.S. imperialists that illuminated the longstanding, fundamental tensions between the American traditions of white supremacy and egalitarianism (King and Smith 2005). While many anti-imperialists believed in equal representation for Filipinos/as, most of white society at the turn of the twentieth century took white supremacy for granted in general, leaving the idea of citizenship beyond the realm of possibility. However, there were two popular types of white supremacy. One form was rooted in social Darwinism, which supported the theory of the "survival of the fittest" and accepted racial "extinction" as part of the course of social development. The other was rooted in NeoLamarckianism, which believed in the changeability of nonwhites and their potential for achieving greater "civilization" through exposure to "white civilization" and its teachings. Although both forms of white superiority believed in the superiority of white civilization, their differences led down different paths for shaping U.S. imperialism (Murphy 2015). The conflicts anti-imperialists and Filipinas/os incited contributed to conditions that made formal U.S. empire less appealing to both social Darwinist and NeoLamarckian white supremacists. The development of other forms of more radical anti-imperialism further "helps to explain why the enthusiasm for empire was so short-lived" (Schirmer 1972).[5] Ultimately, pressure from Filipinos/as and anti-imperialists created challenges that made empire difficult. Although instead of stopping imperialism altogether, these challenges made a transition to neocolonialism more appealing. As a result, *formal* U.S. empire was short-lived in comparison to other formal empires and interventionism and neo-colonialism became the favored route, starting with Theodore Roosevelt.

Imperialism is an enduring historical phenomenon that demonstrates changes in race relations, racial violence, as well as the complexities of how resistance to imperialist policies helped shape those very policies. Taking into account the power of U.S. exceptionalism narratives, I define imperialism as the political system of unequal economic and cultural relations carried out and enforced through racist exceptions and narratives of exceptionalism and where violence enforces the agenda at home and abroad. The racialization of

U.S. political institutions at home and abroad was so embedded in both white supremacist and democratic egalitarian traditions that it usually went unquestioned. The imperialism of the United States and other European empires normalized racial violence and advanced a racialized state-focused power. Gayendra Pandey (2006) describes the process:

> The colony, [Achille Mbembe] writes, following Fanon, is "a place where an experience of violence and upheaval is lived, where violence is built into structures and institutions. It is implemented by persons of flesh and bone, such as the soldier, the . . . administrator, the police officer, and the native chief. It is sustained by an imaginary—that is, an interrelated set of signs that present themselves, in every instance, as an indisputable and undisputed meaning. The violence insinuates itself into the economy, domestic life, language, consciousness. It . . . pursues the colonized even in sleep and dream." What one has here, he suggests, is the *"spirit of violence."* This spirit "makes the violence omnipresent; it is presence—presence not deferred (except occasionally) but *spatialized, visible, immediate, sometimes ritualized, sometimes dramatic, very often caricatural.*" (p. 11, my emphasis)

I agree with Pandey in defining the experience of the colony in terms that emphasize how normative the experiences of violence are for the colonized *and the colonizer*, rather than only territorial relations. One cannot experience the colony from any standpoint without encountering the "spirit of violence" even though those encounters will be different for the colonized and the colonizer.

Given that violence is central to the entire experience of imperialism, it is surprising how little studies of empire focus on how colonial violence influences the metropole, such as with reactions to promote global human rights. It was the exceptionalist narratives that provided justifications for colonial violence and codified legal racist exceptions that both normalized and formalized the practices of violence. For the United States, this process became legitimated through the exceptionalist narratives of benevolent assimilation and the white man's burden.[6]

The white man's burden resonated for proponents and critics of empire alike. I join scholars who have critiqued U.S. exceptionalism as fantasy, but I explore how the fantasy of exceptional narratives, especially benevolent assimilation and civilization (see further), normalized colonial violence in the Philippines by institutionalizing U.S. practices and policies into racist exceptions. In other words, these may have been narratives, but they had material consequences. Rather than seeing American exceptionalism as simply narrative, I bring into focus how imperialists suspended the norms for enfranchised whites and applied the norms of violence and disenfranchisement for people of color in the new colony—a seemingly obvious point, but often just taken for granted. Starting with the habitual, dehistoricized use of the white man's burden as common parlance for imperialism (Murphy 2009), the cultural aspect of different types of exceptionalism and the emotionally charged nature of anti-imperialist responses deserve historicized, empirical attention. It was not coincidental that the subtitle of Kipling's poem "The White Man's Burden" was "The United States and the Philippine Islands," or that the subtitle is rarely mentioned.[7] I argue that when U.S. and European empires cited the white man's burden, they had in mind the exceptional beliefs and fantasies about white civilization. Indeed, my contention is that the core problem of the ethical witnessing of anti-imperialist leaders was that they did not try to undermine the racist underpinnings of U.S. exceptionalism, but instead tried to rework and refocus it, causing them to lose many of their natural allies. And in deploying these exceptional narratives, imperialists were able to maintain their claims that the United States held the highest values of "civilization" and the American people were, in the words of Mr. Dooley, "grr-reat" indeed.

For progressive anti-imperialists, the United States was messy and imperfect but worthy of the promise. This promise is why AIL President Moorfield Storey stated there could be "no middle ground" between political equality and tyranny. There could be no racist exceptions and a true democracy. In Boston, Faneuil Hall, the center of abolitionist activity, carried symbolic meanings for subsequent campaigns for liberty. A speaker at the first meeting of anti-imperialists invoked this symbolism of freedom to establish their legitimacy and place them in this tradition of American history. Anti-imperialists also adopted abolitionist practices, such as petitions to Congress, public meetings, and general social agitation. No longer fighting Jim Crow only at home, they were now protesting U.S. despotism thousands of miles away across an ocean, not just south of the Mason-Dixon line. Like abolitionists before them, anti-imperialists made the argument that even as far away as the Philippines, despotism degraded democracy at home. Still, physical distance that created extensive time lags in communication from the colony presented real hurdles for anti-imperialists, who had to argue against what had already happened in the Philippines often months before.[8]

In the chapters that follow, I outline the anti-imperialists' political sphere. By pairing scholarly discussions of U.S. imperialism with protest, I situate anti-imperialists in the world where they worked. Highlighting the tension between anti-imperialists' and imperialists' perceptions, I bring into the picture what made their commitments at times deeply emotional. Structured chronologically, the book is organized into two parts that travels the course of the anti-imperialist movement. Each chapter focuses on a different aspect of how anti-imperialist debates affected U.S. imperialism and modified anti-imperialists' ethical witnessing.

Part I, "The White Man's Burden in a World of Empires," outlines the world where debates between anti-imperialists and imperialists took place in order to set up the historical context in which the anti-imperialist coalition formed. Chapter 1, "Anti-Imperialists and Ethnical Witnessing" traces the first major anti-imperialist campaign, analyzing how disparate anti-imperialist social positions created multiple anti-imperialisms that offered unification solely around the bottom line opposition to imperialism. Focusing on the Treaty of Paris and the AIL, this chapter applies an intersectionality framework that tracks across race, class, and gender. By analyzing actors' social positions and relationships to violence, we see the differences in the emotional excitement that motivated multiple anti-imperialisms. Chapter 2, "Sacred Democracy and the Presidential Election of 1900," details the trials and tribulations of the second major anti-imperialist campaign, the unsuccessful quest to elect William Jennings Bryan as president. Anti-imperialists used diverse and ultimately polarizing tactics to gather as many supporters as they could, in particular, influential citizens. They debated the distinctions of civilization with each other, with imperialists, and later fought the indifference of the U.S. public. Drawing these distinctions was not merely a matter of parsing words or refining ideas, they held material consequences for the legal development of U.S. democracy as well as the U.S. treatment of Filipinos/as and sovereignty over the Philippines. But, other issues at stake were more interesting to the U.S. public, such as the economy and domestic race relations, which caused many potential supporters to shy away from Bryan. Ultimately, anti-imperialists were unable to consolidate their constituents around a problematic candidate, and many initial supporters of anti-imperialism fell away after Bryan's defeat.

Part II, "From Tracking Public Opinion to Tracking the Law," traces the third and final campaign in which anti-imperialists consolidated their agenda to focus on exposing violence in order to right the wayward path of U.S. imperialism in the Philippines. It details the efforts to document the violence through the formation of a transnational advocacy network with prominent Filipinos/as and the use of soldiers' letters to lobby lawmakers. Finally, they succeeded in generating a major Senate investigation. Chapter 3, "The Senate Investigation on Affairs in the Philippines," discusses the Senate investigation and its aftermath. It follows the anti-imperialist activists who investigated and prepared soldiers to testify about the extraordinary violence before the SIAP. In so doing, they intended to reveal the suppressed facts and set the agenda for public debate around the injustice of the U.S. military violence in the Philippines. It then traces the three main topics of the hearings themselves—violations of the rules of war, the water cure, and reconcentration. The investigation revealed the differences in how anti-imperialists and imperialists framed these topics, the former as atrocities and the latter as exceptions. An abrupt halt to the investigation left the anti-imperialists spinning their wheels, struggling to keep it going so that they could continue sharing the shocking testimony to awaken the public from their indifference. Chapter 4, "Tracking Benevolent Assimilation," considers the anti-imperialists' efforts to continue tracking events in the Philippines and keep the U.S. public informed after the failure of the SIAP. Rather than remain at the mercy of the censored press, they obtained first-hand information. Anti-imperialists sent three different Americans to the Philippines to report back home. They also expanded their networks with nationalist Filipinos/as and utilized Filipino newspapers to obtain and verify information and further critique racist violence.

The conclusion of the book discusses the unintended consequences of anti-imperialist protests in shaping U.S. imperialism. Learning from their failures, many of the activists shifted their "anti" focus to advocate for the rights of disenfranchised groups, beginning new organizations like the National Association for the Advancement of Colored People and Women's International League for Peace and Freedom. They would continue their ethical witnessing, forging ahead a path of human rights.

## NOTES

1. The Moorfield Storey Institute. Moorfield Storey, March 2, 1920. "Who Was Moorfield Storey?" by Damon Root. *Reason*. December 2007. Retrieved June 16, 2017, http://files.meetup.com/1617413/storey%20booklet.pdf.

2. For more on ethical witnessing, see Paula Ioanide's (2015) *The Emotional Politics of Racism: How Feelings Trump Facts in an Era of Colorblindness* and F. Ishu Ishiyama's (2000) Keynote Address, "Toward Organizational Maturation: Active Witnessing for Prejudice Reduction," Transcending Boundaries: Integrating People, Processes, and Systems.

3. See appendix for discussion of methods and lists of sources.

4. Meanwhile, the Platt Amendment would make Cuba a legal protectorate.

5. Mugwumps were political independents who used their votes to influence particular issues. See Robert L. Beisner. 1968. *Twelve Against Empire: The Anti-Imperialists, 1898–1900*. New York: McGraw-Hill Book Company.

6. The rhetorical structure of the "exception" normalizes democracy as the rule (for enfranchised citizens, that is, whites, especially men) and allows exceptions for certain uses of violence (against the disfranchised, i.e., people of color and sometimes white women and working-class, white men). Indeed, empirical studies of violence reveal the historically racialized, gendered, stratified nature of violence in U.S. democracy (e.g., see Richard Drinnon. 1980. *Facing West: The Metaphysics of Indian-hating and Empire-building*. Norman and London: The University of Oklahoma Press; see also, Richard Slotkin. 1992. *Gunfighter Nation: The Myth of the Frontier in Twentieth-Century America*. New York: Atheneum). These democratic exceptions fall on the backs of nonwhite subjects, historically making it less likely that they will mobilize around the frame of the "myth of rights" until there have been

legal wins for civil rights (see, Stuart A. Scheingold (2004 [1974]). *The Politics of Rights: Lawyers, Public Policy, and Political Change.* Ann Arbor, The University of Michigan).

7. The fact that the white man's burden is so often referenced as shorthand for imperialism while the history of the Philippine-American War is so commonly unknown evidences a contemporary imperialist schema still impressing a politics of memory—or rather a politics of forgetting and ignoring.

8. Racist exceptions continue to shape the United States today, in the implications of the U.S. prison system; the exceptional applications of the law, such as "stand your ground," drug laws, and cases of police brutality across race (Michael Brown, Eric Garner, Walter Scott, Tamir Rice); and changes to the Voting Rights Act of 1965. One needs only to investigate black sites or ponder the naval base at Guantánamo Bay to see the lingering implications of U.S. racist exceptions abroad. With this book, I seek to reinstate the history of the Philippine-American War and the anti-imperialists into the broader U.S. historical narrative. In mapping the legacy of racist exceptions to its origins, I reveal more of the nation's messy imperfections and the unrelenting work toward its promise of democracy. To achieve a truly multiracial democracy, racist exceptions must be identified, recognized, and acknowledged in order to work through and abolish them, because, as Storey phrased it, between tyranny and equality there is "no middle ground."

could be argued here that some Filipinos did not internalise the standard beauty ideals posed by the Spanish and Americans. Aguinaldo's words may $\longrightarrow$ suggest that he views Filipinos and black Americans as the same and that there shouldn't be a division — they all should have a common goal — that is to fight against the mistreatment of coloured people.

But another side of the coin could be the notion that this internalised colourism that is so prevalent in the Philippines today could be a result of resentment against black Americans for their lack in solidarity.

# Part I

# A WORLD OF EMPIRES AND THE WHITE MAN'S BURDEN

To understand what anti-imperialists were up against, it helps to get a sense of the bigger picture. U.S. imperialists and anti-imperialists were inventing themselves in a world of empires. The intra-imperial and inter-imperial fields best frames how Western fantasies of white supremacy were embedded in ideas of civilization, even justifying violence through racist exceptions. Historical sociologist Julian Go (2003) applies imperialism to Pierre Bourdieu's field theory, which frames social, political, and cultural phenomena, like classical music or academia, as structured networks of relationships that use others in the field as reference points. He does this to make distinctions between the intra-imperial field, within an empire, that is, between the metropole—or center of the empire—and its colonies, and the inter-imperial field, which is between empires (e.g., Great Britain and the United States), both fields which are characterized by "competition, contest, and exchange" (p. 16). Emilio Aguinaldo, the leader of the Philippine revolution, strategically used the comparison of the intra-imperial field, between the colony and the metropole, to convince black American soldiers that their mistreatment at home paralleled U.S. treatment of the Filipino people, and they should, therefore, lay down their arms against Filipinos and support their cause. And a few did. While Aguinaldo used this field to counter racist violence, imperialists used them to justify it.

In order to understand the characteristic (Stoler 2006) and particular exceptionalist narratives that developed during the imperialist Philippine-American War, we need a map of the political ground they traversed (Pease 2009: 57). Beliefs in white supremacy informed exceptionalist fantasies about U.S. superiority that allowed imperialists to exercise a self-satisfied indifference and dismissiveness in the face of racist violence, like lynching, against blacks—a logic then extended to Filipino/as as nonwhites. For anti-imperialists, the hypocrisy and betrayal of believing in U.S. and white moral superiority while instigating (or dismissing) racist violence inspired critiques of exceptionalism and sharpened their advocacy for representative government and democratic rights for Filipinas/os. It also sharpened their condemnations of violence almost concurrently administered by other empires, including Great Britain in South Africa (against the Boers) and in China (against the Chinese Boxers), as well as Spain in Cuba.[1]

In the following pages, I first show the inter-imperial field and how exceptionalist narratives and violent practices developed simultaneously, as empires not only *competed* over the status of being exceptional but also *exchanged* violent practices, creating racist exceptions. Next, I show the intra-imperial field and the violence that emerged out of civilizing projects that enacted comparably violent treatment of people of color across the U.S. Empire. In response to colonial resistance in the Philippines and anti-imperialist protests, this exceptionalist violence crystallized into the policies of benevolent assimilation that codified new, legal racist exceptions and manifested the policies of U.S. Empire with which Filipino/as and anti-imperialists were forced to contend.

Western nation-states have considered empire to be the marker of peak civilization and power for millennia. When some empires, including Spain, weakened at the turn of the twentieth century, the United States began strengthening its empire with strategic territorial acquisitions that include Hawai'i, Puerto Rico, Cuba, Guam, Samoa, and the Philippines. Other empires in the Pacific, with which the United States shared the inter-imperial field, served as points of comparison when U.S. imperialists fantasized developing a different kind of empire. American imperialists and anti-imperialists understood the development of U.S. Empire in the Philippines, Puerto Rico, and Cuba as a way of competing with Spain, Great Britain, China, and Japan over territory, and the moral high ground of civilization. But with revelations of U.S. violence in the Philippines, debates over benevolent assimilation and other exceptionalist doctrines that fantasized U.S. exceptionalism flared at home.

Since 1823, the United States had used the Monroe Doctrine to claim preferred trade agreements. Puerto Rico and Cuba, the last two Spanish colonies, were close to U.S. territory, so Spain presented the greatest threat to U.S. trade interests, which made the U.S. very interested in the Cuban revolution. When Cuba started a revolutionary movement against Spain, historical events coincided with U.S. interests to promote U.S. Empire.

Additionally, reports from Cuba described Spain's shockingly horrific use of violence against Cubans, especially the tactics of a man named General Weyler. Weyler was nicknamed "the butcher" for the violent tactics he used against Cuban revolutionaries, including the reconcentrado policy, which involved indiscriminately burning homes and fields, destroying villages, and reconcentrating the surviving population into monitored camps. The American public was outraged by these reports, and President McKinley objected strongly to what he viewed as the unequivocally "cruel" practice of reconcentration. He acknowledged in his first message to Congress that although reconcentration was rationalized "as a necessary measure of war" in order to cut "off supplies from the insurgents" the base immorality of it required the United States to make a "firm and earnest protest" as "[i]t was not civilized warfare," but a war of "extermination" (as quoted in Kramer 2006:153). The U.S. public therefore widely supported the government's deployment of the *USS Maine* to Havana to allegedly survey the situation.

When the warship was damaged in an explosion, the United States had all the reason it needed to officially go to war with Spain, ostensibly to aid the Cubans in their quest for independence. The Spanish-American War lasted only a few months, ending in Manila Bay, the Philippines, and making Commodore George Dewey and Theodore Roosevelt national heroes. Because it was relatively short and successfully freed the Cubans from Spanish tyranny, the war became known as America's "splendid little war," a phrase inspired by John Hays, American Ambassador to Great Britain. In a letter congratulating then Colonel Theodore Roosevelt, Hay wrote, "It has been a splendid little war, begun with the highest motives, carried on with magnificent intelligence and spirit, favored by that Fortune which loves the brave."[2] In the letter, Hay went on to praise Roosevelt for his success in the war, admitting Roosevelt had been right to take part in its leadership and was reaping the "glory."

What is often curiously left out of this triumphal story is that the Cubans were not alone in their quest for independence. In 1896, Filipino nationalists began to stage their own rebellion against Spain. Their leader, Emilio Aguinaldo, believed he was coordinating with U.S. forces to defeat Spanish troops in the Philippines. Aguinaldo even returned from exile in Hong Kong with Dewey on the *USS Olympia* to help coordinate with the Americans. Aguinaldo believed that the United States would offer the Philippines independence, not that his country would trade one colonial occupier for another. Little did he know that the U.S. officers in the Philippines had staged a mock battle with Spain in Manila, having previously agreed that Spain would surrender to the Americans, not the Filipinos (Luzviminda 1987).

When Aguinaldo learned the terms of the Treaty, he alleged U.S. officers in Manila had betrayed him. It became clear to Aguinaldo and the revolutionary junta in Hong Kong that the United States was not even going to grant protectorate status to the Philippines as it had agreed to do in Cuba. Rather, they seemed to intend to keep the Philippines as a U.S. colony. Anticipating the necessity for defense against a new occupier, Filipino military forces gathered around U.S.-occupied Manila. For Filipinos/as nationalists, the supposed ally of the United States turned to an enemy.

In the months before the U.S. Senate actually ratified the Treaty of Paris, emotional political debates erupted over what the relationship would look like with the Philippines and, for anti-imperialists, how imperialism corrupted the country's democratic traditions and ideals. Meanwhile, tensions rose between American and Filipino military forces until, finally, war began on February 4, 1899. Imperialists had a twofold problem: they were forced to justify the backhanded course in the Philippines to an influential domestic opposition at the same time as they had to configure their own purpose and agenda in the Philippines where the U.S. military faced armed Filipino nationalists on their own terrain.

Imperialists argued foremost that taking and keeping the Philippines was a strategic necessity, constitutional or not, for the United States to compete in trade with Asia (Go 2003; Kramer 2006; Miller 1982; Rosenberg 1982; Schirmer 1972). Most importantly, control of the Philippines would allow the United States to use Manila as a fueling station and point of entry for trade with China (Miller 1982; Rosenberg 1982). Claiming benevolence as a secondary rationale for empire, U.S. imperialists set out to distinguish themselves from the brutality of other empires, like Spain and Great Britain. The United States would supposedly demonstrate a more civilized imperialism.

Across the inter-imperial field, the exceptionalist narrative of the white man's burden expressed views of civilization, such that: indigenous groups needed to be controlled and organized according to Western standards. This narrative helped rationalize the violent tactics used by imperial powers whose key military figures, such as Spain's General Weyler in Cuba, and Great Britain's equally infamous Lord Kitchener in South Africa during the Boer War, became familiar to Americans for the outrageous violence committed against the Cubans and the Boers. In fact, General Weyler became one major reference because of his infamous use of torture, starvation, and reconcentration camps against the Cubans. For instance, journalists described the incredible violence committed by the United States in the Philippines in terms of "Weyler-like tactics" and "Weylerian procedures" (Kramer 2006: 170, 293). Then, Lord Kitchener became another reference for the unimaginable violence as he employed concentration camps in South Africa during the Boer War, which also started in 1899. The U.S. public came to see Weyler and Kitchener as synonymous with organized brutality. There was the world of empires in which imperialists and anti-imperialists emerged. Anti-imperialists called attention to the U.S. military's extraordinary violence by invoking these names as shameful shorthand for wanton violence, the antithesis of how many Americans viewed ideals of civilization.[3]

U.S. imperialists primarily compared their plans for U.S. empire with Great Britain. When South Africa's Boers, descendants of Dutch settler-colonizers, took up arms against the British settler-colonizers in South Africa, the U.S. military was already involved in armed conflict in the Philippines, and both supporters and opponents of U.S. imperialism paid close attention. While U.S. critics often referred to British policies against the Boers as "extermination," a practice with residual shame that carried over from the Indian Wars in the West and Midwest (Drinnon 1997; Slotkin 1992), others had a more positive take. The *Boston Herald* reported on November 19, 1899, that Lord Kitchener's plan for South Africa, "harsh though it appears to be, appeals to officials of the war department, and during the coming campaign . . . no mercy is to be extended to those in active rebellion or who give aid and comfort to the insurgents" (as quoted in Schirmer 1972: 226). On November 20, 1899, the *Boston Globe* reported that those officials in the War Department explained the appeal of Kitchener's plan to use reconcentration. They explained that the only "hope" for "suppressing the guerilla warfare" was if "Filipinos are forced to leave the country districts and settle in the towns where they can be kept under the eye of the military authorities" (as quoted in Schirmer 1972: 226). They all used the inter-imperial field to make sense of this new imperialist endeavor, both in exchanging violent tactics and in providing the rationales for the violence.

While many anti-imperialists were outraged over the U.S. military violence and did their best to publicize and protest it, especially after 1900, U.S. officials, in turn, kept it quiet through censorship. Instead, they vilified Filipino insurgents as savage and publicized the education and civilization the United States was benevolently bringing them. This strategy successfully achieved an immobilizing indifference on the part of most of the American public, who were interested in domestic issues rather than violence in the Philippines (Nichols 2011).

At the same time as many liberal U.S. elites ignored what leaked about U.S. atrocities, as anti-imperialists termed them, in the Philippines, they continued to express disappointment in Britain's use of violence against the Boers, which they associated with Kitchener. Their disappointment was fueled by white supremacist beliefs that Anglo-Saxons were the heralds of "civilization" and, therefore, morally should practice self-restraint rather than savage violence—even though these beliefs weren't applied at home.

Well-known writer and anti-imperialist sympathizer Caroline Pemberton observed the racial lines that were drawn around many white anti-imperialist sympathies, using the inter-imperial field and the Boer War as her lens. In an 1899 letter to AIL leader Herbert Welsh, she referred to a new story she was writing, *Stephanie the Black*, in which she tied together the issues of racism at home and the war in the Philippines. She struggled to make sense of the contradictions between the American public's outrage over the violence against the Boers and relative silence on U.S. violence against Filipinos/as.

> Most intimately connected is I believe this problem with our shameful conduct in the Philippines. If the people of those islands were white, we could sympathize with their struggle for independence as we sympathize with the Boers. When shall we outgrow this hideous arrogance that is in our blood toward all whom the sun has browned? *The liberty of the Anglo-saxon[sic] is for himself alone.*"[4] (my emphasis)

Pemberton suggests that racism was *the* significant determinant of how U.S. Americans felt about the Philippine-American War.

While the Boer War raged on in South Africa and the Philippine War continued in the Philippines, the Boxer Rebellion broke out in China, affecting both the United States and Great Britain. As Americans grappled with racialized colonial relationships on three different fronts in places many had never heard of previously, there were increasingly new connections and comparisons for them to consider and with which to understand the ever-changing world across the inter-imperial field. Chinese nationalists, known as Boxers, began fighting Western Christian missionaries from the United States and Great Britain in 1900. The western missionaries in China played a similar role to those in Hawai'i: they went abroad to evangelize but also paved the way for U.S. trade (Jung 2006; Miller 1982; Rosenberg 1982).[5] The United States had benefited from Great Britain's colonial ventures in Chinese ports, which had resulted in preferential treaties for the United States, as Great Britain's "junior partner" (Miller 1982: 4). The open door policy with China essentially allowed the United States to practice nonterritorial imperialism (Kramer 2006; Ninkovich 2001; Schirmer 1972).

Because American imperialists saw China as a vast outlet for trade, they justified the colonization of the Philippines for its strategic geographical position. In an influential speech on "Our Philippine Policy" in 1900, Indiana Senator and imperialist Albert Beveridge declared that China offered "illimitable markets" and such opportunities should not be abandoned, hence the importance of the Philippines.[6] It was no coincidence, then, that the United States allied with Great Britain to put down Chinese nationalist resistance, which also provided security for accessing Chinese markets.[7]

Protests against U.S. and European trade agreements had been increasing within China and Japan (Kramer 2006). The Boxer Rebellion was a significant event for Protestant missionaries and capitalists hoping to further penetrate the Chinese interior. Chinese nationalists taking up arms against them was a disturbing prospect for conducting effective business. By 1900, imperialists were finding it more difficult to justify the war in the Philippines to American citizens (Schirmer and Shalom 1987). But Beveridge's speech in Congress invoking China's markets and Anglo racial superiority helped rally imperialist supporters. He asserted:

> Our largest trade henceforth must be with Asia. The Pacific is our ocean. More and more Europe will manufacture the most it needs, secure from its colonies the most it consumes. Where shall we turn for consumers of our surplus? Geography answers the question. China is our natural customer. [. . .] The Philippines give us a base at the door of all the East.

He continued,

> It will be hard for Americans who have not studied them to understand the people. They are a barbarous race, modified by three centuries of contact with a decadent race. The Filipino is the South Sea Malay, put through a process of three hundred years of superstition in religion, dishonesty in dealing, disorder in habits of industry, and cruelty, caprice, and corruption in government. It is barely possible that 1,000 men in all the archipelago are capable of self-government in the Anglo-Saxon sense.

The year following Beveridge's speech, the U.S. sent troops who were stationed in the Philippines to put down the Boxers in China, supporting his claim that the Philippines were a base not only for trade but also, as subsequent history would reveal, for significant military operations.

Additionally, Beveridge addressed the inter-imperial concerns of Russian and Japanese power with regard to China. He observed:

> Russia's Chinese trade is growing beyond belief. She is spending the revenues of the Empire to finish her railroad into Pekin itself, and she is in physical possession of the imperial province of Manchuria. Japan's Chinese trade is multiplying in volume and value. She is bending her energy to her merchant marine, and is located along China's very coast; but Manila is nearer China than Yokohama is.[8]

Five years after this speech, Japan would defeat Russia in a war over Pacific imperialist control. This defeat would send a ripple effect of concern over the white man's burden, and losing footing in imperialist control.

But at this point, U.S. imperialists put benevolent assimilation policies at the center of their justifications for colonizing the Philippines. The narrative went like this: unlike European empires, which were understood to simply exploit the resources and labor of their colonies, the United States would benevolently "civilize" the "savage" Filipino/as and tutor them in the ways of democracy (Go 2007; Murphy 2014), a classic paternalistic rescue narrative. Rather than focusing on the problems of violence in their midst, they changed the topic to focus on their "upliftment" programs, much as white supremacists had with the problem of lynching. This was not surprising given the significant overlap between white supremacists and imperialists at the turn of the twentieth century. Sidestepping the hypocrisy of racist violence at home allowed them to continue to rationalize racist exceptions that permitted breathtaking violence in the new colony.

To anti-imperialists, like the AIL leader and lawyer Moorfield Storey, notes taken from Great Britain's violence against the Boers and Spain's violence against Cuba by conservative imperialists was "no guide for us in this case," given these empires recognized the "law of might" and the "right of conquest," which McKinley had already labeled as "criminal aggression."[9] Even so, conservative imperialists continued to look to other empires *and* drew intra-imperial inspiration for policies in the Philippines from previous exclusionary tactics and violence against nonwhites that had taken place at home, such as settler colonialism, slavery, the Monroe Doctrine, and the annexation of Hawai'i. Storey confronted these intra-imperial comparisons in a broadside titled, "Our New Departure." Making a few "general observations," he argued,

> [F]irst, [. . .] our practice in the past is no argument for a new departure from the true path. Precedents may make law, but not morals. [. . .] Our whole treatment of the colored race for years was in violation of our principles, and we paid bitterly for our sin. The Declaration sets up the standard to which we should conform. Our failures in the past are to be regretted, not repeated.[10]

While many anti-imperialists agreed with Storey that these sins had been paid for dearly in the Civil War, the tradition of them paved a path for much of the white public's support for colonial interventions in the Philippines. And so, progressive anti-imperialists drew on the impassioned anti-slavery arguments of abolitionists and Lincoln as well as critiques of genocide and extermination that originated in the context of the Indian Wars.

That all sides drew on intra-imperial history to make their case shows the colonization of the Philippines was not a standalone event, but another iteration of a long-standing tension that has stood at the crux of U.S. identity since its colonizing and anti-colonial origins. To this point, Storey reminded his readers that Europe's empires were not to be emulated, given they "all claim the right to govern men without their consent, and sell territories without consulting their inhabitants" and that America was founded "upon a denial of that right." Referencing past struggles for freedom, Storey framed it in appeals to American exceptionalism and human rights.

Let it be remembered that it has ever been the pride and boast of America that the rights for which we contended [in our revolution and in the Civil War] were rights of human nature?

A result so astonishing [as a Philippine colony] should lead you to reconsider the arguments on which it rests. It is no answer to say that our purposes are benevolent, and that we shall use this power wisely. It is a question of right.[11]

Even while activists like Storey lobbied critiques and presented arguments for ethical witnessing in terms of human rights, legal exceptions that rationalized racist violence were still a routine aspect of expanding the U.S. Empire. For instance, by the time the Philippine-American War began, the genocidal Indian Wars of the 1880s were over, but the project of "civilizing" the Indians and containing them on reservations was still an ongoing priority for missionaries and educators. In fact, Storey cited case law on Indian rights to make his case for Philippine independence. Many of the officers in the military had begun—and indeed made—their careers in those wars against Indians (Slotkin 1992). In the Philippines, they drew upon these prior experiences, including forcing Indians to relocate onto reservations. Meanwhile, white lynch mobs were increasingly terrorizing black Americans (Wells 1997). These domestic racial crises became another essential lens through which anti-imperialists and imperialists understood and argued over the violence in the Philippines.

For example, along with addressing competition across the inter-imperial field, Beveridge's speech on Philippine policy, quoted earlier, compared racist violence across the intra-imperial field as well. Beveridge was one of the anti-imperialists most odious adversaries. He asserted that the Indian Wars in the Midwestern United States should have been more "continuous" and "decisive," and suggested that "Our Indian wars would have been shortened, the lives of soldiers and settlers saved, and the Indians themselves benefited had we made continuous decisive war; and any other kind of war is criminal because ineffective." In other words, effective war meant using any means necessary to win quickly and decisively, including what many, even in his day, called extermination and genocide. This vision of "decisive" war framed military justifications of the violence against Filipinos/as, which officers referred to with the military terminology of "total war" (see chapter 6 for more on rules of war). As a social Darwinist, Beveridge did not self-consciously or shyly use the language of "extermination" to express his purpose. Rather, he went on to suggest that such extraordinary violence offered "lasting peace." Imperialists like Beveridge unapologetically advocated for violent methods of putting down a revolt of people of color, if they went against the will of the U.S. government. While methods of extermination were obviously revolting to anti-imperialists, for imperialists like Beveridge, it was a logical fulfillment of his racist interpretations of social Darwinism.

On the other hand, NeoLamarckian racism was a hopeful, paternalistic racism. It promoted a supposedly softer version of U.S. Empire, by suggesting that Filipinos/as would eventually be able to learn the ways of democracy through exposure to and training in American-style colonial education and governance (Go 2007; Murphy 2014). In the Philippines, this cultural logic, which Paul Kramer (2006) calls an "inclusionary racial formation," touted the capacities of Filipinas/os for *future* self-governance while lamenting their present shortcomings (Kramer 2006: 192, my emphasis). The benevolent assimilation idea took shape amid the civilizing projects that racialized Filipinas/os as savage or barbaric and then attempted to assimilate them to white cultural standards through education and governance.

Anti-imperialist leaders positioned themselves in the abolitionist legacy and saw white Southerners as culpable for the racist imperialism in the Philippines. However, many Southern whites were also considered anti-imperialist or anti-expansionist at the time because they wanted to prevent the United States from including additional non-white groups within the nation. The widow of Jefferson Davis, the former president of the Confederacy, was one such person. In "The White Man's Problem: Why We Do Not Want the Philippines," she made intra-imperial connections, categorizing herself as both an "anti-imperialist," who opposed the government taking the Philippines, and an "anti-expansionist," who saw no benefit to adding the Philippines to the United States. Her objection was based on the problem of race in the United States:

> For my own part, however, I cannot see why we should add several millions of negroes to our population when we already have eight millions of negroes in the United States. The problem of how best to govern *these* and promote their welfare we have not yet solved.[12]

She shared no interest with imperialist racists in obtaining the Philippines in order to control a nonwhite population, rather she would keep the United States as white as possible as a more insular racist, given the continued "problem," as she framed it, of figuring out what to do with "negroes" at home.

Many black men were lynched on the basis of unfounded accusations of consorting with white women, but politics was also a common cause for lynching in ways that particularly resonated across the intra-imperial field. In some areas of the South, black political participation was enough to be lynched. One infamous lynching occurred in Wilmington, North Carolina, in November 1898, just as the debate over the Philippines was heating up. When the established middle-class black population ran candidates for public office, enraged whites killed dozens of black community members and burned the building that housed the black newspaper office. This violence drove the elected black officials and white allies out of the community (Schirmer 1972). The violence spread to South Carolina when a small number of enfranchised blacks tried to vote, and "Before nightfall ten blacks were killed; five lay dead all day long by the roadside, four others were lynched in adjoining woods" (Schirmer 1972: 101). Newspapers in the North came out against the Southern violence.

Underscoring the intra-imperial connections, the anti-imperial *Boston Advertiser* noted, "The white man's government of the North Carolina pattern is precisely the government which so-called expansionists hope to put in operation . . . in the Philippines" (as quoted in Schirmer 1972: 101). The *Memphis Commercial Appeal*, a Southern paper, had a different take, asking, "How are we going to govern the Philippines, Hawaii, and other new possessions? Peaceably if we can; or like the white men are doing in the Carolinas, if we must, but govern them we will" (as quoted in Schirmer 1972: 101-102). The analogy between lynching and the violence in the Philippines hung so heavy, in fact, that President Roosevelt, in a Memorial Address at Arlington Cemetery on May 30, 1902, alleged the silence on lynching was hypocritical of critics of the violence in the Philippines. He went on at length to speak against the lynchings at home as far worse than the crimes committed by the U.S. military in the Philippines, stating that the violence in the Philippines was "shamelessly exaggerated" and that lynchings at home deserved far more "condemnation."[13]

Lynching was also at issue in the Philippines, where Emilio Aguinaldo followed U.S. newspapers, staying up on their characterizations of both the war and domestic racial issues (Silbey 2007). Aware of the lynching problem, he exploited it to the advantage of his cause utilizing the intra-imperial field. He used the especially incendiary lynching of Sam Hose, to attract and recruit black U.S. soldiers. Hose was lynched in April 1899 by a white mob in Newnan, Georgia, who burned him at the stake because he was accused of raping the wife of his employer, which he consistently denied. While burning was a common form of lynching, Hose's attackers went even further, dismembering, cooking, and selling his body. Schirmer (1972) described the horror of the event in *Republic or Empire*:

> "small pieces of bone went for 25 cents and a bit of liver crisply cooked for 10." When the news of the lynching spread to nearby Atlanta, the railroad put on special excursion trains to take nearly 4,000 whites to the affair. Arriving too late for the burning, they returned home with souvenirs. (Schirmer 1972: p. 146)[14]

Given these realities at home, it is a wonder Aguinaldo succeeded in only recruiting a dozen or so troops.

In fact, two Black volunteer regiments served in the Philippines, though it was much to the chagrin of many of their white counterparts. Aguinaldo's tactics, which included flyers and broadsides, especially targeted them. And although he was able to draw only a dozen or so, the disaffected soldiers received a lot of media attention (Jacobson 2000). One notorious case of desertion involved David Fagen, of the Twenty-fourth Infantry, who deserted

> in November 1899, evidently after coming across a placard from Aguinaldo addressed "To the Colored American." "It is without honor that you are spilling your costly blood," such broadsides proclaimed. "You must consider your situation and your history, and take charge that the blood ...of Sam Hose proclaims vengeance." (Jacobson 2000: 252)

Fagen deserted the U.S. military, joined the Filipinos, and led his own regiment. His regiment was later captured by the U.S. military, and he was beheaded (Jacobson 2000).

Filipino nationalists also utilized the intra-imperial field, taking note of the successful tactics the Boers used against the British and employing them against the U.S. military (Kramer 2006). Filipinos/as were on guard as to how the racist history of the United States could come into play against them as subjects of the United States. Along with their attempts to communicate with U.S. soldiers in the Philippines, the leadership in Hong Kong also made contact with prominent anti-imperialists in the United States, exchanging information and even visiting the United States to educate the American public (De Ocampo 1977; Zwick 1998). These collaborative activities with Filipino nationalists led imperialists to label American anti-imperialists as traitors.

The description thus far briefly depicts the world of empires in which anti-imperialists and imperialists lived. The rationales for and against U.S. involvement in the Philippines developed through comparing U.S. empire with other empires and using racial fantasies of people of color at home and extending them onto Filipinas/os. Sharing the inter-imperial and intra-imperial fields provided the same reference points for imperialists and anti-imperialists as they developed their views by defending their positions using exceptionalist narratives. And these narratives took on new life when overlaid with social Darwinism, NeoLarmarckianism, the white man's burden, and manifest destiny. The peculiarities of U.S. domestic racism hung heavy over the development of U.S. colonial racializations of Filipinos/as. These racist fantasies provided the parameters for how U.S. exceptionalism and benevolent assimilation could be imagined.

In fact, these exceptionalist narratives gave legs to racist legal exceptions, whereby nonwhite groups were included within the sovereignty of the United States but excluded from full political participation, in a prime example of "states of exception" (Agamben 1998; Agamben 2005). These were the exact policies put forth by imperialists as benevolent assimilation legitimated the use of violence against nonwhites. Thus, nonwhite groups in both the metropole and colony were excluded from the body politic of the United State via disenfranchisement and the denial of citizenship, even as they were included within the parameters of government control through recourse to violence and confinement. This paradox underlies imperialist—and anti-democratic—relations and continues today.

Given the historical facts of the Philippine-American War do not match up with the dominant exceptionalist narrative of leaders of the Free World has made it convenient to erase that war from common accounts of U.S. history, which has significant implications for U.S. Americans and our imaginations about U.S. global involvement today. Matthew Frye Jacobson (2000) aptly frames the conflict over the memory of the Philippine-American War, suggesting that "the states are quite high for Americans' national self conception" since the history of the Philippine-American War and the anti-imperialist protests have been disremembered. Because of this, "Americans adopt a broken narrative" where "Manifest Destiny and continental expansionism" are placed "adrift from 'modern' U.S. history" which "obscures the extent to which the modern state was built, and modern nationalism generated" upon imperialism. The result has been that "U.S. involvement in global affairs" is mystified today, with the history leading up to these affairs boxed away deep in the proverbial shadows (Jacobson 200: 263–264).

Clearly, understanding the history of the Philippine-American War involves more than seeing it simply as an overlooked or even hidden war. To fully understand its implications requires reckoning with this period as a fundamental moment where U.S. imperialist state formations, such as racist exceptions, were reformulated and institutionalized. Framing the history this way sheds much needed light on modern imperialist moments that seem mystified, such as when American Samoan's were still seeking and being denied U.S. birthright citizenship in 2015.[15] But, truly reckoning with this history could also help us understand racist fantasies that still allow police despotism in cities across the United States to occur with little consequence and the modern prison industrial complex. No less important, this reckoning could also help us understand the racist fantasies of whites that are promoted by the fear of a truly multi-racial democracy and the wish to harken back to a time when white racial power was more solidified so as to "Make America Great Again."

## NOTES

1. Exceptionalist narratives, like benevolent assimilation, traversed the intraimperial field, from U.S. metropole to colony, and framed interventions in the Philippines as *necessary consequences* of the inter-imperial narrative of the white man's

burden, which was to "uplift" the Filipino/a people, and therefore helping to justify incredible violence, like the water cure and the burning of entire villages, by enacting racist exceptions. U.S. exceptionalism also traveled across inter-imperial fields, as imperialists framed U.S. empire as not only different from but also better and more moral than other empires like the Spanish or British. At the same time, however, imperialists exchanged and refined their practices of military violence, like reconcentration camps and the water cure, across those same inter-imperial fields.

2. Hay to Roosevelt, July 27, 1898. "Shown In His Own Letters." *Scribner's Magazine.* 1919. Edited by Edward Livermore Burlingame, Robert Bridges, Harlan Logan. Vol. 66, p. 533.

3. For more on the symbolic meaning and use of reputations see Gary Alan Fine, "Thinking about Evil: Adolph Hitler and the Dilemma of the Social Construction of Reputation," in *Culture in Mind: Toward a Sociology of Culture and Cognition,* edited by Karen A. Cerulo (New York: Routledge, 2002).

4. Letter from Caroline Pemberton to Herbert Welsh, November 15, 1899. Herbert Welsh Papers, Hatcher Graduate Library, Special Collections Library. Although in her letter she says this book will be about "Stephanie," it was ultimately published in 1899 as *Stephen the Black.*

5. Justifications for the United States taking Hawai'i as a colony and later as a territory also cited proximity to China and China's purportedly infinite possibilities for trade given the size of its population (Miller 1982).

6. Albert Beveridge, "Our Philippine Policy." *Congressional Record,* January 9, 1900.

7. Troops stationed in the Philippines were conveniently rerouted to Hong Kong to help put down the fighting (Kramer 2006). See pp. 349–350.

8. Albert Beveridge, "Our Philippine Policy." *Congressional Record,* January 9, 1900.

9. Moorfield Storey, *Our New Departure: 1. Letter to a Friend, October 21, 1899 2. Speech at Brookline, October 26, 1900* (George H. Ellis, Printer: Boston, MA, 1901), p. 5.

10. Storey, *Our New Departure.*

11. Ibid., p. 7.

12. Mrs. Jefferson Davis, *The Arena.* New York. Jan–Jun 1900. Emphasis in original.

13. President Roosevelt, "Memorial Day Address." May 30, 1902.

14. This was likely the lynching that so affected Du Bois to write *The Souls of Black Folk* and express his double consciousness. DuBois referenced one such souvenir in a store front window.

15. Pema Levy, "An Federal Appeals Court Just Denied Birthright Citizenship to American Samoans Using Racist Case Law." *Mother Jones,* June 5, 2015. http://www.motherjones.com/mojo/2015/06/appeals-court-denies-birthright-citizenship-american-samoans.

# Chapter 1

# Anti-Imperialisms and Ethical Witnessing

Morrison Swift dreamed of the equality promoted by both democracy and socialism. He wrote, "Any form or degree of domination has a like tendency. It fosters the degrading sense of superiority, contempt, arrogance, aloofness, the domineering spirit, all of which canker the superior man's nature. It prevents the growth of brotherliness—the highest idea of civilization; of equality—the basis of democratic evolution; of the American spirit—the essence of the American spirit being equal opportunity of development for all" (1899). Swift framed his critique of imperialism through one narrative of American exceptionalism, contrasting imperialism's "sense of superiority" and "domineering spirit," to the unique "American spirit" of democracy and "equal opportunity of development." Swift's critique draws on an astute observation of emotional dispositions that often goes overlooked. Diagramming a relationship between emotions and politics, he argues that this "domineering spirit" maintained the feelings of superiority and inferiority, which were, and are, essential to maintaining hierarchies (Collins 2004). Swift was far from the only anti-imperialist to connect emotions and politics; indeed, the range of anti-imperialist views clearly delineated varying emotional dispositions.

I argue that examining the connection between anti-imperialists' emotions and politics illuminates the origins of the diverse—and competing—politics within the movement. It also provides space for empathic practices of "looking at where the other is coming from"—a skill that also needs consciously cultivated today. While scholars have not always taken this approach seriously, today there is more interest and acceptance of the idea that although emotions are not necessarily based in facts, they still help shape reality, sometimes at the expense of facts. Collective emotions are a social force that powerfully shapes the perceptions under which we operate in our own version of reality. The degree to which we are able and willing to see other perspectives is the degree to which we are able to foster a shared reality, rather than insular, parallel, realities. For instance, our self-righteousnesses may feel good and energize our engagement with causes but that serves a different purpose than cultivating coalitions, as anti-imperialist leaders hoped to do. Therefore, this chapter focuses on the emotions of key groups of anti-imperialists at the beginning of the Philippine conflict. To do this, we will observe their own accounts of their actions, the actions themselves, and the emotional language they used to describe their feelings. I think the current moment has shown us the necessity for better empathic understandings of one another, not only for the power of emotions in subverting what are considered relevant facts. Ethical witnessing by way of empathic emotional connections to one another showed to be transformative for anti-imperialists personally and politically.

Anti-imperialist emotions raged during the Senate debates over the Treaty of Paris early in 1899. Believing that the future of the United States was at stake in deciding how to handle the Philippines, senators passionately disputed over issues of commerce, military strategy, and government. Meanwhile, 8,000 miles away, Filipino and U.S. forces were in a hostile standoff after the Benevolent Assimilation Proclamation (BAP) was disbursed on January 1st. The hostile standoff boiled over into war when shots were prematurely fired. With this, the anti-imperialists lost their first major political battle. In a crushing defeat, two days after the fighting began the Treaty was ratified, by one vote.

It also made the BAP legal under U.S. law, further outraging anti-imperialists who were now more determined than ever. Mobilizing a tenuous alliance of diverse anti-imperialists, they organized the AIL to oppose the Philippine-American War and the new U.S. acquisition of the Philippines. The AIL brought together Democrats and Republicans; white supremacists and believers in equal rights across race; men and women; the upper classes as well as laborers.

Histories of the AIL have focused mainly on the elite white men from the northeast who made up its leadership (Beisner 1968, 1970, 1973; Foner and Winchester 1984; Hoganson 1998; Jacobson 2000; Lasch 1958; Markowitz 1976; Reyes 1971; Schirmer 1972; Tompkins 1970; Welch Jr. 1973, 1979). This is understandable, given their influence and the plethora of readily available archival sources. However, I expand the record to include anti-imperialist white women, black men and black women, and members of the working class, finally making visible the entire unwieldy field of anti-imperialism at the turn of the twentieth century. These previous studies of the anti-imperialists have argued that they were racist or provincial (Lasch 1958, 1973). These overgeneralizations obscured the various racisms at play within the white leadership and how the movement's complexity and competing racisms affected its activism (Go 2004; Jung 2006). Most problematically, however, these overgeneralizations erased the influential work white women and women and men of color contributed to the movement.

Mending this gaping hole, I take a closer look at race, class, and gender differences within the AIL and the larger movement. By considering the emotional dispositions expressed in their anti-imperialisms, I am able to show how different social locations generated differences in beliefs. It should not be surprising that social positions informed distinct anti-imperialist perspectives. Furthermore, it should not be surprising that the white leadership were unable to acknowledge how social location informed their own view of anti-imperialism, because from that height of privilege, it was observed as a universal standpoint. We will see this evidenced in the following pages by their emotional expressions in political debates. However, in the places where they employed compassion that allowed them to empathically listen to other anti-imperialists' perspectives, they created mental space for a more expansive transformation of their views.

Selecting categories for an intersectional analysis is both a theoretical and methodological question. Including all possibilities (e.g., political affiliation, religion, age, generation, education, region, race, class, gender, sexuality, and citizenship status) can dilute and detract from the narrative and the analysis. Since previous literature has already focused on the political differences of party and different positions on nationalism, I primarily focus on race, class, and gender, given that these areas have been overlooked theoretically and historically. Yet, this choice raises its own methodological challenges. It was surprisingly easy to find personal documents for many of the elite white men involved in the movement. The well-archived organizational documents of the AIL represent their involvement as well. The preservation and organization of which should largely be credited to Maria Lanzar, a Filipina student who gathered and donated them when she wrote her dissertation at the University of Michigan in the late 1920s. The organizational documents include activities of the elite white women who were affiliated with the official organization—though I had to use creative archival tactics to track the full extent of their involvement. However, evidence for working-class anti-imperialisms of both whites and people of color was harder to obtain. They were only obliquely mentioned in AIL documents, but fortunately labor newspapers were booming between the 1880s and 1940s. Therefore, I searched newspapers for public statements of their anti-imperialist positions and looked into the archival papers for public figures like Ida B. Wells and W. E. B. Du Bois, which availed nothing on this particular moment of anti-imperialism.

The uneven availability of sources creates challenges for telling an equally represented and weighted story. Often, more questions are raised than can be answered. I think this makes it all the more important and worthwhile to include the story of other anti-imperialists beyond elites, to purposefully include those groups of people who were underrepresented in their time and continue to be underrepresented in histories today. Therefore, I fill the gaps in the history to the best of my ability, realizing this choice of limited inclusion may leave the reader (and the writer) wanting more information about those underrepresented groups, especially black men and women.

The sources I have been able to recover shows that the AIL was at the center of the movement. While white women and people of color, both individually and in groups, tried to correspond and coordinate with the organization, the AIL *officially* excluded them categorically but utilized their activism on the side. Therefore, many of these excluded anti-imperialists acted on their own, writing to newspapers and organizing independently within their community. Excavating these sources that expand the views of the movement, I provide a history that recovers the work of women and people of color, showing both local and national aspects of anti-imperialists' organizing efforts as well as how anti-imperialists worked at the individual and group level.

The excited responses of the anti-imperialists and the stonewalling of imperialists marked a stark contrast. Anti-imperialists expressed personal indignation *and* worked to incite greater public indignation as the United States traveled farther down the path of imperialism. Imperialists, on the other hand, expressed Swift's earlier description in this chapter of "domination . . . superiority, contempt, arrogance, [and] aloofness"—a cultivation of disregard.

Studying emotions as a category of social analysis (rather than psychological analysis) has been accepted in both history and sociology (Barbalet 2002; Collins 2004; Denzin 1984; Hochschild 1983; Reddy 2001; Stearns and Lewis 1998; Stearns and Stearns 1988; Thoits 1989; Williams 2001). Yet, until fairly recently[1] most social scientists have avoided using emotional expressions as any kind of evidence. Sewell (2005) suggests that social scientists seem to fear being tainted by the "irrationality, volatility, subjectivity, and ineffability that we associate with [emotion]" and that studying emotion will call into question our own "scientific objectivity," but, if this is the case, avoiding the study of emotion out of fear (how ironic), it not good social science either—especially if "emotional excitement is a constitutive ingredient of many transformative actions" as Sewell maintains and with which I agree (p. 248). Analyzing the relationship between emotion and cognition in the "doings and sayings" (Scheer 2012) of historical actors enhances an intersectional analysis of their actions and allows us to examine the role of emotions in larger social transformations—showing that moments of compassion and connection led to the transformation of their perspectives.

Anti-imperialists expressed their different anti-imperialisms through emotional language (Scheer's category of "sayings") and performances (her category of "doings"), which together I refer to as emotives because of the action the words elicit.[2] At the same time, I look at the silent indifference and self-admiring defensiveness of imperialists, akin to stonewalling, also as emotives that determined the emotional currents with which anti-imperialists navigated. For historical sociologists, what people do and say are often more revealing for explaining events than what they actually *think* about what they are doing or saying. Without much self-awareness, what we think about what we do and what we actually do can diverge to a surprising degree.

Inspired by both Pierre Bourdieu (1993) and William Reddy (2001), Monique Scheer (2012) suggests that there are "four kinds of emotional practices that make use of the capacities of a body trained by specific social settings and power relations . . . mobilizing, naming, communicating, and regulating emotion" (p. 193). *Mobilizing* emotions incite us to action. *Naming* emotions categorize and typify emotional experiences and actions. *Communicating* emotions perform or display the emotions we are experiencing or want to elicit in others. *Regulating* emotions are the behaviors that constitute the social scripts of normalized, or expected, emotional behaviors. For anti-imperialists and imperialists, mobilizing, naming, communicating, and regulating emotions all came into play as they enacted and organized their views that stemmed from their social position. In the subsequent sections, I demonstrate how social position informed how these political emotions came into play in the development of unique anti-imperialisms.

## ABIDING ALLIANCES

The anti-imperialist movement brought together individuals and groups from multiple social positions (see table 1.1). According to the AIL secretary's report of February 10, 1899, the "membership of the Anti-Imperialist League [was] considerably over 25,000."[3] However, since only "men able and willing to work" were granted formal membership, and the assumption that members were to be white went "without comment" (Jung 2015: 29), these numbers omit the women and people of color involved in affiliated auxiliary organizations as well as those who supported the main organization.[4] Using archival collections of active AIL members, previous scholarship that accounts for black and working-class anti-imperialists (Gatewood 1975; Schirmer 1987), and newspaper articles, I have recovered the activities of white women and people of color in the history of anti-imperialism.[5] For instance, in the same report that provided the membership numbers earlier, the AIL noted that a committee of women in Cincinnati had put together an anti-imperialist petition with the names of over 2,000 women. The information is there, but someone had to find it notable and track it down.

**Table 1.1   Anti-imperialist Coalition in 1899**

| |
|---|
| Progressive Republicans (George Hoar) |
| Mugwumps (political independents) |
| Conservative Democratic leaders |
| Progressive Democratic leaders (William Jennings Bryan) |
| Business leaders (Andrew Carnegie) |
| Former abolitionists (Charles Sumner) |
| Liberal Religious Groups (Albert Love) |
| Liberal Media (*Springfield Republican, City & State*, labor newspapers) |
| Labor unions (AFL) |
| Labor Leaders (Samuel Gompers, Horace White) |
| Women's organizations (Women's Christian Temperance Union, later Women's International League for Peace and Freedom members, Congress of Mothers, Daughters of the American Revolution) |
| Black leaders (Booker T. Washington, Kelly Miller) |
| Black newspapers (*Freeman*) |
| Academics (William James, Jacob Schurman, William Graham Sumner) |

## "National Honor": Anti-Imperialist Elites

New England elites who self-identified as anti-imperialists were concerned about the contradictions between democracy and imperialism, but some politicians and southern elites aligned with anti-imperialist politics because of their racist beliefs, leading them to reject the idea of more people of color from the Philippines joining the United States and further complicating the "race problem."[6] Manifest Destiny had been the call earlier in the nation's settlement history, and imperialists increasingly invoked it again during the late 1890s as an exceptionalist narrative to justify imperialist interests in Hawai'i, Cuba, Puerto Rico, Samoa, and the Philippines (Jacobson 2000; Rydell 1984; Tompkins 1970). These policies offended many Republicans and Independents, who believed in self-determination and held a vision of America based on the ideals espoused in the Declaration of Independence (Beisner 1968). They also worried many southern Democrats, who believed there was already a "race problem" (in the vernacular of the day) in the South that would be further complicated by bringing other nonwhite peoples into the republic (Lasch 1973). As a bottom-line opposition to taking the Philippines, anti-imperialism bridged divisions of political party and ideology.

The most well-known anti-imperialists were these white men from elite backgrounds. For instance, the leaders of the movement were academics, politicians, lawyers, and businessmen. Beisner's (1968) list of anti-imperialists includes "Ex-Presidents Benjamin Harrison and Grover Cleveland," as well as senators, representatives, political independents called Mugwumps, and clergymen.[7] Mark Twain was another ally. Keenly aware of their societal status, many of these figures held prejudices that corresponded with an elite social position. For instance, at one point when his feathers were ruffled the

AIL Secretary Erving Winslow insulted the offending parties as "obscure persons of obscure ancestry," an epithet that could only hold bearing among elites.[8]

Two key subsets of these leaders were Mugwumps and Brahmins. Mugwumps were political independents who went from party to party, considering themselves "the heralds of reform, at liberty to use their uncommitted votes to force reform upon the existing political parties, or if reforms were resisted, to threaten the parties with destruction" (Beisner 1968: 7). Most earned their name for leaving the Republican Party for the Democratic Party because of financial corruption. They were WASP elites with particular ideals for the nation that reflected the moral and cultural interests of what they viewed as their heritage and legacy. As such, they had concerns about the contributions of new European immigrants and the working classes to the nation: "the Mugwumps felt dislike and contempt not only for swarming immigrants and striking railroaders but also for the methods and manners of the businessmen of the age" (Beisner 1968: 12). Boston Brahmins (who were not necessarily Mugwumps in earlier elections) were upper-middle-class white men descended from Puritans and Pilgrims and connected with New England's wealthy mercantile sectors (Schirmer 1972). Their particular brand of anti-imperialism corresponded with their Brahmin social position, which instilled deep beliefs in political independence and support for reformist policies. They were engaged citizens, who enjoyed the unquestioned empowerment of formal and informal citizenship.

Gamaliel Bradford, one of these Boston elites, made the initial call for a meeting of anti-imperialist men at Faneuil Hall in June 1898 (Schirmer 1972). Faneuil Hall was a significant part of Boston's political culture including its reform movements, and for progressive Bostonians, the building itself summoned the "emotional excitement" (Mukerji 2006) of a tradition of advocating for equality and liberty. For the elder statesmen and women of the anti-imperialist movement, Faneuil Hall particularly invoked transformative memories of town hall meetings during the abolitionist movement. Bradford directly evoked these memories in the *Boston Evening Transcript*:

> If free speech is to be suppressed in Massachusetts, if Faneuil Hall is to be converted into a *silent tomb*, if the spirit of Wendell Phillips and William Lloyd Garrison—sorely needed to avert a slavery worse for Massachusetts at least, we had better find it out now. If enough men will join with me to secure the hall, I for one, will stand up and have my say against the *insane* and *wicked ambition* which is *dragging this country* at least to *moral ruin*. (as quoted in Schirmer 1972: 73, emphasis added to note the emotive language)

Knowing his audience, Bradford expressively attempted to regulate and mobilize their emotions with the image of a silent and indifferent Faneuil

Hall, which would represent the stonewalling of democracy. For these men, many of whom grew up knowing soldiers of the Revolutionary War and participated in the abolitionist movement, the Constitution, U.S. democracy, and liberty were sacred tenets that transcended personal interests. Deviating from these tenets created a political and symbolic identity crisis for them as Americans.

Deeply identified as American citizens, these elites expressed their anti-imperialism through emotions ranging from debilitating depression to mobilizing outrage. The mobilized began to organize. As insiders with fully included citizenship, their anger did not require justification. From their perspective, they were acting in the interest of the country, which was also in their own interest. And, their leadership made anti-imperialism a viable political position across the board. Their confidence and empowerment also shaped one of their interventions: chronicling what they saw as the truth of events in the Philippines for the historical record.

John J. Valentine, an AIL vice president and president of the Wells-Fargo Express Company, argued that what was happening in the Philippines was "A Question of National Honor." The supporting evidence he used was to chronologically outline state documents that showed the U.S. betrayal of Emilio Aguinaldo. He concluded:

> The case stated to a point is simply this: We asked the assistance of the Filipinos as allies and they complied effectively. The Filipinos asked us for our consent to their independence. We refused. Hence the American-Filipino war.
> LET FACTS BE SUBMITTED TO A CANDID WORLD![9]

Though words like "simply," "facts," and "candid" bespeak a cool rationality that Valentine aimed for in making his case, the capitalization and punctuation of his last emphatic sentence communicate the emotions he felt and intended to elicit in others, which was outrage over the duplicity.

### "Throwing Washington Overboard": Socialist Radicals

For anti-imperialists, like socialist Morrison Swift, the AIL was far too conservative (Welch Jr. 1979). William Appleman Williams (1972) has argued that it would be more accurate to call the AIL anti-colonial imperialists, rather than anti-imperialists (as they called themselves). This label—or in today's expression neocolonialist—would have applied to some anti-imperialists. However, it was not the leadership's main reason for opposing imperialism. Their position had much more to do with the democratic and ethical ideals described in the previous section (Beisner 1968; Tompkins 1970).

Nevertheless, the comparative conservatism of much of the AIL leadership was a problem for their radical anti-imperialist contemporaries. Mocking the arrogance of imperialists, influential socialist Daniel de Leon attacked their selective use of American exceptionalism, noting that they only invoked the sacredness of the American past when convenient or expedient. Writing for *The People* in 1898, he pointed to the hypocritical contradictions between imperialist critiques of socialism and anti-imperialism:

Capitalism, threatened from behind by the Social Revolution, turns around to the uprising Proletariat, and with a *sanctimonious scowl* invokes the past as a sacred thing, to be worshipped and bowed down before. *What?!* Does the Socialist Movement want to break with the "time-honored" habits of the land? *What?!* Shall the principles of Americanism, *consecrated by the Revolutionary Fathers*, be done away with? *What?!* In *horror* the Pillars of Society *throw up their arms*, and the *conviction leaps from their eyes* that, as the Socialists have no reverence for the past, they must be *wiped out*. [. . .] Among the most venerated figures in the land, Washington holds very generally a leading place; to him our capitalist politicians, professors and parsons have ever turned; his words have again and again been quoted; and among the bad things imputed to the bad Socialists more than once has an intention to "repudiate Washington" been mentioned. And yet, what do we see now?

In Congress, in the press, in the pulpit, the Washingtonian warning against entangling alliances, conquests, etc., now frequently uttered against the plan to keep the Philippines, take Hawaii, etc., etc., is met with, what? With nothing short of a *sneer* at Washington, a declaration amounting to pronouncing him a "back number," in short, by *throwing him overboard*.

Washington, these same recent devotees of the past now say, could not have foreseen the changed conditions in which we now live; Washington, they tell us, wrote and spoke and thought in other and for other times; Washington, in short, is not now of any account.[10] (emphasis mine to note the emotives)

Where Valentine used emotives sparsely, de Leon sprinkled them lavishly throughout his treatise to mobilize supporters, communicate his position, and regulate the emotions of both critics and sympathizers. He noted that imperialists and anti-imperialists alike invoked an exceptional past. But anti-imperialist leaders referenced the past to critique the imperialist disregard for the rule of law and sins against the republic. To de Leon, liberal anti-imperialists worshiped the past and Washington, imperialists used tradition expediently, concurrently disregarding tradition as inconvenient and irrelevant to the times. However, socialists sought a new kind of future based on more egalitarian principles of economics (rather than just government) and were off the historical trajectory altogether.

Although many radical anti-imperialists believed the "mugwump" anti-imperialists were "anti-colonial imperialists" (Williams 1972), whose anti-imperialism was a cover for their belief in an informal empire based on trade, this was not the case for all anti-imperialists nor the AIL. As Beisner (1968)

observed, many anti-imperialists did not even consider the "economic implications of imperialism, and those who did almost invariably subordinated
them to moral, racial, historical, and constitutional considerations" (p. 87).
This understandably frustrated economically radical anti-imperialists. After
all, the "Gilded Age" was noted for its incredible income inequality, com-
parable to the dramatic economic inequality of today. Given socialists were
already far more critical of contemporary politics, de Leon's use of emotion
to emphasize his points reflected his social position as he questioned both
leading anti-imperialists but especially the hypocrisy of imperialists.

## "War Is Hell": White Working-Class Anti-imperialists

The anti-imperialist views of many working-class whites centered around
their family and friends in the military. In 1898, as the Spanish-American
War came to an end and the Philippines took the military center stage, the
widespread support for war began to wane. Public opinion shifted toward
bringing the troops home, especially in regions where soldiers and their rela-
tives lived (Schirmer 1972). In fact, letters from soldiers fueled the opposition
to the Philippine-American War. While some soldiers conveyed their own
opposition to the war in their letters, others believed the military's violent
tactics were justified (Schirmer 1972).[11]

When the fighting between U.S. troops and Filipino nationalists began,
family members and state officials from California, Pennsylvania, South
Dakota, Tennessee, Oregon, Minnesota, and Nebraska actually requested that
volunteer regiments be sent home (Schirmer 1972). In March 1899, soldiers
from the Tenth Pennsylvania stationed in the Philippines wrote to family and
friends that the government was even suppressing information and underre-
porting the death rates for volunteers. As a result, family and friends began
organizing to have the troops returned home (Schirmer 1972).

In April, "[r]elatives and friends of Oregon volunteers, supported by
newspapers of that state, called for the return of the Oregon troops, 'who
never enlisted for such a war' " (Schirmer 1972: 150). The South Dakota
governor wrote emphatically to President McKinley "that the Philippine war
was 'repugnant to the fundamental principles of government,' and that South
Dakota men were being held in the army against their will" (Schirmer 1972:
150). Several hundred parents of the First Nebraska Regiment "demanded
that 'the government send back home those who have not contributed their
*precious fever-stricken or bullet-torn bodies* to enrich the soil of Luzon' "
(Schirmer 1972: 151, emphasis mine to highlight emotives). While these parents and their representatives may not have been highly educated elites, their
family members were on the front lines. They emotionally communicated
their perspective on the war from their direct experience. Their contribution

to the anti-imperialist cause lay in communicating both their opposition and their personal suffering in hopes of eliciting the transformative emotion of empathy. Their emotives aimed to elicit this empathy and regulate emotions by making it clear that they believed that their family members were being used.

The volunteers for the Spanish-American War signed up to free the Cubans, from their perspective. They had not anticipated fighting in the Philippines, and their support for the war also continued to wane. Schirmer (1972) quotes Herbert Myrick, vice president of the Phelps Publishing Company and publisher of the Orange Judd Farm Weeklies, who claimed "'an utter absence of imperialist spirit among the rank and file of the people throughout the West and South . . . the unpopularity of the war increases with each Western boy who is killed or wounded,' " and "'each mail from Manila'" (p. 150). In fact, the increasing disillusionment of the soldiers became a problem for the McKinley administration when the vast majority of soldiers chose not to re-enlist after the government called for 100,000 more soldiers; in April, the government admitted that only about 7% of the volunteers planned to re-enlist, despite being offered $500 as a re-enlistment bonus (Schirmer 1972). Even for working-class soldiers, money was not enough of an enticement to stay on.

In 1899, the AIL published the groundbreaking *Soldiers' Letters: Being Materials for the History of a War of Criminal Aggression*, in which they organized and compiled published letters from soldiers. Writing to those back home, soldiers described the policy of "taking no prisoners" and reported on the "progress of this goo-goo hunt," using a new racist epithet for Filipinos that prefigured the similar racialization of Vietnamese as "gooks" (see Roediger [1994] *Towards the Abolition of Whiteness*). Some letters expressed distress at the U.S. treatment of the Filipino/as, which was no more benevolent than Spain's, as well as general confusion over the war. Arthur Vickers, a sergeant in the First Nebraska Regiment, wrote, "I am not afraid, and am always ready to do my duty, but I would like some one [*sic*] to tell me what we are fighting for." Not fear, but political confusion was the cause of his lack of support. On the other hand, General Reeve, "lately Colonel of the Thirteenth Minnesota Regiment," knew exactly what he didn't want to fight for:

I *deprecate* this war, this *slaughter* of our own boys and of the Filipinos, because it seems to me that we are doing something that is *contrary to our principles* in the past. Certainly we are doing something that we should have *shrunk* from not so very long ago.[12] (emphasis mine)

Reeve communicated his emotions through language designed to express his open opposition to war from his social position as a military officer, both naming his personal feelings ("deprecate") and eliciting feelings in others to incite them to an anti-imperialist position. Despite the paternalistic imperialist discourse of the white man's burden, soldiers were clearly more than symbolic tropes of American martial masculinity for family members and friends; indeed, they were powerful evidence of the problems with the war.[13]

In addition to soldiers, workers and union members at home offer another important working-class, anti-imperialist perspective. After the ratification of the Treaty of Paris, anti-imperialists began to look beyond the ranks of the elite to strengthen the anti-imperialist coalition. Early on, they turned to unions to gather support. In a speech at a Chicago Peace Jubilee on Oct. 18, 1898, American Federation of Labor President Samuel Gompers asked:

> If the Philippines are annexed what is to prevent the Chinese, the Negritos and the Malays coming to our country? How can we prevent the Chinese coolies from going to the Philippines and from there *swarm* into the United States and *engulf* our people and our civilization?[14] (emphasis mine)

Gompers, inspired by his racism, went on to suggest that forcing U.S. rule on Filipinos/as would create a surplus of cheap labor, but those workers would be "ruled and killed at the convenience of the very small minority there, backed up by our armed land and sea forces." He concluded:

> When *innocent men can be shot down on the public highway* as they were in Lattimer, Pa., and Virden, Ill., *men of our own flesh and blood*, men who help to make this *homogenous* nation great, because they *dare ask for humane conditions* at the hands of the moneyed class of our country, how much more difficult will it be to *arouse any sympathy*, and *secure relief for the poor semi-savages* in the Philippines, much less *indignation at any crime* against their inherent and natural rights to life, liberty, and the pursuit of happiness? (emphasis mine)

Contrasting the violence experienced by "homogenous" white workers in the United States with the potentially greater racist violence that could be committed against Filipino/as, Gompers centered his racist anti-imperialist views on the difficulty of generating "sympathy . . . much less indignation" for Filipino/a workers. He used emotive language to mobilize his followers, communicate his position, and regulate emotions in support of white labor as well as to elicit support for anti-imperialism.

On March 21, 1899, Gompers was the main speaker at an anti-imperialist meeting at the Tremont Temple in Boston, where he "warned that 'if peace cannot be secured in any other way, the time is coming when federated labor will refuse to make implements that are intended to strike down their fellow-men' " (as quoted in Schirmer 1972: 139). But although he was one of a long list of names for the original vice presidents of the AIL and initially spoke out strongly against imperialism, Gompers refused to endorse William Jennings Bryan's candidacy for president when he ran on an anti-imperialist platform.

Newspapers that focused on organizing workers or had a more socialist bent related the Philippines to workers and a capitalist society fraught with violence. The *Social Democratic Herald*, which was associated with Eugene Debs and the Social Democratic Party, was one of the earliest media outlets to make these connections. It strategically connected the use of violence in the United States (including lynching) and the Philippines by listing a single day's violent newspaper headlines and exposed the contradictions of the civilized/savage discourse in a column titled "Capitalist Civilization."[15] These newspapers also published letters from soldiers in the Philippines and directly criticized the administration's call for more troops, doing their part to advocate against soldier reenlistment.[16] In a speech in support of the candidacy of Bryan, Gamaliel Bradford referred to government violence against striking workers, stating, "The rich in this country are beginning to distrust the multitude and get ready the sword for their protection. The danger of violence is not from below, but from above" (as quoted in Schirmer 1972: 206–208). Those seeking working-class support for the anti-imperialist movement thus established regulating emotions through social scripts that appealed to the all-too real threat of violence "from above" at a time where there was growing inequality between the wealthy few and the working classes.

And yet, the labor press was not all of the same mind. Even as many in the labor movement joined the rest of the country in a jingoist fever over liberating the Cubans, the *American Freeman* ran critical poems, such as "We Are Savages," and "Sham Soldiers"[17] as early as 1898. It also ran articles claiming that the army would be a good place to recruit for the revolutionary cause and charging it with suspect recruiting tactics for recruiting criminals in exchange for suspended sentences.[18] Using a populist tone, the paper based out of Kansas also repeatedly published articles about soldiers being exploited by the government. In contrast, the *National Labor Tribune* celebrated U.S. military victories in the Philippines, after the liberation of Cubans, though it also criticized the expansionist policies of the U.S. government.[19] One of the tamer labor newspapers, the *Journal of the Knights of Labor*, became increasingly critical of the U.S. war in the Philippines over the course of 1900 criticizing Congress for approving the request for a 100,000-man standing army and publishing a soldier's letter titled "War Is Hell."[20]

Working-class anti-imperialists were motivated by distress and outrage that friends and family were fighting a war with changing rationales. Workers realized they were the ones being asked to fight the war, so they wrote to their representatives and local newspapers to uncover the violence censored by mainstream newspapers.[21] From the outset, their arguments focused on the actual *experience of the violence* of war in contrast to the elites who focused on the ideological contradictions between imperialist violence and democratic principles. While most working-class anti-imperialists weren't leaders in anti-imperialist political organizations, the men were still enfranchised citizens, who could influence the political positions of their worker organizations through their "doings and sayings." Connecting working-class experiences to the breakdown of democratic principles of governance created a space for transformation between anti-imperialist leaders and working-class anti-imperialists.

## "Cold Consolation": Black Anti-imperialists

If the empathetic connection of workers' rights and violence was key to white working-class anti-imperialism, similar connections between lynching and imperialism mobilized black anti-imperialists to take a principled stance on the war in the Philippines. While white anti-imperialist leaders in Boston were progressive in comparison to their contemporaries, they still largely capitulated to the norms of the time when it came to racial segregation. Clifford H. Plummer, a Boston attorney and secretary of the National Colored Protective League, embodied this position when he proposed a "colored auxiliary" to the AIL in the summer of 1899. The white AIL voted to cover the expenses for the first meeting, which was held on July 17.[22] Like working-class white anti-imperialists, Plummer compared imperialism to black experiences with violence. Discussing the potential organization with the press, he compared McKinley's refusal to speak out against the lynching of blacks in the south to the president's aspirations for the "negroes" in the Philippines (Schirmer 1972). At the inaugural meeting, the attendees connected McKinley's stonewalling of lynching with his war in the Philippines. The meeting was attended by Boston blacks and whites like William Lloyd Garrison, and "the assembly passed resolutions condemning McKinley for his war in the Philippines and for his silence on lynching" and officially founded the "Colored National Anti-Imperialistic League," with Jerome Riley as President, although the group was still widely known as the "colored auxiliary" (Schirmer 1972: 172).[23] Other organizations formed by black men, many of which had cross membership, included the "National Negro Anti-Expansion, Anti-Imperialist, Anti-Trust, Anti-Lynching League," started by businessman and newspaper publisher H.J. Scott, a businessman and newspaper publisher, in Cairo, Illinois, and the "Negro National Anti-Imperial and Anti-Trust League" (Foner and Winchester 1984: 167).

In *Black Americans and the White Man's Burden*, Willard Gatewood, Jr. (1975) noted that "[w]hether he favored or opposed expansionism, the white

American was also likely to interpret the issue in racial terms; however, his approach bore little resemblance to that of the black citizen" (p. 182). The social position of black anti-imperialists allowed them to make empathic connections between the racist violence of lynching and the war against Filipino/as. Often the connection was historical, as when "at a meeting of Boston's black citizens to commemorate the 129th anniversary of the death of Crispus Attucks, speakers attacked Anglo-Saxon colonization and opposed killing Filipinos because they were 'fighting for just what our forefathers sought thirty-five years ago' " (Schirmer 1972: 138).

In the pamphlet, "The Effect of Imperialism Upon the Negro Race," Howard University mathematics professor Kelly Miller, who later edited *The Crisis* with W. E. B. Du Bois, delineated connections between the deteriorating conditions of blacks at home and the plight of Filipinas/os abroad, claiming that "The whole trend of imperial aggression is *antagonistic* to the feebler races. It is a revival of racial *arrogance*" (my emphasis).[24] Naming the mercurial nature of the attention blacks endured in attempts to obtain citizenship rights, Miller attempted to regulate emotions by eloquently pointing out the hypocrisies:

> [The black man] has been the incidental beneficiary of two *revolutionary waves of feeling* which swept the current of *popular sentiment* outside of its accustomed channel. He moves up and down in the scale of *national regard* as the mercury in a thermometric tube reaching *blood heat in seasons of excitement,* and sinking to the *freezing point in times of tranquility and repose.* [. . .] The Revolutionary fathers did not dare apply the logic of their principles. They *lacked the courage* of their conscience. (my emphasis)

Like the white elite anti-imperialists, Miller focused on the political implications of imperialism, relating it to the social position of blacks:

> The charge of denying 'the consent of the governed' is hurled back and forth between the parties with the resilience of a bounding ball. One says to the other: "Although we suppress the negro in the South, you shall not suppress the Malay in the Orient." The other replies: "You are stopped from protesting by your first admission," and then turning to the negro, it says coyly: "Because those fellows suppress black men in Louisiana, you ought to resent it by helping us suppress brown men in Luzon." Between the two, the brother in black, or rather the *brother in colors*, finds *cold consolation* indeed. The negro is thus placed politically *between the devil and the deep sea.* (my emphasis)

Highlighting his sentiment of empathic connection for "brother in colors," Miller goes on to argue that blacks should not accept any political compromise that grants them voting rights in the South at the expense of Filipinos/as unless they want to betray the hope of extending rights to all citizens. Miller critically named the emotions of his anti-imperialist position and communicated a political view rooted in the social position of a black anti-imperialist in hopes of regulating the behaviors of other blacks vis-a-vis opposition to imperialism in a manner of connection with Filipinos/as that was quite different from the emphases of working-class white anti-imperialists, socialists, or elites.

And yet, black leaders had varied responses to the anti-imperialist movement. Booker T. Washington privately declared his support for anti-imperialist efforts in a letter to the New York AIL,[25] but he also publicly declared his opposition on the basis of already existing "race problems" (Gatewood 1975). Although W. E. B. Du Bois became a self-identified anti-imperialist by the 1920s, at the turn of the century he was not inspired to be involved with AIL and remained focused on the domestic issues facing African Americans. Although the anti-imperialist analyses of black men ranged from radical to moderate, they were all rooted in a critique of spreading race prejudice beyond already-existing U.S. "race problems" with Indians and blacks (Gatewood 1975). The urgency of black anti-imperialists was to convey the unbreakable link between racism and imperialism.

Like working-class, white newspapers, anti-imperialist, African-American newspapers were a powerful voice for the sentiments of their constituencies through editorials and letters from soldiers. The virulence of the Jim Crow laws that had spread across the South in the 1890s provided another context for them to compare the shared plights of the people of the Philippines and people of color at home. Like the rest of the black community, the newspapers saw the Philippine-American War and U.S. expansion more generally as part of a larger race question (Gatewood Jr. 1975).[26] As the War Department called for "colored" troops and organized "colored" regiments led by white officers, anti-imperialist papers challenged the idea of people of color fighting other people of color on behalf of whites,[27] especially when their own demands for protection and recognition of their rights at home continued to go unheeded.[28]

Newspapers frequently published analyses of the situation that traversed the intra-imperial field, comparing the treatment of those in the Philippines with blacks at home. For instance, in a June 1899 letter to the *Washington Post*, Archibald Grimke wrote, "From *sad* experience the negroes have known well what *cruel and oppressive* treatment the dark races of the Filipino archipelago will surely receive at the hands of the American nation in the event of their final *submission to or subjugation* by it" (my emphasis).[29] In recognition of the racist hypocrisy of Kipling's poem "The White Man's Burden," replies entitled "The Black Man's Burden" sprung up by the dozens across black newspapers (Gatewood Jr. 1975). One version by H. T. Johnson, editor of the *Christian Recorder*, expressly addressed the inter-imperial experiences of violence suffered by Cubans, Hawaiians, Filipino/as, blacks, and Indians under the United States:

Pile on the Black Man's Burden.
    'Tis nearest at your door;
Why heed long bleeding Cuba,
    Or dark Hawaii's shore?
Hail ye your fearless armies,
    Which menace feeble folks
Who fight with clubs and arrows
    And brook your rifle's smoke.
Pile on the Black Man's Burden
    His wail with laughter drown
You've sealed the Red Man's problem,
    And will take up the Brown,
In vain ye seek to end it,
    With bullets, blood or death
Better by far defend it
    With honor's holy breath.[30]

Communicating his sorrow and indignation of the Black Man's Burden, Johnson showed a common plight of violence for people of color under the United States. While black men did have formal U.S. citizenship, Jim Crow laws were continually stripping away their rights and lynchings were on the rise. Johnson foregrounds this continued black oppression when he ironically urges his interlocutors to "Pile on the black man's burden/ His wails with laughter drown." As both victims and resisters of injustice and violence, black writers like Johnson could easily empathically connect personal experience with that of Filipinos/as, and this ability and willingness to connect shaped their anti-imperialist views.

Alice Smith-Travers published an incisive rejoinder to Kipling's poem, also titled "The White Man's Burden," in *The Freeman*, a black Indianapolis newspaper, on March 4, 1899. She too focused on the intra-imperial horrors of violence, but without irony, focusing on lynching and slavery of Filipinos/as along with the "Judas"-like behavior of the United States. She made plain the racist links between exceptionalism and violence:

"Take up the white man's burden!"
That causes the heart to quake
As we read again with horror,
Of those burnings at the stake,

Of white caps riding in the night,
And burning black men's homes,
Of the inmates shot as they rush out
And the awful dying groans,

Of crimes that would outnumber
Those in the foreign Isle,
Committed by heath[*sic*] people
"Half devil and half child."

Then free those Filipinos[*sic*] people,
From the accursed rule of Spain,
And put on them the shackels
Of a haughtier nation's reign.

With "Judas" acts in every form,
Conceivable by man,
And the thirst for blood, and greed for gold
Is surely the white man's plan.[31]

Although lynching was a criminal activity under U.S. law, by and large it went unenforced when committed against blacks. Smith-Travers also flipped the script on the white man's burden, putting the white men and their violent behaviors as those "half devil and half child." Again, she used her social position to empathically connect with the experience of Filipinos/as, which informed her anti-imperialist position.

Black anti-imperialist newspapers were not the only ones to utilize the intra-imperial field in their arguments about the Philippines. At the opposite end of the political spectrum, racist white imperialists compared Filipinos/as to Indians and blacks as a potential race problem in the United States. Unlike the more reformist or progressive imperialists who wanted to civilize the Filipinas/os, these imperialists had no qualms about uncritically lumping together all people of color—no exceptions required. Meanwhile, the AIL tried to frame U.S. imperialism in the Philippines in terms of the American Revolution, much as the abolitionist movement had thus framed slavery. John Edward Bruce, a widely respected African American journalist and political writer (Crowder 1994), wrote to *The Colored American* under his pen name Bruce Grit:

There you have it. The Tagals or Filipinos, have an *American Weyler* on their hands in the person of General Otis. He believes they are *inferior* to Americans (white), and he is going to *crush* them if he can, because of their resistance to the armed authority of the United States and to the arbitrary attempts of this government to force upon them a system of government which they do not want. In their resistance to this effort of the United States and its *"humane"* policy in the Philippines in what respect are they different from the American colonists who, a hundred years ago resisted the attempt of Great Britain, which arbitrarily sought to make laws for them *without their consent,* and *persistently denied* them the right to participate in the making of those laws. (emphasis mine)[32]

Overall, the anti-imperialist ire of black citizens was powerfully fed by the increased lynchings at home, juxtaposed with black troops fighting against other people of color abroad being similarly denigrated. As Gatewood Jr. (1975) put it, they fully understood that "any government that could not or would not protect its own citizens from atrocities was in no position to become the standard-bearer of enlightenment among other people" (p. 199). The racism of the Philippine-American War was central to the black anti-imperialists' perspective, informed by their social position and communicated chiefly and emotively through their empathic distress over lynching and the spread of racial oppression.

## "Moral Feeling": White Women Anti-imperialists

In *Republic or Empire* (1972), one of the most thorough histories of the anti-imperialist movement to date, Daniel B. Schirmer notes the expansive outreach of the Boston reformers to obtain support across race, class, political party, and region—and the limits of that outreach: "[t]he elected leadership of the Anti-Imperialist League gave evidence of this policy in all save one respect: it included no women. Evidently even the pressing need for anti-imperialist unity could not subdue this stubborn prejudice" (p. 17-18). Still, women made themselves a presence in the movement from the very first anti-imperialist meeting at Faneuil Hall, where "[t]he papers noted . . . that nearly half the audience were women" (p. 75). Although they were blocked from full membership and thus unable to serve as elected leaders, women were quite active in the AIL behind the scenes and in anti-imperialist causes of their own accord. Most of the women directly involved with the AIL were white and middle class, which enabled them to make significant monetary contributions to the movement. Women's anti-imperialist writing and speeches focused on both the morality of the war in the Philippines and its transgressions against liberty, to which they, like Filipino/as, lacked full access under the U.S. government.

Like black men, white women from the Midwest and the East Coast formed auxiliary organizations of the AIL since they were excluded from full membership.[33] The women's auxiliary of the Boston AIL petitioned other women for support in 1899, appealing, like the white elite men, to their American history and values:

> We, women of the United States, earnestly protest against the war of conquest
> into which our country has been plunged in the Philippine islands. We appeal to
> the Declaration of Independence, which is the moral foundation of the constitu-
> tion you have swore to defend, we reaffirm its weighty words.[34]

Other women's organizations, such as the Women's Christian Temperance
Union (WCTU), the Congress of Mothers, and the Daughters of the American Revolution (DAR), took official anti-imperialist stances and offered their
support to the AIL.[35] Each of these groups worked from their own position
and issues, with the WCTU educating its members on international affairs
and violence in the Philippines, which they attributed to prostitution and
liquor (Papachristou 1990).

Many women used poetry to express their anti-imperialist views. At the
turn of the twentieth century, poetry was a legitimate and powerful public
medium (Harrington 2002; Nelson 2001), just as appropriate for political
expression as letters to the editor and was therefore allotted specific space
in newspapers. Though both women and men expressed their political views
through poems, the less direct format of poetic imagery gave women, who
were still disfranchised citizens, a more conventionally acceptable public
outlet for civic participation. The sentimental lyric of poetry at the time
foregrounded personal emotions, which also allowed women to address
the emotional costs of the war from their perspective, including the loss of
democratic liberty and morality in the face of "criminal aggression." In 1900,
the New England AIL published a volume entitled *Liberty Poems: Inspired
by the Crisis of 1898-1900*, whose publication was underwritten by Mary
Pickering, a substantial AIL donor (Zwick 2005).[36] *Liberty Poems* included
seventy-six anti-imperialist poems, most written by anti-imperialist leaders
and thirteen authored by women, testifying both to the importance of poetry
in allowing emotional expressions of political positions in the movement and
the participation of women.

Social activist and Hull House founder Jane Addams is still cited today
as one of the AIL's most well-known vice presidents.[37] But she also helped
to found the Chicago affiliate of the AIL, and lent her name to the cause
early on when she spoke at the Chicago Liberty Meetings on April 30, 1899.
According to the annual report of the AIL, the meeting, which overflowed the
Central Music Hall, was "attended by some ten thousand people."[38] Adams
opened her speech, which was published as "Democracy or Militarism," by
declaring that "None of us who has been reared and nurtured in America can
be wholly without the democratic instinct. It is not a question with any of us
of having it or not having it; it is merely question of trusting it or not trusting
it." Continuing to focus on national political principles, Addams asked, "Are
we going to trust our democracy, or are we going to weakly imitate the policy

of other governments, which have never claimed democratic basis?" She then argued that "political code" and "moral law" lost all meaning outside of real world relations. But while many anti-imperialists argued for a kind of isolationism, she suggested that the situation in the Philippines must extend "our nationalism into internationalism," for "unless it has thrust forward our patriotism into humanitarianism we cannot meet it." Addams further stated that "peace" cannot be "abstract dogma" but must come as "a rising tide of moral feeling" that engulfs "all pride of conquest." She went on to credit workingmen with having incited the cause for peace and with having the most to lose under a militaristic policy.[39] From her perspective, we can see how white women could be more open to internationalism rather than only focus on a parochial nationalism given their limited access to the government, even as they supported the inclusive ideals of the United States.

If Addams was the most well-known anti-imperialist woman leader, there were also many others lesser known. Josephine Shaw Lowell was the first woman elected vice president of the New York AIL (other prominent members included Andrew Carnegie, Carl Schurz, Mark Twain, William Dean Howell, and Samuel Gompers), in 1901.[40] When individual chapters of the AIL started organizing of their own accord, they also began making exceptions for women like Lowell. Lowell had lived with her husband in military camps during the Civil War and subsequently devoted her life to philanthropic and reform work in New York. Like Addams, she was a seasoned and connected reformer when she joined the anti-imperialist cause.[41]

Well into her sixties, she remained deeply involved in the organization, providing strategic and financial support, and especially, emotional support for her friend, Secretary Edward Ordway.[42] She gave opening and closing remarks at multiple meetings. In her prolific correspondence with Ordway (the most of any anti-imperialist), she humbly made suggestions as to the best and most effective course of action. She agitated for more protests and public demonstrations against imperialism, specifically requesting something akin to what was done during the abolitionist movement.[43] Lowell also wrote newspaper editorials in support of William Jennings Bryan's anti-imperialist presidential campaign,[44] encouraging women to "pray and work to revive in the hearts of the people love of liberty."[45]

One of her favored tactics was gathering petitions with the names of prominent U.S. Americans in supporting particular issues against the imperialist involvement in the Philippines. This became a common practice used by the New York AIL and elsewhere. For instance, the Philadelphia AIL still used *Who's Who of America* by 1902 to determine whom to send their pamphlets.[46] Although she gave considerable time and money to the anti-imperialist cause, she was also aware of Anglo-Saxon gender politics of women's involvement in such activities. Lowell believed that keeping her name off petitions and other public matters would help to gain more support for anti-imperialism than taking credit for her activities. Therefore, she asked to have her name left off many petitions, even though her work had been critical in making them happen.[47] She also feigned ignorance at how much money she was donating so as to convince Ordway to take her frequent and generous donations. Her activism exemplifies the networking practices of AIL leaders who shared the Anglo-Saxon social position (characterized by being white, middle or upper class, progressive, and politically paternalistic). Her racialized and gendered performance of Anglo-Saxonism determined the way she identified and utilized resources as well as her focus on connecting influential white men to the cause.

In nearby Massachusetts, Mary Storer Cobb helped form a chapter of the AIL in Northampton, for which Mary Emma Byrd, professor of astronomy at Smith College, served as secretary,[48] and prepared soldiers to go before the Senate Investigation on Affairs in the Philippines in 1900.[49] Under the pseudonym "A Massachusetts Woman," Helen Wilson published her findings on the military reconcentration policy from a fact-finding mission to the Philippines sponsored by Boston anti-imperialist Fiske Warren.[50] Clemencia Lopez, sister of Sixto Lopez, who was initially the main Filipino contact for U.S. anti-imperialists, also played a significant role in the U.S. movement after 1900.

As early as 1899, Boston anti-imperialist Edward Atkinson noted that having influential women in public leadership roles would help the AIL gain the support of organized women's groups (Hoganson 1998). Herbert Welsh also made efforts to engage women activists, pointing out to AIL President Moorfield Storey that well-known women would be helpful for organizing other women.[51] Although no formal plans were ever made to involve women as a group, over time individual white women were increasingly granted the symbolic office of vice president of the AIL.[52] Women expressed their anti-imperialist views from their social positions and expected gender roles: as moral stewards, mothers of soldiers, and, like men, advocates for democracy. Their poetry and speeches used emotional imagery to mobilize through eliciting empathic connections and to invite their audiences to question the rationales for why Americans were at war in the Philippines.

## AIL OUTREACH

The AIL attempted to obtain support from white laborers and blacks opposed to "race prejudice," especially early in their organizational efforts, rooting their appeals in acknowledgments of how imperialism would affect each group. George S. Boutwell, President of the Boston and then the American

AIL, spoke at labor and union meetings about how the imperialist issue especially affected laborers. In the campaign against the re-election of William McKinley, Boutwell addressed the laboring classes, focusing on the sacrifices they had to make for the unjustified and ongoing war in the Philippines, which continued at an "enormous cost in men and money": "Who are to furnish the men and by what means is the army to be kept in the field? The laboring population must furnish the men, either by voluntary enlistments or through a process of conscription."[53] Asking whether the "unnecessary" war in the Philippines actually roused "patriotism" in anyone and whether "laboring people" were "prepared to accept" either "alternative," he targeted McKinley as a faulty leader for whom laborers paid the price. In another address, Boutwell summarized the AIL's outreach:

> To me the context of 1900 is not doubtful. We are summoning and summoning successfully, the laboring and producing millions from every field of industry, and while we shall appeal to them upon the higher *considerations of justice*, of duty, of *regard for the rights of others*, we shall not hesitate to appeal to the selfish interests of those who are most concerned in preserving for themselves the share of independence and power which the laborers of America have enjoyed.[54]

Characterizing the "higher considerations" of principle above those of "selfish interests" of social position was easy for him as a man of relative privilege, for whom real-world concerns of full representation, "power," and "independence" were not at question. A more charitable reading would suggest that he at least recognized their right to a "share of independence and power." Nevertheless, the underlying strategy included fostering empathic connections that would support justice and the rights of others.

In reaching out to black anti-imperialists, AIL leaders had to take into account their historical loyalty to the Republican Party, the party of Lincoln, the Emancipation Proclamation, and the end of slavery. Asking blacks to vote against McKinley and for Democratic candidate William Jennings Bryan, who had taken racist positions against blacks in the South, was no small request. AIL leaders with historical ties to abolitionism and the Republican Party, such as George Boutwell (in fact one of the founders of the Republican Party), Thomas Wentworth Higginson, and William Lloyd Garrison, Jr., thus made the most public appeals to black voters. In an open letter, they warned that the "imperialistic Republican Party of today is not the liberty-loving party of that name which set the American negro free forty years ago," so black voters were no longer beholden to it, and "henceforth" the "American Negro must . . . think for himself." Summoning the rhetorical power of the Civil War for their side, they stated that "we fought" to "get rid of" the "doctrine" that argued "the natural supremacy of the Anglo-Saxon," and it was "too soon to see such a theory brought up again" to justify a war against "darker races."[55] Another appeal used the lens of racist oppression to suggest that the argument for "race war" hurt not only blacks but also whites. They observed, "Every day in the Philippines is already training our young American soldiers to the habit of thinking that the white man, as such, is the rightful ruler of all other men," for in the letters soldiers wrote home, they called Filipino/as "niggers." "Freedom," these AIL leaders argued, "is to become, for the new Republican Party, a matter of complexion."[56]

White laborers, black men and women, and white women all offered their largely unsolicited support to the cause of anti-imperialism and the AIL. Each group in their own way related their anti-imperialist views to their social position. As such, they also found characteristic ways to argue for empathic connections to the plight of Filipinos/as that molded their version of ethical witnessing.

## Transformative Emotions: Connecting across Differences

Transformative emotional experiences, like experiencing racist violence or protesting it, foster a critical posture toward social structures, or, in Bourdieu and Wacquant's (1992) terms, "an awareness of symbolic violence," and allow for alternative thinking that replaces the *unthinking*, or taken-for-granted, reproduction of the social structure. Understanding the relationship between social position and the obliviousness that accompanies privilege along with emotional openness to recognizing one's blind spots in the transformation of personal views helps explain the expansion of the oppositional consciousness of white anti-imperialists that was originally expressed in the work of black anti-imperialists. The more conventional ideologies of white anti-imperialists attempting ethical witnessing had to expand to acknowledge the points of view of black anti-imperialists and Filipinos/as in order to be sustained.

When actors internalize the arbitrariness of cultural domination as the natural order, blaming themselves or others for their domination, they perpetuate the symbolic violence, which is key to the legitimation of physical violence, often unthinkingly. One would expect anti-imperialist racisms to serve as a kind of symbolic violence in this way, but it is also possible for actors to stake a claim to critical space, or in other words raise their consciousness, such that they can resist symbolic violence. Black anti-imperialists neither denied nor ignored structural domination, but rather used the experience of structural domination to critique the complacent, self-admiring notions of "civilization." Through critical and reflexive analysis of their experiences with civilization, they came to their anti-imperialist views. By sharing their perspective with white anti-imperialists, some of whom were able to empathically connect, they helped lay the groundwork for white anti-imperialists' transformation. which also helped transform the movement as we see especially in the third anti-imperialist campaign.

## Static Emotions: Stonewalling the Experiences of Others' across Differences

In contrast, racist white imperialists and anti-imperialists minimized or ignored the connections between physical violence against Filipinos/as and the increased lynching of blacks. According to Bourdieu (1993), what appears to be merely an emotional tone of indifference and an impulse to forget are crucial to the reproduction of domination through what Jung (2004) refers to as "tacit nonrecognition."[57] This is not just unthinking. Stonewalling is an active stance of indifference and disavowal, which are also crucial to the routine reproduction of domination.

For example, for many whites, the idea of civilization was never seen as a problematic as an organizing system based on racial superiority. Most whites rarely questioned it on a fundamental basis. Furthermore, progressive whites saw democratic practice as part of the march of civilization and its ideals were rarely questioned. Civilization was both ambiguous and so taken-for-granted that everyone, at least vaguely, knew what was meant when invoked. Thus, invoking civilization as a goal could evoke notions of equality and inalienable rights *as well as* justifications for white supremacy. Therefore, civilization discourse was grounds for both connecting across social position as well as stonewalling.

Historically, civilization and democratic practice have been fraught with elitism, racism, and sexism. But these discourses also have justified protests for a more equitable society. The application of democracy was central to both anti-imperialist and imperialist arguments, with the one questioning whether the U.S. had the right to force the Philippines into democracy and the other insisting that an eventual democracy was a benevolent improvement for the Filipinas/os.[58] The social positions of anti-imperialists were particularly central to their views on the traditions of U.S. democracy and its future formation, which were profoundly shaped by anti-imperialist racisms. Social location also determined the material resources and networks through which they were able to express their views and get those views heard. However, imperialists were focused on maintaining the racial status quo, not advocating a social change that would mean a more fully realized racial democracy. In both stances, emotions played a role in mobilization/immobilization, communicating their perspective, and attempts for regulating the perspectives of others.

Although this chapter takes a less traveled path in the political and socio-historical literature by using the case of anti-imperialist thought and the AIL to analyze the relationship between social transformation, empathic emotions, and social positions, I have argued that this path leads us to more thorough understandings of the differing anti-imperialisms and the personal transformation of anti-imperialist leaders in the AIL overtime. Focusing on emotional motivations as well as how those actors articulated their emotions to empathically connect with Filipinos/as facilitates a more dynamic analysis of the constitution of inequalities within the anti-imperialist movement and in the larger political field. This analysis, in turn, establishes how the schisms within the movement unfolded. Understanding emotions as relationally structured and structuring to both facilitates social transformation and social stasis, as in the case of stonewalling through indifference, and can further help to see how key moments of transformation unfold (Sewell 2005), as they did in the presidential election of 1900 the focus of the next chapter.

## NOTES

1. It's worth noting that the 2018 American Sociological Association meeting's theme was "Feeling Race: An Invitation to Explore Racialized Emotions."

2. Some literature on class, race, and gender has addressed emotion—though more often research on emotion has addressed women's experiences quite self-consciously (e.g., Hochschild's [1983] *The Managed Heart*). More recently, historical scholarship has taken up emotion as related to class (Barrett 2002) or ethnicity and race (Diner 1998; Janiewski 1998). Sociological studies of social movements have also contributed to the study of emotion (Berezin 2002; Goodwin, Jasper, and Polletta 2001; Jasper 1998). The interdisciplinary study of emotion has elaborated and deepened understandings of their biological and social characteristics (Denzin 1984; Thoits 1989; Williams 2001). I am solely interested in the social characteristics here.

3. Annual Report of the Anti-Imperialist League, February 10, 1899, Record Books of the Anti-Imperialist League, Vol. 1, Maria Lanzar-Carpio Papers, Hatcher Graduate Library, University of Michigan, Ann Arbor.

4. Ibid.

5. I have not been able to recover enough archival sources to include a section dedicated solely to the anti-imperialist activities of black women. However, I include what I have recovered in the section "Cold Consolation: Black Anti-imperialists."

6. Mrs. Jefferson Davis, *The Arena*. New York, Jan–Jun 1900. This article provides just one example of this line of argument.

7. "Among the Democratic anti-imperialists were presidential aspirant William Jennings Bryan, representative Champ Clark, senators Ben Tillman and Arthur

Gorman, and former cabinet officers Richard Olney and J. Sterling Morton. Republican anti-imperialists included three New England senators, George F. Hoar, Eugene Hale, and Justin Morrill, House Speaker Thomas Brackett Reed, and John Sherman, who served as Secretary of State in 1897–1898 before retiring and entering the ranks of the opposition. . . . The many reformers and political independents who flocked to the banner of anti-imperialism included in their numbers Carl Schurz, E. L. Godkin, Charles Francis Adams, Jr., Moorfield Storey, Gamaliel Bradford, Henry Demarest Lloyd, Jane Addams, and Horace White.

In an age when the general public paid respectful attention to the sayings and doings of university presidents, David Starr Jordan of Stanford lent substantial aid to the anti-imperialists while a more erratic and lukewarm attitude was expressed by Cornell's Jacob G. Schurman, Michigan's James B. Angell, Northwestern's Henry Wade Rogers, and Charles W. Eliot of Harvard. Other academic figures in the movement included Yale's William Graham Sumner, William James and Charles Eliot Norton of Harvard, Hermann von Holst of the University of Chicago, Graham Taylor, Thorstein Veblen, and Bliss Perry. Representing the clergy were Edward Everett Hale, Henry Codman Potter, Henry Van Dyke Charles H. Parkhurst, Theodore Cuyler, and John Lancaster Spalding" (Beisner 1968: x–xii).

8. Letter to Erving Winslow from Jacques Lee. February 23, 1920. Charles Edward Armory Winslow Collection. Yale University Library.

9. John J. Valentine, "Forcible Annexation: Criminal Aggression: Benevolent Assimilation A Question of National Honor-Official Documents for Future Historians." San Francisco, CA, 1899.

10. "Throwing Washington Overboard." *The People*, June 28, 1898.

11. Either way, anti-imperialist leaders used their reports as sources of information to learn of the situation in the Philippines.

12. *Soldiers' Letters: Being Materials for the History of a War of Criminal Aggression* (N.p.: Anti-Imperialist League, 1899). Anti-Imperialist League Papers, Swarthmore Peace Collection.

13. Although this was surely also a point of pride for many of the family and friends of soldiers, admiring them for what they symbolized to the nation.

14. Samuel Gompers, "Imperialism-Its Dangers and Wrongs." October 18, 1898. William Jennings Bryan et al., *Republic or Empire? The Philippine Question.* Chicago: The Independence Co., 1899.

15. "Capitalist Civilization." *Social Democratic Herald,* March 25, 1899.

16. "100,000 More: Need for More Butchers to Slaughter Philipinos [*sic*], Wholesale Murderers Needed," and "Letters from Soldiers." *Workers Call,* April 22, 1899.

17. "We are Savages," and "Sham Soldiers." *American Freeman,* May 28, 1898.

18. "The Cry of the Poor." *American Freeman,* July 30, 1898.

19. "Fighting for Liberty: The Philippine Insurgents Insist on Suspecting Us: Bloody Battle at Manila: Our Boys Fought Splendidly and the Filipinos Left Thousands Dead Upon the Field—Dewey Assisted." *National Labor Tribune,* February 9, 1899; "Iloilo Taken. Further Victory for American Troops Over Filipinos." *National Labor Tribune,* February 16, 1899; "Permanent Army Increase Beaten." *National Labor Tribune,* March 2, 1899; "Labor's Voice of Protest. Agitation Against the

Imperialistic Policy Started. Ringing Circular to the K. of L." *National Labor Tribune.*

20. "A Standing Army" and "War is Hell!" *Journal of the Knights of Labor,* November, 1900.

21. The degree to which they joined anti-imperialist organizations is still in question as the papers for AIL chapters in the west and middle west are not available, if they exist.

22. AIL Meeting Minutes, July 18, 1899. Record Book Volume I, University of Michigan, Maria Lanzar-Carpio Papers.

23. "Negroes Protest." *Boston Globe,* July 18, 1899.

24. *Springfield Republican*, September 7, 1900. "Immortal Doctrines of Liberty Ably Set Out by a Colored Man The Effect of Imperialism Upon the Negro Race." In *The Anti-Imperialist Reader: Volume I From the Mexican War to the Election of 1900,* edited by Philip S. Foner and Richard C. Winchester.

25. Letter dated May 14, 1901, Box 1, Edward Ordway papers, New York Public Library.

26. *Christian Recorder,* February 9, 1899. "Filipinos' Troubles." In *The Anti-Imperialist Reader: Volume I From the Mexican War to the Election of 1900*, edited by Philip S. Foner and Richard C. Winchester.

27. "The Negro Should Not Enter the Army." *Voice of Missions 7,* May 1, 1899; *The Freeman,* October 21, 1899. "Colored Soldiers Should Not Fight in the Philippine War." In *The Anti-Imperialist Reader: Volume I From the Mexican War to the Election of 1900*, edited by Philip S. Foner and Richard C. Winchester.

28. *Christian Recorder*, June 29, 1899. "Let the Negro Protest." In *The Anti-Imperialist Reader: Volume I From the Mexican War to the Election of 1900*, edited by Philip S. Foner and Richard C. Winchester.

29. "Colored Troops in the Philippines." *Washington Post,* June 19, 1899.

30. H.T. Johnson, "The Black Man's Burden." [AME] *The Christian Recorder,* March 1899.

31. Alice Smith-Travers, "The White Man's Burden." *The Freeman* (Indianapolis), March 4, 1899.

32. *The Colored American,* April 8, 1899. "An Unjust War." In *The Anti-Imperialist Reader: Volume I From the Mexican War to the Election of 1900*, edited by Philip S. Foner and Richard C. Winchester.

33. Jim Zwick, "Illinois Women's Anti-Imperialist League," and "Women's Auxiliary of the Anti-Imperialist League." http://www.boondocksnet.com/ai/people/illinois_womens_ail.html. Printed November 2006.

34. Women's Auxiliary of the Anti-Imperialist League, "Women Make an Appeal/ In Behalf of the Foundation Principles of the Republic." *Springfield Republican,* May 30, 1899.

35. Moorfield Storey Papers, Library of Congress; Edward Ordway Papers, Manuscripts Division, New York Public Library; Record Book Vol. I, Anti-Imperialist League, Maria Lanzar-Carpio Papers, Hatcher Graduate Library, University of Michigan, Ann Arbor.

36. Jim Zwick compiled "Ladies for Liberty: Women's Poems Against Imperialism and War" dedicated to Mary G. W. Pickering, who "paid the entire expense of publishing the [*Liberty Poems* volume]." Jim Zwick, "Ladies for Liberty: Women's Poems against Imperialism and War." http://www.boondocksnet.com/ail/lit/powe ms_by_women.html. Printed in November, 2006.

37. Other recognizable names of women involved with the AIL or anti-imperialist writings include Mary Emma Byrd, Alice Thatcher Post, Lucia Ames Mead, Fanny Garrison Villard, Elsie Clew Parsons, and Caroline Pemberton.

38. Report of the Secretary of the Anti-Imperialist League, Record Books of the Anti-Imperialist League, Vol. 1 (1899), Maria Lanzar-Carpio Papers, Hatcher Graduate Library, University of Michigan, Ann Arbor.

39. Jane Addams, "Democracy or Militarism." *The Chicago Liberty Meeting: Liberty Tracts, Vol I,* April 30, 1899. Central Anti-Imperialist League: Chicago.

40. Anti-Imperialist League Papers, Swarthmore Peace Collection, Swarthmore College.

41. Newspaper clipping, undated. Herbert Welsh Papers, Special Collections, Hatcher Graduate Library, University of Michigan.

42. Edward Ordway Papers, Manuscripts Division, New York Public Library.

43. Edward Ordway Papers, Manuscripts Division, New York Public Library.

44. Josephine Shaw Lowell, "Two Reasons in Favor of the Election of William Jennings Bryan." *City and State,* September 13, 1900.

45. Josephine Shaw Lowell, "What Shall It Profit a Man or a Nation?" *The Public 3,* November 3, 1900.

46. Box 61. Herbert Welsh Papers, Historical Society of Pennsylvania.

47. Ibid.

48. Jim Zwick, "Suffrage and Self-Determination: Women in the Debate About Imperialism." http://www.boondocksnet.com/ai/wj/In; Jim Zwick, ed. *Anti-Imperialism in the United States, 1898–1935.* http://www.boondocksnet.com/ai/ (September 8, 2005).

49. Mary Storer Cobb Papers, Massachusetts Historical Society.

50. "A Massachusetts Woman in the Philippines."

51. Letter dated February 4, 1902, Box 1, MSLOC.

52. Maria Lanzar-Carpio, *The Anti-Imperialist League.* University of Michigan, Dissertation, 1928.

53. George S. Boutwell, *Address to the Laboring and Producing Classes of the United States.* Chicago: American Anti-Imperialist League, 1900.

54. George S. Boutwell, "The President's Policy-War and Conquest Abroad, Degradation of Labor at Home." *Liberty Tracts,* No. 7. Chicago: American Anti-Imperialist League, 1900.

55. Thomas Wentworth Higginson, William Lloyd Garrison, and George S. Boutwell, "To Colored Voters." *Chicago Broad Ax,* October 27, 1900, 1.

56. Thomas Wentworth Higginson, William Lloyd Garrison, and George S. Boutwell. "Address to the Colored People of the United States." *Voice of Missions* 8, November 1, 1900.

57. A common critique of Bourdieu's theories is his lack of attention to social transformation, and, following, his over-deterministic analyses. Unlike Jeffrey Alexander (1995), I do not think this is necessarily a fatal flaw in his theories. Some actors, as part of their habitus, consider themselves to be agents of influence and are highly active in the field of opinion. Anti-imperialist leaders were such agents. Additionally, sometimes efforts to reproduce social structures are at odds with each other. This was the case for anti-imperialists concerned with preserving democratic practice and the Constitution of the United States and imperialists concerned with expanding U.S. control and influence abroad. Agents become involved in the field of opinion and put forth counter-hegemonic arguments. The particular arguments of these actors derive from social position and their collective tenor of discourse stems from emotional excitement.

58. These arguments formed a "field of opinion" (Bourdieu 1993), designating a material outlet for tensions between contradictory understandings of an event or policy. The field of opinion is where "heterodoxy," or the counter-hegemonic discourse that challenges the normalization of "doxa," and where "orthodoxy," or the hegemonic discourse of the status quo trying to protect that which preserves the dominant order of things, take place.

## Chapter 2

# Sacred Democracy and the Presidential Election of 1900

Jane Addams addressed the crowd in the historic Central Music Hall at the Chicago Liberty Meetings in April 1899. Addams was the headliner for her day. She stated, "To 'protect the weak' has always been the excuse of the ruler and tax-gatherer, the chief, the king, the baron; and now, at last, of 'the white man.' "[1] Throughout the speech, she made clear that she believed there was a direct link between despotism, white "superiority," and benevolent assimilation. The Liberty Meetings were held over the course of a few days and with well-respected, anti-imperialist leaders speaking to the crowds. Addams was the only woman. The AIL reported that over 10,000 people attended the meetings, bringing the political position of anti-imperialism to a bona fide political movement. At the same time as the Liberty Meetings, AIL leaders also worked to organize anti-imperialist constituents behind a single presidential candidate, as this chapter outlines. Because of the competing political camps within the movement, no single candidate could make everyone happy. Their challenge was to figure out who could get the most votes and have the best possibility of defeating McKinley. Therefore, they strategically chose to focus on the continued mobilization of the movement around the status and appeal of their leaders.

Over the course of the self-identified anti-imperialist movement, anti-imperialists organized around three major campaigns: defeating the Treaty of Paris and nullifying the BAP, beating imperialist President William McKinley in the presidential election of 1900, and informing the American people about what was happening in the Philippines. Each of these campaigns marked a different stage in the development, character, and constituencies of the movement. This chapter covers the more commonly known second campaign and the trials and tribulations of working to elect William Jennings Bryan as President. A sense of responsibility as citizens and ideas of civilization shaped the choices and constraints that characterized *the network-ing practices* of the White Anglo-Saxon anti-imperialist leadership, which are the central focus of this chapter. As part of their elitist social position, they recognized and utilized the power of networks and reputations to wield influ-ence, and their core beliefs compelled them to focus their activism on persons with more influence in government.

However, chapter 1 showed how anti-imperialist supporters came from all strata of society and were motivated to fight imperialism for different, often competing, reasons. For instance, anti-imperialist black men and women, white women, political radicals, and laborers argued against imperialism through varying empathic appeals that connected to the plight of Filipinos/as with positions that foregrounded the injustice of the violence, especially the racism involved with the violence. Meanwhile, the appeals of white male AIL leaders were based on abstract principles, namely the contradictions between democracy and empire. The AIL nevertheless organized a loose coalition across these ideological differences, through meetings, petitions, and letters-to-the editor, which harnessed the widespread outrage against imperialism. For a moment leading up to the Presidential election of 1900, the coalition grew into a social movement with momentum.

To anti-imperialist leaders, the exceptionalist rhetoric of benevolent assimi-lation policies, which started with the BAP and the Treaty of Paris, was a reprehensible discredit to the United States. In fact, imperialism only expanded the most abusive parts of America's political traditions. Yet inescapably, exceptionalism was embedded in ideas of civilization that informed AIL strate-gies in each of their three major campaigns. Therefore, I think it is important to go beyond questioning whether aspirations and claims to exceptionalism is simply good or bad—after all, sometimes being mediocre or among the aver-age is nothing to celebrate—in favor of questioning how it both limited the possibilities of imagination and was creatively used as a tool for liberation. The contradictory positions within the anti-imperialist coalition forced its members to compromise with each other if they hoped to obtain their goals. The AIL leadership's whitewashed notion of civilization ultimately kept black men and white labor voters both uninspired by the movement and at the margins. This whitewashed idea of civilization also solidified a core group of white activists with a shared worldview of democratic representation.

Civilization discourses included ambiguous, polysemic cultural ideas about the morals and values of societal institutions. In turn, civilization framed the emotional sentiments that imbued debates over imperialism with a tone of moralism. For imperialists, this tone stemmed from ideologies of racial hierarchy. Imperialist leaders practiced an expansive paternalistic ide-ology of civilization that focused on the "progress" of racialized subjects. This imperialist ideology manifested policies that extended U.S.-style educa-tion to inform and to civilize (whether it was blacks in the South, American

Indians in the West, or Filipino/as in the Philippines). Such sentiments coincided with their domineering spirit, enacted through regulating emotions of stonewalling that included indifference, aloofness, arrogance, and contempt, which was accepted and expected when dealing with the demands and requests of nonwhite subjects. For white American imperialists, their own supposed superiority was the foundation of their politics in the Philippines so maintaining their standards for civilization in their own interests went without question (Jung 2004). This was the routine part of their social reproduction of U.S. state racism. Benevolence, however, was a worthwhile by-product that furthered their beliefs in their own white American exceptionalism. A multicultural democracy was nowhere on their radar.

The moralistic tone of the anti-imperialist leaders emerged out of an ideological conviction in U.S. democracy that transcended party politics. As fully enfranchised white men, anti-imperialist leaders held the ideals of democratic practice as sacred, meaning it was a belief that not only went beyond party politics but also transcended the everyday competitions of political belief or societal status. They also fervently believed in their *responsibility as citizens* to maintain and protect democratic governance. If they were not victims nor perpetrators of imperialism, they could only hope to be rescuers of democracy.

Therefore, against the imperialist push to extend civilization, progressive anti-imperialists developed anti-imperialist doctrines for civil rights, liberty, and freedom rooted in the Declaration of Independence and the Constitution. Some of them even began to develop internationalist arguments for a more inclusive human rights that went beyond nation-state boundaries, eventually coming to the point of arguing for political enfranchisement of nonwhites across U.S. imperialist fields. As self-designated heralds of civilization motivated to do their ethical witnessing, they communicated their feelings of outrage and indignation over the imperialist disregard for democratic practice and principles of republican government to elicit mobilizing emotions in other whites with full citizenship. They used their emotions as resources to help build and sustain the movement. They believed American democracy was in peril and sought to protect their standards for civilization even as imperialism progressed; although the ethical witnessing to Filipino/a subjugation was the AIL leaders bottom-line duty, self-determination was their ultimate goal.

## LOSING RIGHTS AT HOME

In the run-up to the election of 1900, anti-imperialists framed their cause as a defense of democracy, a rhetoric rooted in the ethical witnessing traditions of white abolitionists, guarding self-representation and freedom of speech. As leading anti-imperialist senator George F. Hoar expressed it:

The blood of the slaughtered Filipinos, the blood and the wasted health and life of our own soldiers, is upon the heads of those who have undertaken to buy a people in the market, like sheep, to treat them as lawful prize and booty of war, to impose a government on them without their consent, and to trample under foot not only the people of the Philippine islands, but the principles upon which the American republic itself rests.[2]

The righteousness of the anti-slavery tradition provided roots for fighting violent anti-democratic impulses. Hoar used this descriptive language to emotionally mobilize his contemporaries as well as regulate them through the guilt of culpability if they remained unmoved. In fact, for Hoar, the act of trampling Filipinos equated trampling the principles of the American republic. The sanctity of Filipino life and the sanctity of American democracy were intertwined for progressive Anti-imperialist leaders. As early as March 29, 1899, the AIL in Boston published an official letter by the Massachusetts Senator, George F. Hoar, where he laid out what the anti-imperialists' next course of action, after the defeat of the Treaty of Paris, should be. He stated in part,

I hope every effort will be made to give the people full and accurate knowledge of the facts which are so carefully withheld or perverted by the organs of the imperialistic policy. The information which we get as to the events in the Philippine islands comes almost wholly from sources interested in the prolongation of the war, or from irresponsible and unscrupulous adventurers.[3]

Gathering accurate information on events in the Philippines was tantamount to the AIL's subsequent campaigns. Hoar went on to cite evidence from his own experience regarding the censorship of his words from being sent to the Philippines from Hong Kong. The information presented in the news and government reports of events happening on the other side of the globe was already called into question. After all, the war in the Philippines came on the heels of the Spanish-American War, where the quality of the William Randolph Hearst and Joseph Pulitzer newspapers' stories had also been questioned. Therefore, anti-imperialists also defended democracy at home by opposing the censorship of information going to and from the Philippines.

By spring, letters from soldiers in the Philippines were filtering back to family members (and then making their way to the press) documenting wanton violence against Filipinos as well as the disillusionment of soldiers who had volunteered to fight Spain, not guard Filipinos.[4] In turn, family members of volunteers, already skeptical of the war became increasingly vocal in bringing the troops home from the Philippines (Schirmer 1972). Many anti-imperialists in the Midwest were family of soldiers in the Philippines. In late April 1899, some of these women in Nebraska sent a telegram, intercepted by the censor, telling their soldiers, sons and husbands, not to reenlist.[5]

Upon learning from what he deemed "good authority" that family members of a Nebraska regiment were not able to send letters to their soldiers via U.S. mail, Edward Atkinson hatched a plan to test the suspected censorship.[6] Already one of the more daring anti-imperialists, Atkinson set out to test the mail system by sending a letter to Secretary of War Russell Alger requesting to send pamphlets entitled "The Hell of War," "The Cost of a National Crime," and "Criminal Aggression" to the officers and privates in the Philippines. He received no reply. In the meantime, he went ahead and sent the pamphlets to Admiral Dewey, President J. G. Schurman (Cornell University) and Professor Dean C. Worcester (University of Michigan), who were both members of President McKinley's First Philippine Commission, General E. Otis, General Lawton, General Miller, and J. W. Bass (correspondent for *Harper's Weekly*). All the pamphlets were seized.

Writing to Secretary of the Treasury Lyman Gage, Atkinson said he had not yet contacted soldiers as accused, but that he found it a good suggestion (Schirmer 1972). Atkinson notified the Boston press of his plan to send the pamphlets directly to the soldiers at the same time as he notified the Executive Committee of the AIL. Behind the scenes, the AIL leadership discussed how to deal with Atkinson as a public relations problem. They soon announced that he had acted at his own behest and not in his capacity as an AIL vice president. Atkinson learned through the press that the Attorney General was going to charge him with *treason* and the Postmaster General planned to seize his pamphlets again. These developments sparked another furious debate in the press over censorship at home as well as what constituted "seditious" acts.

In a letter to the Attorney General on May 5, Atkinson stated that "profound indignation" was the cause of his actions:

> Moved by a sense of profound indignation at such a state of affairs [censorship] and for the purpose of ascertaining whatever or not the United States mails were or were not open to the citizens of the United States residing in Manila, I addressed at once on April 22nd a letter to the Secretary of War.

Then he firmly asserted his determination to continue in his efforts:

> It is said that the circulation of these pamphlets in the United States will be permitted. I shall continue to use the United States mail for their transmission in this country not as a matter of permission but as a matter of right.[7]

As a prominent white man granted the formal and informal rights of a full citizen, Atkinson communicated his indignation and how this outrage had mobilized him to act to protect his rights and the rights of other citizens in practice. His emotional expressions, his "doings and sayings," were also regulating in that they were designed to test the limits of rights and elicit outrage in others if it proved that U.S. citizens were in fact losing their rights at home. His own shock over censorship led him literally to push the envelope to see how far it would safely go, as he geared his behavior to protecting the right to free speech.

In a letter to the *New York Times*, Atkinson said that he had not anticipated much interest in his pamphlets, given the "excited state of the public mind" in support of war, but 60,000 copies of the documents had been put in circulation since the beginning of the controversy, and he expected that number to rise to 100,000.[8] Given the debate in the press, he continued, he no longer needed to send pamphlets to soldiers in the Philippines as they could gather their content from the coverage of the controversy in the *Times*—an ironic comment because the *Times* had sided with the government in labeling him a disloyal traitor.

Atkinson made much of this irony. After that article in the *Times*, the administration soon pulled back on its persecution of Atkinson, becoming aware that they were doing more to publicize his anti-imperialist works than simply ignoring him would. In a June 8, 1899, letter to subscribers of the "Anti-Imperialist," a periodical Atkinson started, he wrote, "There has been a sudden cessation of the attack of the Administration papers upon myself personally, which I regret. I think it had become evident that the more bitter this attack the wider the influence of my own work."[9] If Atkinson had at first felt ostracized and abandoned by his fellow anti-imperialists, he soon received letters of support praising him for moral leadership and courage.

In fact, Atkinson received letters requesting his pamphlets and supporting "the noble stand which [he had] taken against 'Criminal Aggression' "[10] from eighteen different women, many offering donations to the anti-imperialist cause as well as offering to circulate the pamphlets. This is worth noting as no other AIL member had so much support from women over a particular issue as Atkinson did over the issue of freedom of speech. While women were citizens, they did not yet have the right to vote. Supporting leaders, like Atkinson, was one way to exercise their citizenship. Additionally, newspapers printed letters to the editor from men in support of Atkinson. In the end, Atkinson's "radical" tactics (as the executive committee lamented) communicated his outrage at the breech of rights involved in censorship. Atkinson's intervention revealed how imperialism threatened not only the civil rights of Filipinos/as, but also the civil rights of U.S. citizens at home. Indeed, it struck to the heart of the country's core democratic institutions.

His intervention also revealed the initial conservatism and networking preferences of the AIL leadership, as they initially distanced themselves from him as an organization. The New England elites, especially those with significant influence like Charles F. Adams, Jr., were greatly averse to the kind of attention Atkinson generated, preferring to work more quietly through established political channels. Once they saw the public supporthe actually garnered for the AIL, however, the rest of the leadership changed their tune and came out in support of Atkinson.

After the Atkinson Affair blew over came another instance in mid-July of 1899. U.S. newspaper correspondents in the Philippines began making public claims that the military in the Philippines was also censoring news sent back to the United States. Not only were they suppressing information, they were also framing the news with an unlikely optimism about the Philippine War (Foner and Winchester 1984). Correspondents in Manila from the *New York Herald, New York Sun, Chicago Record, Chicago Tribune,* the *Associated Press,* and the Publishers' and Scripps-McRae press associations, "sent, by way of Hong Kong" a statement about the military situation and the military censorship of the situation in Manila.

> We believe that owing to official dispatches from Manila, made public at Washington, the people of the United States have not received a correct impression of the situation in the Philippines, and that the dispatches presented an ultra-optimistic view not shared by the general officers in the field.
>
> We believe these dispatches incorrectly represented existing conditions among the Filipinos respecting internal dissension and demoralization resulting from the American campaign and the brigand character of their army.
>
> We believe the dispatches err in the declaration 'that the situation is well in hand,' and the assumption that the insurrection can be speedily ended without a greatly increased force.
>
> We think the tenacity and purpose of the Filipinos have been underestimated and that the statements are unfounded that the volunteers are willing to give further service.
>
> The censorship has compelled us to participate in this misrepresentation by excising or altering uncontroverted statements and facts on the plea, as General Otis stated, "that they would alarm the people at home,' or 'have the people in the United States by the ears."
>
> Specifications: The prohibitions to send hospital reports and the number of heat prostrations in the field; the suppression of full reports of field operations in the event of their failure; systematic minimization of naval operations, and the prohibition to send complete reports of the situation.[11]

The anti-imperialist press responded to the correspondents' protests by widely condemning the censorship in Manila. The *Springfield Republican,* one of the most outspoken and consistent anti-imperialist papers, and the Baltimore *American,* reported on the censorship by the administration in October of 1899.[12] Having already suspected that the news reported in the United States on the Philippines was questionable, anti-imperialists were ready to assess the situation through the best sources at their disposal, soldiers returning from the Philippines. At the same time, they had to mobilize anti-imperialist voters around an anti-imperialist candidate for president if they wanted to truly stop U.S. Empire in the Philippines.

## DETERMINING AN ANTI-IMPERIALIST
## PRESIDENTIAL CANDIDATE

On the heels of another censorship scandal, they made a large and concerted push for an anti-imperialist presidential candidate. The AIL also focused on keeping anti-imperialists mobilized, through letters soliciting funds, petitions, and networking. An initially successful strategy was to target reputable individuals in the hopes of using their influence to get others to join the cause. Along with the texts of letters, speeches, and treatises, the AIL published lists of signatories, speakers, authors, and its vice presidents. *The number of names lent legitimacy to the cause, but so did the names themselves, for well-respected and influential names helped the AIL obtain its own reputation and influence.*

This strategy also had a price. By focusing on members with influence and respectability, the AIL lost its potential to inspire a wider base of blacks, labor, and more women. With this strategy, the AIL leadership focused and limited their intended audience to elite white men like themselves. Networking with each other and arguing with other prominent white men, they excluded logical allies. It is worth reminding, however, that many, if not most, of these allies were disenfranchised.

Previous studies of the anti-imperialist movement have established the importance of the second AIL campaign during which anti-imperialists were especially active in the political arena, as befits a presidential campaign. It was during this second campaign that they strategically sought support from highly respected citizens to bolster the influence of the movement and the organization (Beisner 1968, 1970, 1973; Foner 1958; Schirmer 1972; Tompkins 1970; Welch Jr. 1979). These studies duly note the reputations, the public influence, as well as the wealth of many AIL members and vice presidents. However, they have only briefly discussed the self-conscious strategy of networking in the AIL, often taking for granted the cultural formation of the AIL and then dismissing it as an elitist organization within the larger field of conflicting anti-imperialist sentiments (Kramer 2006).

If we turn a sociological lens onto the AIL's initial organizing strategy, we see that its tactics emerged out of the intersectionality of race, class, and gender positions of its leaders. A masculinist Anglo-Saxon habitus delimited the New England leadership's conceptions of activism *and* vision for democracy. Anglo-Saxon rapprochement between Britain and the United States has often been described as a shared "race instinct" (Miller 1982), or, to put it another way, a sense of a racial-ethnic "in-group" posed against a racial-ethnic "out-group" that excludes everyone else. Anglo-Saxonism was thus ineffective in uniting "white" working classes, including immigrants, who were not included in the Anglo-Saxon class and lineage. In fact, this sense of frater-nity between Anglo-Saxons acted as a deterrent for other aspiring whites (Jacobson 1995; Roediger 2005). In contrast, Anglo-Saxonism worked as an implicit racial justification for imperialism among "English-speaking" people (Dyer 1980), who often took it for granted that they were the pinnacle of civilization (Beisel and Kay 2004). However, the appeal to democracy and the principles of the Constitution, were by definition more inclusive, and therefore, had greater appeal across the board. Like imperialists, they also demonstrated contradictions around elitism and anti-imperialism. However, including the contradictions gave other groups like white women, black women and men, and working-class whites an opening in which they could find common cause with the most influential organization with the greatest hope to stop imperialism. They had no other promising alternatives anyway. It was these latter groups sharing their perspective with the elitist leadership that forged the most lasting transformations of the anti-imperialists, which is covered in third campaign.

But in the second campaign, the AIL initially had a two-pronged organiz-ing strategy. One, as mentioned, centered on networking with other Ameri-cans of significant political influence. Much of their activism on this front entailed rhetorical arguments presented in broadsides meant to persuade other educated, influential whites. But this tactic designed to engage enfranchised citizens increasingly excluded working-class whites and blacks as a target audience, further marginalizing them within the movement. Trying to influ-ence individuals with the power to guide government policies through the vote made sense, but this tactic frayed the fabric of an already weak alliance between anti-imperialists by ignoring their most passionate, committed sym-pathizers. However, had the AIL targeted black women and men and white women, they would have lost support from the racist, sexist, elitist wing of anti-imperialist supporters. Whether or not they liked the choices, they did choose to foster relationships with whites with influence and hoped the masses would follow their lead without other plausible choices of organiza-tional leadership.

The second tactic was to educate the American public on the U.S. govern-ment's intentions for the Philippines by disseminating accurate information. This was clear in Hoar's admonishment of censorship after the defeat of the Treaty of Paris, the Atkinson Affair with mailing the broadsides, and the cen-sorship of the press in Manila. As discussed in chapter 1, many AIL leaders were regarded as Mugwumps, political independents who voted according to single issues rather than party politics and thus were known for crossing party lines. They used their reputations and political unpredictability to help set political agendas according to what they saw as the most pressing issues. In this case, they saw the most pressing issues as better information. While this goal was broadly aimed, the constitution of the leadership pushing it affected the constitution of the movement as a whole.

Many Mugwumps had previously been Republicans (including some party founders like AIL President George S. Boutwell), but they no longer saw the Republican Party as the party of Lincoln, so they crossed party lines to vote their consciences, even if only to make a symbolic point about democratic governance. Anti-imperialist leaders in Congress included both staunch Democrats, such as Senator Edward Carmack of Tennessee, and Republicans, like Senator George Hoar. Although many anti-imperialists were Boston Brahmins, Schirmer (1972) notes that "the Anti-Imperialist League, in the composition of its leadership at least, reflected efforts to set on foot a loose coalition of diverse social forces" (p. 17), as evidenced by the presence of labor, clergy, lawyers, and professors. Notably, all these figures were enfranchised white men, which was further highlighted as the movement grew.

Seeking to expand their base and gather more support from the Midwest, the AIL moved its headquarters from New England to Chicago after the Liberty Meetings in 1899, referenced at the beginning of the chapter. These Liberty Meetings took place on after the ratification of the Treaty of Paris, which anti-imperialists had fearfully anticipated given the recent expansion of the intra-imperial field with the annexation of Samoa and then Hawai'i in 1898 (Beisner 1968). From the meeting at the Central Music Hall emerged the Central AIL. After another national meeting in Chicago in October, the New England and Central AILs merged into the American AIL to maximize the benefits of social networks across regions. This was the apex of its national appeal.

The main vehicles for the AIL's anti-imperialist arguments were broadsides (lengthy pamphlets, often numbering around 100 pages) and speeches pleading the cause of democracy and the legacy of freedom. Titling these texts with antitheses, anti-imperialist progressives made the case that the United States had to choose between "Liberty or Despotism," "Republic or Empire," "Democracy or Tyranny," and "Democracy or Militarism."[13] And while this rhetoric was powerful, it worked best for a specific audience: those who shared the social position of the AIL's elite leadership, with its passion for democracy and belief in civilization.

A few notable individual anti-imperialist leaders made efforts to organize beyond their social networks. Erving Winslow in Boston attempted to organize working-class and Irish groups to take strong anti-imperialist stances, with the result that these groups passed anti-imperialist resolutions and did little else (Welch Jr. 1979). Herbert Welsh commented on the importance of organizing women, by which he meant getting *prominent* women to organize for anti-imperialist causes, but this tactic left white women only partially included as anti-imperialists (Murphy 2009) and furthered anti-imperialist practices that emphasized elites speaking to other elites.[14] Meanwhile, in the South, the greatest thrust of anti-imperialists were motivated by white supremacist racism (Lasch 1973), which, in turn, kept the full inclusion of black anti-imperialists off the wider anti-imperialist agenda, even though some of the key AIL leaders were founders of the NAACP (see Conclusion). Ultimately, leaders continued to engage reformist middle-class or upper-class white men like themselves, and likely voters. Rather than including marginalized citizens as full members, they sought their support in segregated organizations.

In other words, only in the narrowest sense did anti-imperialist leaders try to obtain the broadest base. Instead of addressing the concerns about racism, war, workers, and violence that motivated white and black women, black men, and the working classes, anti-imperialists tried to unify sympathizers around a simple political opposition to imperialism in order to get the widest range of elite white male supporters. As principled as the AIL leaders claimed to be, they were also extremely calculating.

Anti-imperialist politics were by definition reactive and oppositional. Some anti-imperialist leaders, like Charles Francis Adams, Jr., found this problematic (Beisner 1968). Keenly aware of their reputations, elitist anti-imperialist leaders like Adams (a descendant of the Adams presidents) carefully guarded them. For Adams in particular, focusing the movement in negative terms and orienting it toward the past seemed futile. Having something to reach for and dream about, seemed to him more inspirational. But the anti-imperialists whose politics and arguments looked toward the future were the laborers, women, blacks, and socialists marginalized by the elite leadership, including Adams. The elite anti-imperialist arguments that invoked the democratic traditions of the past did not appeal to many workers or small farmers (Markowitz 1976), who had never fully been included in U.S. practices of democracy. Thus, one of the major AIL networking strategies actually worked against their goal of increasing the anti-imperialist membership, resulting in missed opportunities to create a truly diverse interracial movement.

## Dollars or Duty: Selecting a Presidential Candidate

The search for an anti-imperialist presidential candidate unveiled the depth of divisions between anti-imperialists. As Congressional debates about the war in the Philippines continued into 1900, the upcoming presidential election came into focus. Debates over candidates became the most important field for hashing out U.S. imperialist policies, and anti-imperialists began to draw lines and take sides. From a distance of over a century, the choice might seem simple: the populist Democratic presidential candidate William Jennings Bryan came down on the side of anti-imperialism, while President McKinley, up for re-election as the Republican candidate, maintained his support for imperialism and benevolent assimilation. However, party histories and traditions complicated the situation.

In a speech on February 16, 1899, McKinley laid down his imperialist position, expressed via "sacred" assertions of "progress and civilization," "God," and "trust":

> The Philippines, like Cuba and Porto Rico, were intrusted [*sic*] to our hands by the war, and to that great trust, under the providence of God and in the name of human progress and civilization, we are committed. It is a trust we have not sought; it is a trust from which we will not flinch.

Invoking God, McKinley suggested the righteousness of the imperialist mission:

> Congress can declare war, but a higher Power decrees its bounds and fixes its relations and responsibilities. The President can direct the movements of soldiers in the field and fleets upon the sea, but he cannot foresee the close of such movements or prescribe their limits.

Finally bringing in the question of Filipinos/as, he insisted upon the benevolent motivations of imperialism, disingenuously going so far as to disavow politics and economics:

> Could we, after freeing the Filipinos from the domination of Spain, have left them without government and without power to protect life or property or to perform the international obligations essential to an independent state? Could we have left them in a state of anarchy and justified ourselves in our own consciences or before the tribunal of mankind?
>
> Our concern was not for territory or trade or empire, but for the people whose interests and destiny, without our willing it, had been put in our hands.

McKinley went on to deride the idea of asking Filipina/os to consent to being liberated from Spain, using the familiar elite language of moral superiority and utter lack of humility:

> We were obeying a higher moral obligation, which rested on us and which did not require anybody's consent. We were doing our duty by them, as God gave us the light to see our duty, with the consent of our own consciences and with the approval of civilization.[15]

Though Republican anti-imperialists themselves often claimed that same moral superiority, when McKinley said, "We . . .did not require anybody's consent," he was no longer an option for them. They were forced by principle to look elsewhere.

On the other side, Bryan's anti-imperialist speeches were emotive and convincing. In 1898 at a speech in Lincoln, Nebraska, he directly named the economic motivations of imperialism, critiqued the imperialist rhetoric of "duty," and evoked democracy and the American Revolution in support of "rights" beyond the borders of the United States:

> Imperialism finds its inspiration in dollars, not in duty. It is not our duty to burden our people with increased taxes in order to give a few speculators an opportunity for exploitation; it is not our duty to sacrifice the best blood of our nation in tropical jungles in an attempt to stifle the very sentiments which have given vitality to American institutions; it is not our duty to deny to the people of the Philippines the rights for which our forefathers fought from Bunker Hill to Yorktown.
>
> Our nation has a mission, but it is to liberate those who are in bondage—not to place shackles upon those who are struggling to be free.[16]

After the ratification of the Treaty of Paris (which, in the end, he actually voted for), Bryan began to suggest alternatives to colonialism and empire:

> The ratification of the treaty, instead of committing the United States to a colonial policy, really clears the way for the recognition of a Philippine republic. [. . .] Could the independence of the Filipinos be secured more easily by diplomacy from a foreign and hostile nation than it can through laws passed by Congress and voicing the sentiments of the American people alone? If independence is more desirable to our people than a colonial policy who is there or what is there to prevent the recognition of Philippine independence? It is absurd to say that the United States can be transformed from a republic into an empire without consulting the voters.[17]

For Bryan, there were multiple possibilities for the Philippines to obtain independence. The United States taking them did not preclude independence from where he stood. However, for the AIL, it was their worst fear, believing that once the United States would allow itself to take the Philippines, it would not easily let them go. Therefore, from the outset, Bryan was not their first choice for a presidential candidate.

Bryan was also deeply problematic for Republican anti-imperialists, both blacks and whites, who were already split between party loyalty and voting for an anti-imperialist candidate. In comparison to the incumbent McKinley, who was able to set the agenda as well as argue that he was the better candidate for putting "lunch in the lunch pail" at home, Bryan offered "ill-advised" support for a single-tax system and the silver standard (Williamson 1934). On top of all this was his racism against blacks. Although Bryan spoke out against U.S. imperialist involvement in the Philippines, he also spoke out against the rights of blacks. This fact ultimately split the black anti-imperialist vote and the votes of those who opposed colonialism abroad and supported the civil rights of blacks at home, forcing them to choose one issue over the other.

Anti-imperialist sympathy coupled with a bitter disappointment in the Republican Party did motivate some blacks to vote for Bryan. A group of black men from Boston, including Archibald Grimke, Louis F. Baldwin, Robert F. Coursey, Napoleon B. Marshall, I.D. Barnett, and R.A. Connell, wrote an open "Address to Colored Citizens," urging them to vote for Bryan despite his racism. Acknowledging that "the duty of colored men" in the presidential election was "beset with difficulties," and that some would claim that their position showed the "basest ingratitude to the [R]epublican party," they argued that in fact the Republican Party owed gratitude to blacks especially the soldiers who helped win the Civil War, and "[the black man] owes the possession of the ballot, as he owes his liberty, then, to himself alone."

Having forsaken traditional loyalties for tradition's sake, they pointed out that the Republicans were just as racist as the Democrats:

> some may further object that northern republicans are better friends to the negro than are northern democrats. To this objection we reply with all confidence that you are totally and absolutely mistaken. Scratch the skin of republican leaders like Hanna, Lodge, Roosevelt, and McKinley and you will find race prejudice close underneath, an invincible belief on their part in the divine right of the Anglo-Saxon to govern the republic and to subjugate darker races to his despotic rule, all their loud professions to the contrary.

Indeed, a Republican administration had done little for their people:

> Have we more rights today than we enjoyed four years ago? Are we as secure in person and property today as we were four years ago under a democratic administration? You know we are not.

Given their belief that white Republicans had abandoned blacks and the past few years had shown only economic and social decline for blacks, they argued that blacks should take a principled stand against "every act of law-lessness and violence against us by whomsoever because of our color," and in so doing, align with the other people of color who shared their concern for freedom:

Let us rise above our slavery to a recreant party and to the level of a great opportunity, a supreme duty to ourselves, to the imperiled liberties of the country, and to suffering humanity, which cries loudly to us for help from the Philippines, from Cuba and from Puerto Rico. For the Filipinos, the Cubans and the Puerto Ricans, like ourselves, fellow-citizens, are and of right ought to be free. A vote for Bryan and Stevenson will begin a new day for ourselves and the republic, a new day of emancipation from the trammels of party, of better understanding with the rest of the people of the land, North as well as South.[18]

They concluded by asking black voters who could not bring themselves to vote for Bryan to stay home rather than support McKinley and Roosevelt, "who embody all that is oppressive and rapacious in the commercial spirit of the nation." Using the term "slavery" to describe the relationship of the black community to the Republican party and hailing colonized peoples as "fellow-citizens" who deserved to be "free," they powerfully rearranged the political coordinates of the previous decades, highlighting racial solidarity and the limits of current political parties.

Another approach to the uncomfortable choice between McKinley and Bryan was to try to find an alternative to both. Dissatisfaction with Bryan led a group of otherwise Republican-leaning anti-imperialists to organize an anti-imperialist third party. In the summer of 1900, the "National Party"[19] organized a special Liberty Convention in Indianapolis to decide on a presidential candidate. Chicago lawyer and anti-imperialist leader Edwin Burritt Smith presided (Tompkins 1970). Boston reformer and attorney Moorfield Storey was asked to consider running for president on the ticket but declined, believing the only way to defeat imperialism was to defeat McKinley, and a third party could not accomplish this feat (Tompkins 1970). Former President, anti-imperialist, and gold standard supporter Grover Cleveland also declined to run. The National Party finally settled on Senator Donelson Caffery of Louisiana, an anti-imperialist with Republican Party values, but soon after he accepted the nomination, he had to withdraw for personal reasons. This heralded the end of the brief existence of the National Party, which never gained substantial anti-imperialist support. Ultimately, the Chicago Liberty Meetings endorsed the Bryan campaign in April 1899 (Foner and Winchester 1984). The rest of the AIL also endorsed Bryan, but qualified the endorsement by affirming its support for full political and civil rights for black citizens in the North and South (Schirmer 1972).

A 1903 memoir, "The Suicide of a Political Infant," closed the book on the National Party but reminded readers of its impetus:

The two great parties having declared free silver and not Imperialism the issue, the small but respectable minority who set Imperialism first were confronted by a dilemma. It is interesting to see how, in such a crisis, men who agreed wholly in principle, differed widely in action. Senator George F. Hoar, who had denounced Imperialism with a wide-sweeping eloquence that reminded us of Webster and a *moral fervor* that recalled Sumner,—who had voted against every Imperialistic advance, and had characterized, with judicial moderation, the new policy as '*damnable*,' chose nevertheless to stand by the Republican party. On the other hand, many of the leaders of the Anti-Imperialist League, led by Governor Boutwell and Mr. Moorfield Storey, - went to a convention at Indianapolis, on Aug. 14, listened to the warblings of the Prairie Siren, and persuaded themselves that the country could be *saved* by electing Mr. Bryan.[20]

More than anything, most anti-imperialists wanted a viable anti-imperialist candidate, but unfortunately that wasn't enough for the rest of the country. Their belief in the sacredness of democracy came through strongly in the religious tone of the language with which the National party communicated their position.

There were in fact numerous issues at play in the election of 1900. For Bryan, the contest was "democracy against plutocracy, the man against the dollar, republic against empire" (Schirmer 1972: 208). McKinley seemed to agree that the election was about foreign policy, but his advisor Mark Hanna framed the issue as a robust economy in which workers were earning better wages under Republicans than in previous Democratic administrations (Beisner 1968; Schirmer 1972). Although Senator Hoar was a leading anti-imperialist, he was still a Republican party man, so he campaigned against Bryan and the southern Democrats' policy of disfranchising black voters (Schirmer 1972). Anti-imperialists countered that McKinley's imperialist policies fostered racism at home and abroad (Schirmer 1972). Samuel Gompers told a vice president of the American Federation of Labor not to commit to either Bryan or McKinley, but to advocate a policy of neutrality between the parties (Schirmer 1972). While most Irish laborers and labor leaders in Boston, such as Patrick Collins, came out in support of Bryan, organized labor never explicitly supported him, although working people generally did (Schirmer 1972).

Given the worsening economic conditions and increased violence resulting from the rescinding of radical Reconstruction policies in the Democratic-controlled South, McKinley enjoyed significant black support by default. However, while many black leaders chose to focus solely on domestic politics and economic advancement, a few black anti-imperialist leaders in the North did make appeals to black men to vote against McKinley on the basis of imperialism. These included the "Address to Colored Citizens" noted earlier, as well as speeches by Rev. William H. Scott and C. H. Plummer, the two most prominent black anti-imperialists in Boston, who entreated blacks at a meeting at Faneuil Hall to vote against McKinley, especially in states where they had the majority of votes (Schirmer 1972). Scott also specifically targeted Theodore Roosevelt and his claims that black soldiers were cowards on San Juan Hill, while he took the glory for the achievement of that battle (Schirmer 1972). Despite these appeals, however, the majority of black men

**Figure 2.1 This image from the *Judge* magazine dated November 3, 1900, reads "FOR ONE NEGRO AND AGAINST ANOTHER.** DR. JEKYLL 'BRYAN' AND MR. HYDE 'BRYAN,' illustrating Bryan's political embrace of Filipino suffrage and rejection of suffrage for blacks in the South.

heeded their long-standing allegiances, voting for McKinley and the Republican Party.

## Civil Religion and Civilization

Once white anti-imperialist leaders settled on their candidate, they continued to fervently invoke the legacy of U.S. democracy as sacred, a civil religion. Against the imperialist assertions of the "divine rights" of manifest destiny and McKinley's claims that "Providence" led him to take the Philippines, anti-imperialists used sanctity and morality for their own purposes. As they moved on from the outrage that initially mobilized them, treating democracy as a civil religion helped them articulate and foster their political feelings of honor, integrity, and responsibility in terms of a political covenant between the government and the people. They practiced their civil religion by demonstrating these deeply held beliefs about U.S. democracy through moral and religious language (as in the account of the National Party in "The Suicide of a Political Infant," quoted earlier). But this remained a rhetorical fight for the moral high ground between white elites. The truth of the matter didn't matter in terms of dictating outcomes, similar to lessons we are relearning today. What was more influential for outcomes was the ability to navigate and generate political emotions as well as the inability to foster more empathic connections between the majority of white citizens and Filipinos/as.

Meanwhile, blacks and working-class whites were protesting violence against their people and Filipinas/os. Their social positions led to different rhetorical tactics based on different priorities. As imperialism personally affected anti-imperialists in different ways, the delicate tangles of the alliance continued to unravel.

White anti-imperialist elites in the North fostered a discourse that starkly contrasted a "sacred" democracy and a "profane" imperialism (Alexander and Smith 1993). Performing their devotion to democracy as a civil religion placed them in the same political field as imperialists who professed their "sacrifices" for the white man's burden with missionary zeal. Anti-imperialists and imperialists alike attributed their positions to a transcendent ethos (Welch Jr. 1979), which could not be completely explained. The transcendent ethos manifested in grandiose terms like "manifest destiny," "providence," "progress," "liberty," and "civilization." Practicing civil religion allowed actors to appeal to "progress" and "divine" good on behalf of issues they supported or opposed. Bellah (1992) noted that attempts to neatly define civil religion render it an almost futile term. He argued instead that the inherent contradictions and paradoxes of the term were part of the ambiguity of the moral practices it undergirded.

Neither imperialist nor anti-imperialist leaders questioned the tone of religious fervor in their debates; rather, they endlessly vied over the accuracy and efficacy of their religious arguments. For anti-imperialists, civil religion tied civilization and democracy to social resources that bestowed widespread legitimacy on their principled views about democracy and rights. Imperialists believed the successful future of the republic would rely on expanding territory to expand trade, and the people who came along with the territory were projects for civilizing. Civil religion located the debate over imperialism in the white elite political field, rendering the anti-imperialisms of people of color and working people secondary, further alienating those constituencies. Although this was ethical witnessing, in that they worked to use their resources and privileges to benefit the Filipino/a cause of independence, it was an ethical witnessing that stemmed out of emotional stasis by focusing on a self-referencing elitism.

Even as they made their own sanctimonious arguments, anti-imperialists pounced on McKinley's transcendent appeals to God and Providence, taking every opportunity to point out his hypocrisy. Chicago anti-imperialist Edwin Burritt Smith compiled an entire broadside of maddeningly contradictory quotes from McKinley and his administration, using McKinley against himself and historical arguments. One favorite was what Smith called "The 'Providence of God' Theory," which was a section entirely made up of McKinley quotes that showed how the language of the transcendental and sacred enabled imperialists to avoid personal responsibility for choices they made (even though "responsibility" was one of their favorite claims), as if they were mere servants of "Providence" rather than active agents choosing how to implement imperialist policies. (This brings to mind Trevor Noah's brainchild of the Trump Twitter Presidential Library). One such quote was McKinley's claim in October 1899 that "In the Providence of God, who works in mysterious ways, this great archipelago was put into our lap."[21] The hypocrisies of this providential rhetoric also inspired Robert Stevens Pettet's *Columbia's Apostasy: And other Poems and Essays* (1899), with epigraphs quoted from Proverbs and Revelations and a back cover diagram of "Mystical Numbers: A Key of Providence," which further underscored the absurdity of the imperialist rhetoric.

Senator Albert Beveridge, one of the most active and unapologetic imperialists, couched his arguments in terms that conflated racism and religiosity (Bellah 1992). Though he was a leading imperialist, his extreme racist views on extinction often contradicted the views of more moderate imperialists, as Smith showed in his broadside, taking the opportunity to show contradictions between imperialists. While Admiral Dewey, Secretary Hay, Consul Wildman, and Commissioner Worcester found Filipinos/as capable of self-government, sometimes even more so than Cubans, Beveridge considered them

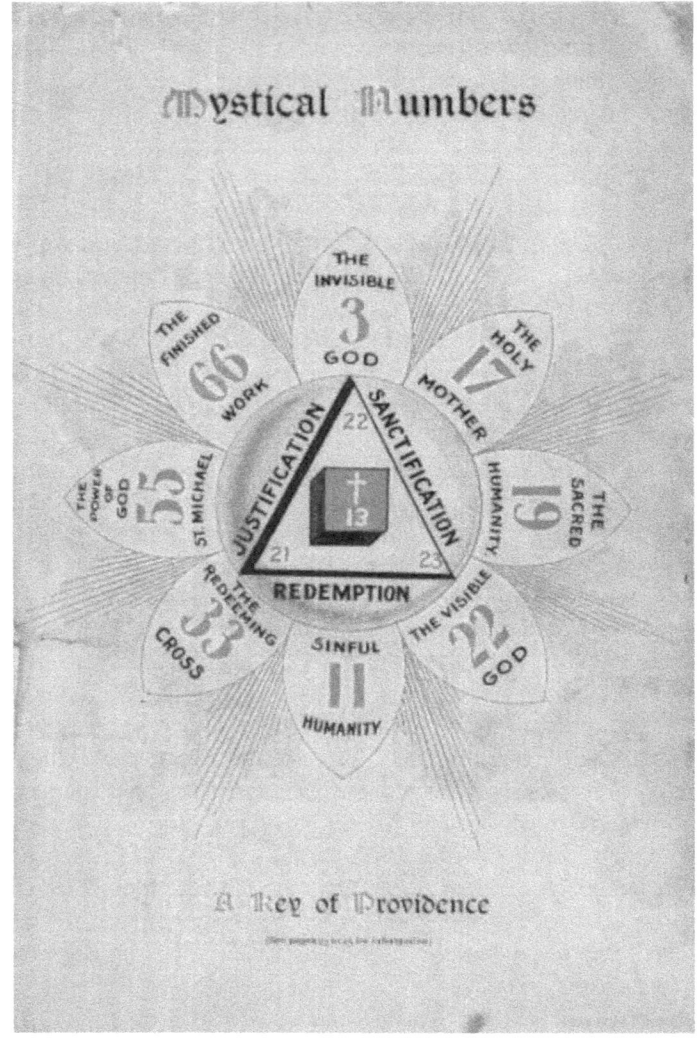

**Figure 2.2 "Mystical Numbers: A Key of Providence."** Back matter to *Columbia's Apostasy: And other Poems and Essays* (1899) by Robert Pettet.

a barbarous race, modified, by three centuries of contact with a decadent race. The Filipino is the South Sea Malay, put through a process of three hundred years of superstition in religion, dishonesty in dealing, disorder in habits of industry, and cruelty, caprice, and corruption in government.[22]

In an address to the Senate in January 1900, after a visit to the Philippines in late 1899, Beveridge surreally conjoined the rhetoric of racism, civilization, and civil religion:

God has not been preparing the English-speaking and Teutonic peoples for a thousand years for nothing but vain and idle self-contemplation and self-admiration. No. He made us master organizers of the world to establish system where chaos reigned. He has given us the spirit of progress to overwhelm the forces of reaction throughout the earth. He has made us adept in government that we may administer government among savage and senile peoples. Were it not for such a force as this the world would relapse into barbarism and night. And of all our race He has marked the American people as His chosen nation to finally lead in the redemption of the world. (as quoted in Bellah 1992)

Beveridge's imperialism was a futuristic vision of the white man's burden, in which God's "chosen nation" had a religious duty to civilize and save the world.

Just after the election, on November 19, 1900, the *Springfield Republican* printed an article that demonstrates how moralism connected to American exceptionalism. The author stated:

Violated moral law sooner or later inflicts its punishment on the violator, in such fashion that he is constrained to acknowledge and repent of the wrong, or else it destroys him. Even favored America can not [*sic*] break with impunity the eternal laws. She is not so great as God.[23]

The Philippine-American War marked one more point at which democratic practice was under dispute among anti-imperialist whites and clearly not radical in its implementation, which alienated and further marginalized black and working-class anti-imperialists. Focusing primarily on the righteousness of their view of democracy, rather than empathic connections to actual humans, undermined the cause. Meanwhile, imperialists used tenets of American democracy to expand the limits of U.S. control and deepen the racialization of state institutions in white supremacy.

## Civilization and "The White Man's Burden"

As the election approached, AIL leaders focused on government officials and voters as their target audience, ignoring most blacks and women. While the anti-imperialist leaders were arguing about civil religion, black men, black women, and white women used their social position to make an intersectional analysis on imperialism's failings for democracy, thus arguing their anti-imperialism on different political, yet overlapping, fields. As the white male elites narrowed their focus to the presidential election, they lost the potential to expand their base given they ignored this activism. For instance, despite the fact that black men had mobilized their own anti-imperialist organization and were prolific in the black press over the relationship between imperialism and race, the AIL did not focus on strengthening these ties. Rather, they saw black anti-imperialist efforts as related to but separate from their own. In contrast, the Negro National Anti-Imperial and Anti-Trust League focused on connecting issues, as its name suggests.

As for white women, two in particular, Jane Addams and Josephine Shaw Lowell, went beyond the typical gendered expectations for women in the AIL because of their influence through their reputations and networks. Addams was a member of the Chicago organization, the American AIL, and is frequently still listed today as one of the AIL's most well-known vice presidents.[24] Addams did lend her name to the cause. She also spoke at the Chicago Liberty Meetings on April 30, 1899. While she supported the anti-imperialist cause, her main efforts remained focused on conditions in Chicago. Lowell worked largely behind the scenes in New York, helping the Secretary of the New York organization, Edward Ordway, organize and strategize. Not only did she help author and circulate anti-imperialist petitions, she also donated generously.

## Women in the Public Debate on Imperialism

Chapter 1 described how women publicly engaged in the debate on imperialism by publishing poems that expressed their anti-imperialist views in newspapers in the metropole as well as letters to the editor in *The Woman's Journal*. Rudyard Kipling's infamous poem advising the United States on involvement in the Philippines, "The White Man's Burden: The United States and the Philippine Islands," which appeared in the February 1899 issue of *McClure's Magazine*, articulated the haughty sentiments of white supremacy and the "duty" to civilize persons of color. It triggered an avalanche of impassioned anti-imperialist poems in response.

Anna Manning Comfort, a leading suffragist, also traced the problem of the "White Man's Burden" across the intra-imperial field, linking lynching, the treatment of Indians, and women's suffrage in her poem, "Home Burdens of Uncle Sam."[25] Some women's poems were included in a volume published in 1900 entitled, *Liberty Poems: Inspired by the Crisis of 1898–1900*, published by the New England AIL. Through poems and letters to the editor, women consistently highlighted the violence being committed in the Philippines and raised the question of women's suffrage by pointing out the hypocrisy of spreading liberty abroad while disenfranchising citizens at home. These women publicly expressed their cynical indignation with regard to "The White Man's Burden," both as women without the vote and as citizens, many of them mothers, with a moral duty as women to show their abhorrence for violence committed in the name of liberty.[26]

**Figure 2.3** *Liberty Poems: Inspired by the Crisis of 1898–1900.* On the inside cover of this anti-imperialist volume is a picture of a trench in the Philippines, with U.S. soldiers standing above the Filipinos they have killed. The volume contains many poems contributed by women and was published through the funding of Mary S. Pickering, one of the most generous contributors to the AIL. Picture taken by author.

## Women's Monetary Contributions

In addition to entering the public debate through criticisms of violence, women with anti-imperialist views, many of them lesser-known, contributed financially to the AIL (Murphy 2009), whose ledgers contain many women's names and donations.[27] Between 1898 and 1902, women gave $7,082, or 29% of the total donations received by the AIL. This figure becomes even more significant when we count multi-millionaire Andrew Carnegie as an outlier category given that over the years he contributed $4,400 or 20% of the total AIL funds. Even with Carnegie included with the men, women's contributions totaled 33%, and men's contributions totaled $10,236, or 47%.[28] In 1899, the year before the election, women's contributions totaled $1445.10, which was 27% of the total budget, while in 1900, the year of the election, they contributed $2551.71, 40.5% of the total budget, and 48% not counting Carnegie's yearly contribution. Although women did not have the legal right to vote until 1920, and were never granted full membership in the AIL, their substantial financial contributions (especially given how much independent expendable income women had at the time) demonstrate their commitment to the cause, and suggest that it would have been worth the leadership's while to pay them more attention.

As well as funding the AIL, women worked together to start a fundraising committee for the Philadelphia anti-imperialist newspaper *City and State*, edited by Herbert Welsh, especially when it was in a tight spot in 1902.[29] That this has been overlooked in anti-imperialist histories of the Philippine-American War reflects the tendency of studies of resistance to treat their subjects unselfconsciously as the "political man" (Ferree and Merrill 2000), despite the fact that, in this movement at least, women were not only there, but indispensable to the few successes the AIL was able to achieve.

## Losing the Election

Despite anti-imperialist support, in the end Bryan lost the popular vote, receiving 6,360,796 votes to McKinley's 7,238,543 (Schirmer 1972). Robert Beisner (1968) wrote:

> It was nearly impossible for any American to leave the polls on election day, 1900, with confidence that he had taken a clear-cut stand on the question of imperialism. The sheer lapse of time had diminished the importance of the issue in the minds of many voters: more than two years had passed since the end of the war with Spain and twenty-one months had elapsed since the ratification of the peace treaty and the beginning of the Filipino rebellion. To others imperialism already seemed an established and unalterable part of the political landscape. (p. 120–121)

For all their railing against imperialism, Democratic policies were not significantly different from Republican policies. Democrats promised to "give" the Filipinos a "stable form of government" and " 'independence' but fail[ed] to offer any timetable for its realization, [. . .] disappoint[ing] those who wanted a pledge of immediate independence" (Beisner 1968: 121–122). The election of 1900 was a critical turning point for the nation, marking the firm establishment of imperialism overseas as well as the decline of the anti-imperialist movement. Imperialists claimed the election as a victory, interpreting McKinley's reelection as a sign of the nation's passive acceptance of imperialist policies. However, historians argue, as anti-imperialists did at the time, that McKinley more likely beat Bryan on the basis of their economic policies. Imperialism in the Philippines took a backseat to economic stability at home (Beisner 1968; Tompkins 1970).

With the defeat of Bryan, ambivalent supporters of the anti-imperialist movement lost interest across all social positions. The consensus of white anti-imperialist leaders was that voting for Bryan had been a distasteful protest against imperialism (Tompkins 1970). Without the clear objective of electing an anti-imperialist president, the movement unraveled. Those who remained active and committed to the AIL were more ideologically aligned with one another and progressive politics. Meanwhile, the AIL abandoned any efforts to maintain the commitments to groups of black anti-imperialists and laborers, while the individual white women who stayed involved did so of their own volition, not because of any organizational efforts.

The remaining committed anti-imperialists formed a smaller, more organized network. It is ironic that, as anti-imperialism lost its conservative supporters, it also lost the active support of more progressive blacks and laborers, given that the AIL changed its focus from the sacred principle of U.S. democracy to the evils of imperialist violence, which had long been the concern of blacks (in comparisons with lynching), laborers (in comparison with violence against labor), and white women (as a moral failing of imperialism). After all, how could one really enjoy democracy if they were under continued threats of violence? But, even as they changed their focus, the leadership still made few efforts to be inclusive in their membership strategies. As the tide changed with Bryan's defeat and the disappointing Supreme Court Rulings in the *Insular Cases*, which determined that the Philippines, Puerto Rico, and Guam were unincorporated territories of the United States, soldiers returned home with more stories of the violent atrocities being committed in the name of benevolence and tutelage. As activists continued to gather these stories, they initiated a new strategy of protest designed to expose the contradictions between imperialist violence and democracy, which became their third and final campaign.

## Strategies of the Anti-Imperialist League

Bryan's defeat and McKinley's promises of benevolent assimilation, economic prosperity, and providence silenced the more conservative anti-imperialists.

This left the movement with fewer differences across racial ideology. The remaining activists formed a leaner and more ideologically aligned anti-imperialist advocacy network. They continued to utilize personal connections with people of influence while also forging networks with elite Filipino/a revolutionaries. They gathered information on U.S. military activities in the Philippines and disseminated this information to the American public. They also used this information to lobby Congress and petition the President, focusing on the legality and incompatibility of imperialist violence, democracy, and benevolent assimilation, putting racist violence in the Philippines center stage.

This core group of activists anchored a more homogenous organization and movement of active, middle-class, white citizens. Although the AIL's initial networking tactics embraced ideological diversity, the organization was never seriously concerned with diversity across social positions. Their networking practices thus further contributed to the anti-imperialist movement's narrow membership. With this transition in membership came a transition in strategy, as the focus of the movement shifted from a historical defense of democratic practices in the metropole to a concerted future-oriented opposition to violence in the colony. With this shift, they were freed from focusing on the priorities of the elite and abstract principles of democracy and able to return to the more empathically connected arguments against imperialism. The progressives of the past had failed to set an affirmative agenda for the future. Only after they lost the election of 1900 did the leadership finally focus on the arguments about violence that progressive women, blacks, and workers had been making all along.

Ellul (1975) claims that "Moralizing is a product of those societies in which the sacred fades out and tends to disappear. It is a weak substitute for that which had been radical, ultimate, and established beyond dispute. The more morality is rational, the further removed it is from the sacred, and the weaker it is" (p. 54). If Ellul's assertion here is accurate, and I think it is with a caveat, the rhetoric of these anti-imperialists reflects how radical elements of U.S. democracy were fading by the turn of the twentieth century, as evidenced in the backlash against radical Reconstruction, increases in lynching, and imposition of Jim Crow laws. The caveat is that the history of U.S. democracy is riddled with both racist violence and radical opposition to racist violence. Though the moralizing was used more successfully to justify imperialism than to block it, civil religion has subsequently been formative in imagining a radicalized democracy in more inclusive and egalitarian directions (e.g., the civil rights movement, which appealed to the "better angels," a phrase anti-imperialists borrowed from Lincoln).

At this point, the anti-imperialist coalition on the verge of a movement transitioned to a smaller group of advocates after the election of 1900. Most histories of the AIL stop here, noting the movement's eventual decline. The leadership's ambivalence over creating coalitions with their natural allies of workers, black women, black men, and whitewomen, limited the possibilities for a broader alliance. While they were not able to utilize the collective energies from these groups, they continued to work with individuals from them. Part II outlines how these dynamics played out in the transition to the third campaign against violence and the movement's efforts to keep policies of benevolent assimilation, at the very least, honest.

## NOTES

1. Jane Addams, "Democracy or Militarism." *The Chicago Liberty Meeting: Liberty Tracts, Vol I.* April 30, 1899.
2. *"Letter" from George. F. Hoar.* March 29, 1899. Published by the Anti-Imperialist League. Swarthmore Peace Collections.
3. Ibid.
4. As Kristin Hoganson's (2001) work has highlighted, many of the volunteers saw the war with Spain as an opportunity to cultivate and prove their masculinity. Initially in the Philippines they were commissioned to keep the peace, not fight (Kramer 2006).
5. "Not Reenlisting." *The Nation,* April 27, 1899. "The Mountain and the Mouse." *City and State*, May 11, 1899. *The Anti-Imperialist Reader* (1984) Edited by Philip Foner and Richard Winchester.
6. Letter to Attorney-General [*sic*] of the United States from Edward Atkinson, May 5, 1899. Edward Atkinson Papers, Massachusetts Historical Society.
7. Letter to Attorney-General [*sic*] of the United States from Edward Atkinson, May, 5, 1899. Edward Atkinson Papers, Massachusetts Historical Society.
8. "The Thinking Bayonet." *New York Times,* June 19, 1899.
9. Moorfield Storey Papers, Library of Congress.
10. Letter to Atkinson from Annie W. Stetson, May 20, 1899, Edward Atkinson Papers, Massachusetts Historical Society.
11. "American Affairs." The Philippine Campaign: The Manila Correspondents' Statement. *The Anti-Imperialist Reader* (1984) Edited by Philip Foner and Richard Winchester.
12. "The Philippine Censorship Abolished." *The Anti-Imperialist Reader* (1984) Edited by Philip Foner and Richard Winchester.
13. See appendix for list of anti-imperialist broadsides.
14. Letter to Storey from Herbert Welsh January 31, 1902. Moorfield Storey Papers, Special Collections, Library of Congress.
15. William McKinley, "Speech at Dinner of the Home Market Club, Boston." February 16, 1899.
16. William Jennings Bryan, "Who Saves His Country Saves Himself." *Republic or Empire,* December 31, 1898.

17. William Jennings Bryan, "Liberty, Not Conquest." *Republic or Empire,* February 14, 1899.

18. "Address to Colored Citizens: Their Political Opportunity: Argument by Boston Afro-Americans in Favor of Mr. Bryan." *Springfield Republican,* October 15, 1900.

19. National Party Papers. Massachusetts Historical Society.

20. National Party Papers, 4. Massachusetts Historical Society. My emphasis to note the tone of the religious language.

21. Quoted in "Republic or Empire with Glimpses of 'Criminal Aggression'" by Edwin Burritt Smith, 1900, *Liberty Tracts*, Vol. 9, Chicago: American Anti-Imperialist League. Box 1, Anti-Imperialist League papers, Swarthmore Peace Collection, Swarthmore College.

22. Ibid.

23. *Springfield Republican*, November 19, 1900. *The Anti-Imperialist Reader*, edited by Philip Foner and Richard Winchester (1984).

24. Other recognizable names of women involved with the AIL or anti-imperialist writings include Mary Emma Byrd, Elsie Clews Parson, Katherine Lee Bates, Alice Thatcher Post, Lucia Ames Mead, Fanny Garrison Villard, Alice Stone Blackwell, and Caroline Pemberton.

25. Anna Manning Comfort, "Home Burdens of Uncle Sam." *The Public 2*, May 13, 1899.

26. A Mother, "A Lament from Kentucky." *The Woman's Journal* 30, February 25, 1899.

27. Moorfield Storey Papers, Massachusetts Historical Society.

28. These numbers come from my calculations based on the information found in the ledger books of the AIL. Moorfield Storey Papers, Massachusetts Historical Society.

29. Box. 71, *City and State.* Herbert Welsh Papers, Historical Society of Pennsylvania.

*Part II*

# FROM TRACKING PUBLIC OPINION TO TRACKING THE LAW

The year 1901 was the time of transition for anti-imperialists. They were forced to regroup after Bryan lost the presidential campaign, and they lost thousands of their supporters. Though the public uproar had died down after the election, anti-imperialists continued to ask whether "the Constitution followed the flag," in the phrase of the day. Even if they could not inspire the wider public, they still demanded definitive answers to questions about the legal status of the new territories. These questions had ramifications for tariffs, not to mention the legal status of their residents.

The AIL and its allies self-consciously worked to influence opinion through three strategic processes: (1) before 1900 (and to some degree after), they developed alliances with prominent public figures to garner legitimacy for the anti-imperialist movement; (2) after 1900, they gathered and shared information from soldiers and Filipinos/as with actual experience of the Philippine-American War; and (3) both before and after 1900, they created outlets for disseminating information—about imperialism writ large and the Philippines specifically—directly to the American public. The political purpose of these efforts shifted after the election. Whereas before 1900, the AIL spent much of their efforts on influencing public opinion through networks and providing information. After 1901, the AIL transitioned their tactics to tracking and influencing the U.S. government and the legality of its violent colonial ventures in the Philippines. Keys to the success of this last project were good information and reliable witnesses.

As 1901 began, the AIL awaited the Supreme Court's decision on the legal status of the territories obtained in the Treaty of Paris. Then in May 1901, the Court issued a series of rulings in what are called the *Insular Cases* because they revolved around the governance of territories administered by the Bureau of Insular Affairs, a division within the Department of War that went on to oversee the civil aspects of the fallout of the wars. With the *Insular Cases*, the Supreme Court navigated a legal path for the formation of a U.S. colonial empire. The justices were notably divided in each opinion, in a five-to-four ruling in the most influential case, *Downes v. Bidwell*. Even the majority disagreed with each other, offering three strikingly different, occasionally contradictory opinions. The rulings, which were considered "judicial legislation" and today would be called "judicial activism" by critics, determined that the new territories were "foreign to the United States in a domestic sense" (*Downes v. Bidwell* 1901), and established them as "unincorporated territories," though what this meant was confusing even at the time.

Ultimately, the ruling established a legal state of exception that made room for a U.S. colonial empire regardless of Constitutional limitations by allowing Congress to make separate laws for unincorporated territories, which were excluded from the provisions and protections of the U.S. Constitution as an exception with a special, newly invented legal status. In other words, the United States could make laws over the territories, but the people living there did not have protected rights under the Constitution. Chief Justice Harlan wrote in his dissent that this "radical and mischievous change in our system of government," whereby "the people inhabiting [these territories] enjoy only such rights as Congress chooses to accord to them—is wholly inconsistent with the spirit and genius as well as with the words of the Constitution" (as quoted in Torruella 2007: 311). Although anti-imperialists (many of whom were lawyers) found the thinly supported ruling in *Downes v. Bidwell* deeply troubling, it did decide lingering legal questions posed by anti-imperialists and wary imperialists. The Philippines, Puerto Rico, and Guam were now part of the United States under the power of Congress, but without the vote.

Two of the most famous responses to the *Insular Cases* came from an anti-imperialist satirist, Finley Peter Dunne and the Secretary of War, Elihu Root. These adages showed how exceptional thinking even permeated the legal consciousness, the doings and sayings about law, of the public. The question the Supreme Court was answering with these cases was essentially whether the Constitution would be applied in the newly acquired territories following the Spanish-American War, or in other words, whether the Constitution followed the flag. In one of his most famous adages, the publican Mr. Dooley, the mouthpiece of anti-imperialist Finley Peter Dunne, stated, "No matter whether th' constitution follows th' flag or not, th' supreme coort follows th' illiction returns."[1] His observation was that the Supreme Court decisions followed the politics of public opinion rather than ethical interpretations of the Constitution that might go against popular political positions. For Dunne by way of Dooley, the problem was that politics ruled the Supreme Court. Indeed, when the Court established the territories as unincorporated, it codified a new legal state of exception that reconciled support for U.S. imperialism in the Philippines with new U.S. law.

The question of whether the Constitution followed the flag was another way of asking whether the expanding empire would be ruled by U.S. law. In discussing the implications from the *Insular Cases*, Secretary of State Elihu Root summarized the Court's opinions: "Ye-es, near as I can make out the Constitution follows the flag--but does not quite catch up with it."[2] Eventually imperialist legal exceptions would be written into U.S. law as the empire expanded. Root was an imperialist, and his point of view showed how imperialist sympathizers could simultaneously disavow that the Constitution did not allow for empire and acknowledge the new state of exception would eventually be legalized, in the statement "the Constitution follows the flag," followed by the amendment "but does not quite catch up with it." It was understood and accepted that the limits, rights, and protections afforded citizens in the Constitution would not be extended to the inhabitants of the new U.S. territories, certainly not initially. For anti-imperialists, the consequences of this muddied exceptional thinking were all too clear. The United States had new unwilling subjects without the rights of citizenship.

As anti-imperialists feared, the Supreme Court had dealt the movement another blow. They had tried their case in the court of public opinion and came up short. By the time the Court handed down their opinions, the AIL reported that it had disseminated 3 million pieces (broadsides, speeches, and articles) of anti-imperialist literature across the United States, 1.2 million pieces by the New England arm alone.[3] In 1901, they published 300 new pieces, including Mark Twain's famous "To the Person Sitting in Darkness," which criticized the exceptionalist imperialist rhetoric of "civilization." Published as a broadside and in the *North American Review* in February 1901, it read in part:

The Blessings-of-Civilization Trust, wisely and cautiously administered, is a Daisy. There is more money in it, more territory, more sovereignty, and other kinds of emolument, than there is in any other game that is played. But Christendom has been playing it badly of late years, and must certainly suffer by it, in my opinion. She has been so eager to get every stake that appeared on the green cloth, that the People who Sit in Darkness have noticed it—they have noticed it, and have begun to show alarm. They have become suspicious of the Blessings of Civilization. More—they have begun to examine them. This is not well. The Blessings of Civilization are all right, and a good commercial property; there could not be a better, in a dim light. In the right kind of light, and at a proper distance, with the goods a little out of focus, they furnish this desirable exhibit to the Gentlemen who Sit in Darkness:

| LOVE,              | LAW AND ORDER,      |
|--------------------|---------------------|
| JUSTICE,           | LIBERTY,            |
| GENTLENESS,        | EQUALITY,           |
| CHRISTIANITY,      | HONORABLE DEALING,  |
| PROTECTION TO THE  | MERCY,              |
| WEAK,              | EDUCATION,          |
| TEMPERANCE,        |                     |

—and so on.

There. Is it good? Sir, it is pie. It will bring into camp any idiot that sits in dark-ness anywhere. But not if we adulterate it. It is proper to be emphatic upon that point. This brand is strictly for Export—apparently. *Apparently.* Privately and confidentially, it is nothing of the kind. Privately and confidentially, it is merely an outside cover, gay and pretty and attractive, displaying the special patterns of our Civilization which we reserve for Home Consumption, while *inside* the bale is the Actual Thing that the Customer Sitting in Darkness buys with his blood and tears and land and liberty. That Actual Thing is, indeed, Civilization, but it is only for Export. Is there a difference between the two brands? In some of the details, yes.[4]

Twain aptly points to the complications inherent in the exceptions of impe-rialism. On the face of it, the promises of the empire's benevolence, which he refers to as Civilization, may seem attractive to sympathetic imperialists and even some in the colony. But even if the promises are indeed desirable (another complicated question), "the Actual Thing," doesn't deliver. Though the imperialists might disavow it, the "difference" between the promises and the "details" of what is delivered resulted in the "export" of a questionable "Civilization," as Twain put it. But despite such powerful rhetoric, the debate on the Philippines never held the public's attention as it did before the 1900 presidential election. The rulings in the *Insular Cases* only further dampened the cause. Because of the decline in public interest, most of the scholarship on anti-imperialism ends the story with the AIL's second campaign of losing the presidential election. Therefore, this is another point of departure for my work, which extensively elaborates the historical record on the third anti-imperialist campaign.

Here is where I contend anti-imperialism transitioned from a movement to an advocacy network and the leadership's ethical witnessing became more interesting. The larger movement lost wider appeal when anti-imperialists operating from a place of static emotions that reproduced the status quo, like elitism and self-referential disconnections from the impact of imperialism on people of color, found there was nothing left for them to work toward in terms of recapturing the past they favored. Other anti-imperialists regrouped to continue their efforts, pivoting their priority from public opinion to the rule of law. With the benefit of hindsight from their losses, they shifted their focus from trying to recapture the democratic advances before the

Philippine-American War, to imagining what U.S. democracy and the Philippines could look like going forward. No longer trying to stop treaties or unseat McKinley, the new goal became Philippine Independence. In so doing, the AIL leaders expanded their ethical witnessing to include the perspectives of those with firsthand experiences of state violence.

Now that imperialism found a codified legal, albeit still questionable, role in the formation of the United States, the AIL began to take a deeper look at the extraordinary violence in the Philippines that black and women anti-imperialists had lamented from the beginning when they interrogated and connected U.S. imperialist policies in the metropole and the colony. State formation is the process where a state accumulates political and economic power that impacts its legal orders and institutions. AIL leaders were determined to limit U.S. imperialist state formation and work for a more expansive democracy, and one of their strategies for doing so was to expose the extent of the racist violence in the Philippines. They hoped that there would be enough people with compassion and principle that proving the outrageousness of the violence would make a difference at the very least in limiting U.S. empire. Still having faith in the rule of law, they believed that showing lawmakers how far out of bounds the U.S. military in the Philippines had gone would incite reform. However, the government leadership strategically stonewalled anti-imperialists by both discursively denying and then institutionalizing racist violence in the Philippines through codifying racist exceptional ideologies and legal states of exception, like the category of "unincorporated territories" institutionalized in the *Insular Cases*.

Anti-imperialists compiled evidence of extraordinary violence to target and track U.S. law. They used emotional appeals to build empathy for Filipinos/as with other lawmakers and the American public. Through reflective and empathic connections, they developed transformative ethical witnessing strategies of using their resources as U.S. citizens with full rights and responsibilities to advance democratic changes to the forming U.S. Empire. Their self-conceptions as "heralds of civilization" shaped their protection of the "national honor" as responsible citizens, and ultimately led them to include and connect multiple vantage points of experience in their investigations with soldiers and Filipinas/os. Therefore, I trace the transnational ties between Filipinos/as and anti-imperialists, showing how they informed practices of ethical witnessing that were forced to change under colonial relations.

## AN INFORMATION CAMPAIGN

With success in promoting the right to accurate information and freedom of expression in the Atkinson Affair, the AIL prepared to turn its networking capacities toward information gathering and dissemination, in particular through utilizing their networks with elite revolutionary Filipino/as and soliciting information from soldiers returning from the Philippines. By fostering networks, the AIL provided the U.S. public and government leaders with information on the Philippines that was more reliable and balanced than anything in the press. In particular, they exposed "criminal aggression" such as the water cure, reconcentration, and other cases of violence, and pressured lawmakers into investigating questions about military rules of engagement, especially with regard to the General Orders No. 100. Their work supported the call for a Senate Investigation on the Affairs in the Philippines (SIAP) in which anti-imperialist senators fought the egregious use of U.S. military violence in the Philippines and the implementation of racist exceptions (see conclusion).

## Filipino-Anti-Imperialist Alliances

To advance their common cause of stopping U.S. colonization, certain members of the AIL and the Central Filipino Committee periodically shared information. These connections gave flesh and blood to the earlier anti-imperialist appeals for empathic compassion for Filipinas/os. However, according to Jim Zwick (1998), who conducted the most extensive research on these interactions, "Because most later studies of the League focused primarily on its activities from 1898 to either the presidential election of 1900 or the official end of the Philippine-American War in 1902, [the] aspect of the League's activities [involving Filipino-Anti-imperialist solidarity], which began as early as 1898 but became more pronounced after 1900, has been neglected" (p. 55). Indeed, the AIL did work with Filipino/as in the United States including Filipino/a students, who were often *pensionados* (government-funded students), throughout its existence (Murphy 2019; Schirmer 1972). This helped not only to oppose arguments that Filipinos were not civilized enough for self-rule but also to spread information about the extreme violence conducted by the United States in the Philippines.

The AIL published multiple statements by Filipino leaders in part to prove the Filipino/a capacity for self-government. According to Zwick (1998), these publications included:

> Emilio Aguinaldo's *The True Version of the Philippine Revolution*, the Constitution of the Philippine Republic and other official documents, the memorials to the U.S. Congress by Philippine Envoy to the United States Felipe Agoncillo, the Central Filipino Committee's address *To the American People* (also distributed by the New England Anti-Imperialist League), numerous letters, pamphlets and addresses written by Sixto Lopez, and a comparison of the views of Theodore Roosevelt and Apolinario Mabini. (p. 71)

The proliferation of diverse authors and texts shows their commitment to giving the Filipino/a people a *direct voice* in the United States, especially when government policies denied them any rights to self-government.

AIL vice president and Bostonian Fiske Warren was the American most involved in developing alliances in the Philippines.[5] To do so, he had to sever his official ties with the AIL in order to preserve the organization's reputation in case he was labeled an "emissary" to the Philippines[6] (although there were more emissaries to come later, which he helped facilitate). Early on Warren traveled with Sixto Lopez to the Philippines and to Hong Kong, where the Filipino revolutionary junta was located (De Ocampo 1977; Reyes 1971). Lopez had been a correspondent for the junta in Britain originally (Reyes 1971). Though the junta eventually excluded him from their activities, he remained an outspoken Filipino nationalist and traveled the United States, speaking out extensively on Philippine issues and debating the terms of "civilization." When Lopez returned to the Philippines in 1901, an article from the *Colorado Springs Gazette* quoted him on his intentions: "My object is to make an impartial investigation of the present conditions in the Philippines and to furnish evidence of the real desires and aspirations of my fellow countrymen."[7] Warren and Lopez worked together until U.S. officials in the Philippines arrested Lopez for refusing to take an oath of allegiance to the United States upon his arrival in Manila with his Australian secretary, Thomas Patterson (who was exempt from the oath as a citizen of the British Empire) and Warren.

While Lopez returned to Hong Kong, Warren went to Manila to get him admitted to the country to see his family as well as to make connections with Americans there who questioned the war. Warren carried out some of Lopez's objectives, including visiting Emilio Aguinaldo, who was held captive by the United States after surrendering. He brought Aguinaldo two diplomas and certificates for conducting a humane war by the Spanish Red Cross.[8]

Anti-imperialists also worked with Felipe Agoncillo and Galicano Apacible, two presidents of the Central Committee who were in direct contact with Emilio Aguinaldo, the military leader of the Filipino forces. They traveled to Washington, D.C., and New York from their base in Toronto to argue for Filipino independence and meet with anti-imperialists (Reyes 1977). Apacible also met with William Jennings Bryan during the presidential campaign (Reyes 1977). Thus, even as U.S. forces fought Filipino nationalists, anti-imperialists and Filipinos/as forged alliances where possible.[9]

Apacible wrote a public letter, "To the American People," to address the U.S. public's lack of confidence in Filipino/a capacity for self-government. In it, he acknowledged the racist conceptions of civilization white Americans held as well as the idea the Filipinos/as were not ready for self-government:

From *The Storey of the Lopez Family* by Canning Eyot 1904 [2001].

We, the Filipinos, are a civilized, progressive and peace-loving people. Many impartial writers and speakers have testified that we are advanced in civilization, that we are capable of improvement, that many of our people for two centuries have enjoyed the advantages of university education, that the number of illiterates among our people is small, and that as artists, scientists, magistrates, generals and dignitaries of the Church, the sons of the Filipines [*sic*], have distinguished themselves greatly and have achieved many positions of eminence especially so in Spain.[10]

In this description of his country and people, Apacible demonstrated an understanding of the contested nature and multiple meanings of U.S. exceptions that revolved around civilization and democratic traditions, publicly interjecting into that debate a powerful Filipino voice that offered clear evidence of Filipino civilization and thus the fallacies underlying those exceptions. The AIL published the letter and disseminated it widely.

Clemencia Lopez, Sixto Lopez's sister, visited the United States as an actual guest of the AIL in 1902–1903 (Zwick 2001). Like her comrades, she spoke to various groups across the United States, disputing the idea that Filipinos/as were insufficiently civilized for self-government. Obviously, Clemencia Lopez was living evidence to the contrary. Her instructors at Wellesley College, where she studied English, used her as an example to convince other white women to support the anti-imperialist cause (Zwick 2001). She also spoke on wartime conditions in the Philippines and made a special appeal to President Roosevelt on behalf of her three brothers, who had been imprisoned by the U.S. military government in Batangas without having any charges brought against them (Zwick 2001).

In a farewell speech at a luncheon given in her honor by the AIL on October 5, 1903, Lopez historically linked the oppression of U.S. blacks and Filipinos/as:

When I planned to return to my native land it never occurred to me that my friends would gather to bid me farewell. Still less could I have expected that the gathering should be presided over by the friend of John Brown [Mr. Sanborn]; that the words of parting should fall from the lips of the son of the Liberator [Mr. Garrison]; that I should see among the guests the secretary of Charles Sumner [Mr. Storey]; and that there should be present *in propria persona* that aged and honored paladin of liberty, Gov. Boutwell. These names became famous at a time when the victim was the *black* man. Now it is the *brown*.[11]

Besides explicitly connecting "the black man" and "the brown," Lopez referenced the connections between anti-imperialists and abolitionists and the tradition of fully enfranchised citizens working toward a more inclusive democracy. Like the other Filipino revolutionaries, especially Apacible (Reyes 1977), Lopez was familiar with the racist history of U.S. democracy and understood the implications of this racism for the chances for democracy in the Philippines under U.S. rule. Zwick (1998) notes that the AIL and the Filipino revolutionaries worked together in a complementary way: they had the same end goals and complementary tactics, even as different nationalist

**From *The Story of the Lopez Family* 1904 [2001] by Canning Eyot.**

agendas motivated their efforts. Overall, developing these transnational ties allowed anti-imperialists to more effectively gather information from Filipinos/as and more successfully send their own emissaries to the Philippines.

## SOLDIERS' LETTERS ON WAR

President of Stanford University David Starr Jordan gave a repeatedly requested anti-imperialist address in 1899 entitled "The Question of the Philippines," in which he stated, "We know nothing of Philippine matters, save through cablegrams passed through government censorship, and from the letters and speech of men of the army and navy" (p. 8).[12] When the Atkinson Affair revealed the level of U.S. government censorship, other anti-imperialist leaders began to gather letters from soldiers to get more information. The result was the AIL's first major publication, the broadside, *Soldier's Letters: Being Materials for the History of a War of Criminal Aggression* (1899),[13] a collection of first-hand accounts of the violence, many of which were compiled from articles previously published in hometown newspapers. The letters conveyed the remorse of some soldiers and the callous disregard of others for the violence they perpetrated and witnessed at the behest of the government's imperialist policies. Most importantly, however, it documented the extraordinariness of the violence.[14] One infamous letter compared the war against the Filipinos to "hunting jackrabbits" and referred to Filipinos as "niggers," a common racist epithet among soldiers.[15] Anti-imperialists used this document to expose the contradictions of benevolent assimilation, supposedly advancing U.S. civilization through democracy and education while also advancing racist brutalities.

The family members of soldiers also played a role in sharing their experiences (see chapter 2). Surprisingly, the wife of a captain stationed in the Philippines broke the story on the military's use of the "water cure" in a letter to a newspaper in the United States. She and her husband worked together as whistleblowers, but thought it better that she expose the story as his wife given that he was a commissioned officer.[16] This story and others like it set anti-imperialists off on a fury of investigations to uncover the violence used by the military as well as the general conditions in the Philippines, which the press at home had not reported.

Herbert Welsh was at the forefront of the anti-imperialist information campaign. An active anti-imperialist, AIL member, and connected insider in Philadelphia reformist circles, the Philadelphia-based Welsh was also the editor of *City & State,* an anti-imperialist newspaper. He was an avid researcher and collected statements in defense of imperialism, which he used in his various publications against their authors, and imperialist policy in general (Welsh 1900). Welsh corresponded tirelessly with other anti-imperialist leaders on the need to investigate and expose the violence committed by the U.S. military in the Philippines, for his foremost issue was racist violence. Welsh organized the AIL information campaign and published his findings in *City & State.*[17] He hired two investigators, Matthew K. Sniffen and J. LeRoy Smith, to contact soldiers and officers and interview them on what they witnessed in the Philippines in order to corroborate reports on the "water cure" and develop a case with which to petition Congress. In response to Welsh's solicitations, other soldiers sought him out to report what they knew.

As early as 1900, Welsh used newspaper accounts from soldiers to piece together events in the Philippines to support his case in the broadside *The Other Man's Country* (Welsh 1900). These firsthand accounts were also used as evidence by Storey and Lichauco (1926) in *The Conquest of the Philippines by the United States 1898-1925.* Describing how the investigations into violence began they quoted Charles Brenner, a private from a Kansas regiment:

> The first investigations which finally resulted from the innumerable letters coming from the soldiers themselves, was the case of Charles Brenner, a private in a Kansas regiment. Speaking of the battle of Caloocan, he wrote to his mother: "Company I had taken a few prisoners and stopped. The colonel ordered them up into line time after time, and finally sent Captain Bishop back to start them. Then occurred the hardest sight I ever saw. They had four prisoners and didn't know what to do with them. They asked Captain Bishop what to do; and he said 'You know the orders,' and four natives fell dead (8)." (p. 130–131)

From the like, the AIL argued the U.S. military was committing violence so heinous that it went against the rules of war, such as taking no prisoners, and these letters provided proof.[18]

Mary Storer Cobb of Northampton, Massachusetts, helped form the Northampton chapter of the AIL (see chapter 2)[19] and also helped with the AIL's national information gathering campaign. The AIL requested an official investigation into the violence by Congress and hoped that the information they compiled would provide evidence for its necessity. Therefore, beginning in 1901, the AIL prepared soldiers to testify before what would become the 1902 Senate Investigation on Affairs in the Philippines. Once it was clear there would be investigations and that they would include questioning on the violence committed by the U.S. military,[20] Cobb prepped soldiers[21] and worked closely with Herbert Welsh on the soldiers' testimonies.[22]

While anti-imperialists solicited information from soldiers in order to ascertain the nature of the slaughter in the Philippines and prove that the U.S. military was breaking the U.S. rules of war, they also believed the soldiers themselves were relatively powerless. The AIL platform at the Chicago Liberty Meetings in 1899 addressed the role of soldiers in the "needless horror":

> We honor our soldiers and sailors in the Philippine Islands for their unquestioned bravery; and we mourn with the whole nation for the American lives that have been sacrificed. Their duty was obedience to orders; our duty is diligent inquiry and fearless protest. We hold that our government created the conditions which have brought about the sacrifice.[23]

Anti-imperialists wanted to be clear that their goal was not to shame the soldiers on the ground, but to expose the shameful "conditions" and "deep dishonor" the government put them in. They believed that the problem stemmed from the complacency and complicity of government officials, such as Secretary of War Elihu Root, and military officials, from the Governor General of the Philippines to the officers in the field. Their position appeared at the top of one of Senator Hoar's 1902 speeches, typed in red for emphasis: "The attempt to subjugate a people striving for freedom, not the American soldier, [is] responsible for cruelties in the Philippine Islands."[24] Their position could not be clearer.

A look at newspapers of the time underscores the influence of anti-imperialist investigations.[25] Before 1901, no newspaper articles focused on the water cure in the Philippines. Between 1901 and 1905, about 180 such articles appeared, with 160 of them published in 1902, the year of the SIAP. The letters soldiers sent from the Philippines to friends and family at home were indispensable to anti-imperialists gathering information on Filipino casualties and the general state of things on the ground. Many of their letters mentioned orders to take no prisoners, as well as burning and pillaging villages, all of which became anti-imperialist rallying cries as the AIL worked to get the attention of the American people and their government.

## Reawakening Lawmakers

Anti-imperialists hoped that exposing the nature of the violence in the Philippines to the U.S. public would again mobilize public support for their efforts, which in turn would force lawmakers to impose and enforce limits on the U.S. military and U.S. policies of colonialism. However, after the *Insular Cases*, the public remained indifferent. Instead, anti-imperialist critiques stirred debates between imperialist and colonial government officials over the limits (or lack thereof) of the racial exceptions that formed imperialist law. As discussed in previous chapters, ideas of civilization helped shape these debates, and having to answer to their own notions of civilization, anti-imperialists brought out questions about where violence in the Philippines fell with regard to: (a) the established laws of war, (b) what were considered the rules of "civilized" warfare, and (c) what was considered within the bounds of a "civilized" society, more generally speaking. They posed these questions to lawmakers as they continued to provide them with evidence of atrocities.

As the anti-imperialists evolved into a leaner network, its most engaged activists attributed the U.S. violence in the Philippines to a normalized and anti-democratic racism. Caroline Knowles (2003) defines what anti-imperialists referred to as vaguely as "race prejudice" more precisely as the "racial grammar" of a society. "Racial grammar" refers to both diffuse interpersonal interactions and more concentrated nodes of racializing resources. Anti-imperialists were especially concerned that the normalization of imperialist racial practices deepened and elaborated inscriptions of racist violence into state institutions.

With limited media coverage of the Philippine-American War in the metropole, the AIL turned to the testimonies of soldiers and Filipinos/as, Filipino newspaper articles, and reports on investigative trips by AIL representatives to contribute new information and evidence to the public debate. As they lobbied government officials, the AIL was able to use concrete accusations to further elaborate the contradictions between imperialism, democracy, and their violent exceptions. By prodding the media and confronting lawmakers, anti-imperialist activists generated widespread agreement over the need for an official investigation of the violence committed by the military against not only Filipino soldiers but also Filipino/a civilians.[26]

## Exposing Criminal Aggression

Filipinos in Iloilo had laughed when the U.S. military distributed the Benevolent Assimilation Proclamation, reported General Miller in his testimony before the SIAP. However, McKinley earnestly intended U.S. citizens and Filipinos/as to believe that imperialism would be implemented in the Philippines with temperance and justice. U.S. imperialism would be different— more benevolent—than other empires, especially recently defeated Spain. That Filipinos/as found it laughable exposed the cracks between what it promised and what Filipinos/as expected would come.

Go (2008) argues that the only substantive difference between American Empire and other empires was not U.S. benevolence, but the fact that Filipino elites negotiated with colonial officials. The Filipino resistance (both revolutionary and diplomatic) forced the colonial government to allow more Filipino participation in colonial institutions than, for instance, in Puerto Rico (Go 2007). But anti-imperialists also played a formative role in shaping the institutions of U.S. empire, forcing imperialists to rephrase and recast their imperialist agenda through legal exceptions in the face of anti-imperialist revelations of the egregious racist violence in the Philippines.

Publicizing letters from soldiers that detailed the violence and racism in the Philippines was only an initial tactic in pursuit of this strategy. Anti-imperialists also cited statistics from reports that showed "the United States [had undertaken] an undeclared practice of taking no prisoners [as seen in] the Filipino battle ratio of five killed to one wounded (the reverse of the usual as confirmation of these reports)" (Schirmer 1972: 226). Indeed, "[w]hat was new at this point was that the McKinley Administration elevated the application of extreme measures [i.e. taking no prisoners], *hitherto unofficial and unacknowledged, into a policy that was official and acknowledged*—from the highest cabinet level through the War Department to MacArthur and the forces in the field" (Schirmer 1972: 227, my emphasis). Stressing the aberrant ratio was a concrete way to establish the extraordinary nature of the U.S. violence in those terms that imperialist lawmakers would have to acknowledge.

Throughout the rest of 1900 and 1901, the AIL continued to leak stories of reconcentration and the water cure to newspapers that were critical of McKinley's policies. After McKinley's assassination in early summer of 1901, Theodore Roosevelt succeeded him in September and was determined to see them through. But though the water cure, burning and pillaging entire villages, and taking no prisoners were not enough to awaken public dissent, they were enough to galvanize anti-imperialists to conduct their own inquiry and, subsequently, to convince lawmakers to conduct an official investigation.

## Investigations into Extraordinary Violence

When anti-imperialists determined that the U.S. was employing reconcentration camps in the Philippines, the AIL executive committee decided to conduct further investigations, appointing Herbert Welsh to head up the effort.[27] Working out of the Philadelphia office of *City & State* with his assistants, Welsh uncovered violent policies through rigorous pursuit of details and multiple sources of corroboration, starting with returning soldiers.

Bolstered by the information Welsh and his team gathered, anti-imperialist Senator George Frisbie Hoar called for a Senate special investigation on the Philippines (Schirmer 1972). In the face of defections from prominent supporters of imperialism, Republicans agreed to an investigation, so long as it stayed under the purview of the Philippine committee, chaired by Senator Henry Cabot Lodge, a Boston Republican, like Hoar, but a strong supporter of imperialism (Schirmer 1972). Finally, on January 14, 1902, Hoar successfully obtained a vote passing a resolution for the investigation. A Maine newspaper quoted his speech that day:

> Now, give us a little light. Take the most zealous men in this body and give us a committee that would hear evidence, put questions, hear both sides and let us know what is the truth. *We are engaged in the unholy office of crushing out a republic, the first great republic ever established in the Eastern hemisphere.* If we had dealt with this people as we dealt with Cuba we should have had today a civilized and happy, peaceful republic, sending their youths to our schools and studying our laws, imitating our example animated by love and affection and gratitude such as no one people on earth ever yet felt for another.[28]

Hoar was an anti-imperialist, but he also had his preferred version of American exceptionalism. After the *Insular Cases*, he thought that the Philippines should have been a protectorate under the United States like Cuba, which would have prevented the atrocities. Meanwhile, colonial administrators in the Philippines, like William H. Taft, who would eventually testify to the SIAP on behalf of the government, keenly watched this political maneuvering. Taking a nod from Hoar's suggestion that Filipino/a youth should study in American schools and learn U.S. law, the following year the Senate passed the 1903 *Pensionado Act*, which sent Filipino youth to the United States to attend schools, study law, and help implement American models of governance and engineering in the Philippines. But before that Act, the SIAP uncovered the terrifying drama still occurring in the Philippines.

The losses in the Presidential election of 1900 and the *Insular Cases* refocused anti-imperialists and forced them to regroup and build on their information-gathering strategies. Some AIL members, like Herbert Welsh, continued to work to disseminate information on violence gathered through their networks with working-class soldiers and elite Filipinos/as. Other AIL members and sympathizers, like Fiske Warren, fostered networks with Filipinos/as to obtain information on the ground in the Philippines. After the AIL losses in 1900 and 1901, the organization began a focused campaign to expose violence and force a public, legal reckoning on the U.S. military's use of racist violence, putting their energies into gathering the details of criminal aggression and benevolent assimilation in order to shed light on the dark corners of these new imperialist state formations.

In acknowledging and using multiple vantage points on events in the Philippines, the AIL formed a core group of activists focused on exposing the violence and debunking what they argued were merely rhetorical claims to benevolent assimilation. By using imperialist violence as a frame to problematize conceptions of civilization, anti-imperialists pressured imperialists to reformulate their justifications for using violence in the Philippines. However, imperialists became more skillful and cagey, employing ambiguities and using the law to develop new kinds of American imperialist exceptions that justified their use of violence. Largely on the basis of ethnicity, with a few exceptions (to the exception), imperialists argued that Filipinos/as were outside the bounds of civilization.[29] Because colonial administrators and military officials also shared an underlying assumption that indiscriminate violence was beyond the bounds of civilization, their logic held that the use of violence was itself exceptional, and was only necessary to control the indiscriminate savagery of Filipino "insurrectos" and "ladrones."[30] In other words, their ideas of civilization allowed them to hold that Filipinos/as were not subject to the rights and protections of existing laws. As the following chapter shows, the SIAP uncovered these beliefs by highlighting the administration's knowledge and tacit approval of the exceptionally violent—and horrifyingly procedural—methods used in the Philippines by the military.

## NOTES

1. Finley Peter Dunne, *Mr. Dooley's Opinions* (New York: R.H. Russell, 1901).

2. Robert L. Beisner, *Twelve against Empire: The Anti-Imperialists, 1998–1900* (New York: McGraw-Hill Book Company, 1968).

3. Report of the Third Annual Meeting of the New England Anti-Imperialist League, November, 1901.

4. Mark Twain, "To the Person Sitting in Darkness." *The North American Review,* Vol. 172, No. 531 (February 1901), pp. 161–176.

5. See Fiske Warren Diaries. Herbert Welsh Papers, Bentley Historical Library, University of Michigan; Herbert Welsh Papers, Hatcher Graduate Library, University of Michigan; Moorfield Storey Papers, Massachusetts Historical Society.

6. Report of the Third Annual Meeting of the New England Anti-Imperialist League, November 1901.

7. "Sixto Lopez Declares His Present Mission." *Colorado Springs Gazette,* August 11, 1901. J.R. Hayden Papers, Bentley Historical Library, University of Michigan, Ann Arbor.

8. Fiske Warren Diary, January 9, 1902, J. R. Hayden Papers, Bentley Historical Society, University of Michigan, Ann Arbor.

9. It is worth mentioning that, as a point of comparison, I have been unable to find any historical reference to this kind of cooperation between advocates of liberty and freedom in the metropole and colony for any other contemporary empire, including Great Britain or Spain. In this way, anti-imperialists were by definition exceptional through their act of connection.

10. *To the American People*, by Galicano Apacible. June 1900. Swarthmore Peace Collection, Philippines Box.

11. Clemencia Lopez, "Reply by Senorita Lopez." *A Farewell Luncheon in Honor of Senorita Clemencia Lopez, October 5, 1903* (Boston: Fiske Warren, 1904).

12. David Starr Jordan, *The Question of the Philippines* (Palo Alto, CA: Printed for the Graduate Club by the Courtesy of John J. Valentine, Esq., 1899).

13. Box 1. Anti-Imperialist League Papers. Swarthmore Peace Collection, Swarthmore College.

14. *Soldiers' Letters: Being Materials for the History of a War of Criminal Aggression*, 1899. Anti-Imperialist Papers, Bound Volumes 1899, Swarthmore Peace Collection, Swarthmore College.

15. Ibid.

16. Correspondence from Herbert Welsh to Storey, January 31, 1902. Moorfield Storey Papers, Library of Congress.

17. Herbert Welsh Papers. Bentley Historical Library, University of Michigan; Herbert Welsh Papers, Hatcher Graduate Library, University of Michigan.

18. Welsh also exposed torture in a broadside, *To Lincoln's Plain People: Facts Regarding "Benevolent Assimilation" in the Philippines*, based on accounts from news stories in the *Evening Post*. One particularly brutal story of torture involved a Major Howze, who was accused in 1900 of committing peculiar tortures and other cruelties on Filipinos, including beating them to death. Anti-imperialists were even

more outraged to learn that General Miles had heard of Howze's practices and only sent an officer to investigate, hoping the incident could stay quietly within the military rather than be made public. This was the reason the story ended up being leaked.

19. Jim Zwick. "Suffrage and Self-Determination: Women in the Debate About Imperialism." http://www.boondocksnet.com/ai/wj/; Jim Zwick, ed. *Anti-Imperialism in the United States, 1898–1935.* http://www.boondocksnet.com/ai/ (September 8, 2005).

20. Senate Investigation on the Affairs in the Philippines. 1902. Congressional Hearings.

21. Mary Storer Cobb Papers, Massachusetts Historical Society.

22. Ibid.

23. *Liberty Tracks.* No. 1. Chicago Liberty Meetings. April, 30, 1899. The Central Anti-Imperialist League: Chicago.

24. Speech of Hon. George Hoar of Massachusetts in the Senate of the United States, May 22, 1902.

25. For instance, see Proquest Historical Newspaper database.

26. Anti-imperialist senators, though outnumbered on the Lodge committee, consistently questioned the burning of villages and the innocence or culpability of villagers.

27. Welsh had already used his newspaper to publicize the violence he discovered in other newspaper accounts from soldiers.

28. "The Philippines." *The Lewiston Daily Sun Journal,* January 15, 1902.

29. The 1904 World's Fair in St. Louis emphasized this point at home (e.g., see Robert Rydell, *All the World's a Fair: Visions of Empire at American International Expositions, 1876–1916* (Chicago: The University of Chicago Press, 1984) and Laura Wexler, *Tender Violence: Domestic Vision in the Age of U.S. Empire)* (Chapel Hill, NC: The University of North Carolina Press, 2004).

30. Insurrectos were leftover from the revolutionary army, while ladrones were understood to be gangs of thieves. Filipino fighters earned this designation after Roosevelt declared the fighting over.

*Chapter 3*

# The Senate Investigation on Affairs in the Philippines

Brigadier-General Jacob Smith ordered his men to wildly "kill and burn" villages in the Philippines in 1901. His exact words were "I want no prisoners. I wish you to kill and burn; the more you kill and burn the better it will please me." His orders were in retaliation to a surprise attack by Filipino fighters. He told his officers that he wanted the area of Samar to become "a howling wilderness," which gained him the nickname, "Howling Jake." The AIL used his orders as glaring evidence of a "take no prisoners" policy, which had previously been understood, but was now clearly articulated in writing. This was by all interpretations against the existing rules of war. With this, they believed they had a clear case for Congress to intervene with the military occupation in the Philippines.

On February 5, 1902, Senator Hoar submitted a petition requesting that the Senate investigate the violence in the Philippines. The petition was signed by "men of letters, scholars, and others," and asked not only that the "truth be laid before the American people" but also be acted upon.

> [I]f the reports be true steps [should] be taken at once to stop reconcentration, the killing of prisoners, the shooting without trial of suspected persons, the use of torture, the employment of savage allies, the wanton destruction of private property, and every other barbarous method of waging war which this Nation from its infancy had ever condemned.[2]

The petition further suggested that troops be directed to treat Filipinos/as as if they were people we would one day "hope to make our friends." This request raised the ire of *The New York Times*. Instead, it claimed that we are dealing with the great body of the Filipinos as persons whom we hope to make our friends. The rebels who are our enemies are their enemies. The chief objects of the anti-imperialist solicitude are these enemies of ourselves and of the Filipino population.[3]

*The Times* framed the subjects of violence not as the Filipinos/as "whom we hope to make our friends," but as "their enemies" as well as "our enemies." This argument rearticulated the petition's distinctions and foreshadowed the exceptional logic U.S. military personnel would invoke when they testified in the hearings.

Even so, the petition successfully secured a Senate Investigation on Affairs in the Philippines (SIAP). The hearings briefly recaptured the public's attention and, more importantly, incited debates that crafted imperialist state formations. By exposing the pervasiveness of violence in the U.S. colonial occupation, imperialists responded by legally codifying racist exceptions in the Philippines. Maria Lanzar's (1928) early work on the AIL highlighted their activity around violence in the Philippines,[4] yet her successors have concentrated on the imperialist excuses for violence at the expense of anti-imperialist efforts to expose it (Jacobson 1995: 2000; Kramer 2006; Welch 1979).[5]

While the moment when imperialists made racist excuses to continue violence in the Philippines is an abhorrent mark on U.S. history, it is also a moment that some citizens both fought to expose and fought to contain racist violence as ethical witnesses. Although they lost, their work in this campaign exposes a pattern deeply embedded in U.S. history, the unfolding of racist states of exception. Because of the scholarly inattention to this anti-imperialist campaign, how their efforts affected U.S. policy-making has not been addressed. Therefore, the legacies from that moment that we live with today, an imperialist curse really, has gone unnoted. The curse is the continued practice of formulating racist states of exception that allow, for instance, the manifestation of legal arguments that codify exceptions for the torture of detainees and refugee camps on the U.S. border that allows for children to be kidnapped from their parents and then abused in detention camps. Legal arguments shield the government and enable these practices. This chapter addresses that historical gap in the hopes of fleshing out how the original pattern unfolded so that we can collectively recognize and free it and, finally, together set out a new, more impeccable course for the future.

The AIL strategy of lobbying politicians to make official inquiries into the violence finally paid off. Once reports from the SIAP became part of the public record, AIL leaders hoped they would again mobilize citizens against U.S. empire, but they would do it regardless. To ensure that the SIAP would address anti-imperialist concerns, Herbert Welsh continued to investigate the "atrocities" in the Philippines and arm senators and witnesses with information (see chapter 4). Welsh and his assistants interviewed soldiers returning from the Philippines to establish what they believed to be indisputable evidence of atrocities. As he gathered information for the official investigations, Welsh simultaneously compiled and published his findings for public consumption.[6] He also continued communication with the officials who were to appear from the Senate committee, also called the "Lodge Committee." The committee was chaired by H. C. Lodge and included imperialist senators—William Allison, Eugene Hale, Redfield Proctor, Albert Beveridge, Julius Burrows, Charles Dietrich, and Joseph Rawlins—and their anti-imperialist colleagues—Charles Culberson, Fred Dubois, Edward Carmack, Thomas Patterson, and George Hoar. Anti-imperialist senators made sure the investigation addressed three issues: (1) the military rules of war, (2) the water cure, and (3) the burning of villages and forced reconcentration.

## RULES OF ENGAGEMENT

During the Civil War, President Lincoln implemented General Order Rules No. 100, also referred to as the Lieber Code (after its primary author, Columbia Professor Francis Lieber), which provided guidelines for U.S. soldiers conducting warfare. These rules were a rhetorical reference point for the narrative of civilization that played out in the SIAP hearings.

The rules stipulated that soldiers should promote and uphold progressive standards of civilization during war. For instance, Article 4 stated,

> As martial law is executed by military force, it is incumbent upon those who administer it to be strictly guided by the principles of justice, honor, and humanity—virtues adorning a soldier even more than other men, for the very reason that he possesses the power of his arms against the unarmed.[7]

According to Article 22,

> as civilization has advanced during the last centuries, so has likewise steadily advanced, especially in war on land, the distinction between the private individual belonging to a hostile country and the hostile country itself.[8]

The rules defined guerilla war and established parameters for capturing property and treatment of prisoners (Maguire 2010). In doing so, they made legal distinctions between "enemy combatants" and "enemy noncombatants," who, in turn, were divided into loyal citizens, who were to be protected, and two classes of disloyal citizens: those who sympathized with the enemy without aiding them, and those who aided them. *Disloyal citizens could experience the "burden of the war" as a commander deemed necessary* (Grimsley 1995: 150). Officers in the Philippines were expected to follow these rules.

In Articles 14, 15, and 16, the rules codified the notion of *"military necessity,"* which determined the limits of acceptable behavior in the field:

14. Military necessity, as understood by modern civilized nations, consists in the necessity of those measures which are indispensable for securing the ends of the war, and which are lawful according to the modern law and usages of war.

15. Military necessity admits of all direct destruction of life or limb of armed enemies, and of other persons whose destruction is incidentally unavoidable in the armed contests of the war; it allows of the capturing of every armed enemy, and every enemy of importance to the hostile government, or of peculiar danger to the captor; it allows of all destruction of property, and obstruction of whatever an enemy's country affords necessary for the subsistence and safety of the Army, and of such deception as does not involve the breaking of good faith either positively pledged, regarding agreements entered into during the war, or supposed by the modern law of war to exist. Men who take up arms against one another in public war do not cease on this account to be moral beings, responsible to one another and to God.

16. Military necessity does not admit of cruelty—that is, the infliction of suffering for the sake of suffering or for revenge, nor of maiming or wounding except in fight, nor of torture to extort confessions. It does not admit of the use of poison in any way, nor the wanton devastation of a district. It admits of deception, but disclaims acts of perfidy; and, in general, military necessity does not include any act of hostility which makes the return to peace unnecessarily difficult.

The ranking officer was in charge of defining "necessity" (Grimsley 1995). Lieber's code defined the treatment of civilians in times of war as a key criteria for civilization and for making the determination of what was done in the field out of "necessity"—a highly subjective determination depending on the officer and his own code of ethics and level of racism.

As codified Western norms for conducting civilized warfare (Maguire 2010), these rules were at the heart of determining in the SIAP hearings whether the violence in the Philippines was standard or exceptional. For instance, the fact that torture for the extraction of information was explicitly forbidden came up repeatedly. When it became clear that these standards were compromised in the Philippines, witnesses and apologists on the committee began rationalizing the transgressions through racist exceptions, which held that *civilized war was required only for civilized people and Filipinos/as were savages.* American leaders made it clear that they believed equity existed only between "equals" (Maguire 2010). The result was that there were two rules of war—those that applied to wars between white people and those comprised of racist exceptions for conflicts that involved nonwhites. The racist division between who imperialists considered civilized or savage also racialized their emotions, such that it shut down their willingness to empathically connect to Filipino/as experiences and allowed them, instead, to stonewall with indifference, disavowals, and ultimately racist legal exceptions. This process went without question. What was left in effect was a deformed and debilitated rule of law.

Nevertheless, the committee had a list of incidents to address. One, mentioned at the opening of this chapter, took place in 1901 and was known as the Balangiga Massacre. Aided by the local population, Filipino guerrilla fighters entered the village of Balangiga disguised as women and attacked U.S. soldiers in their sleep, killing forty-eight. Brigadier-General Jacob Smith retaliated by putting the area under a "kill-and-burn" policy (Ileto 2002; Kramer 2006). In a handwritten message, General Smith famously ordered his soldiers to turn Samar into "a howling wilderness." When Waller asked for clarification of who was to be targeted, Smith sent him verbal orders to shoot every Filipino male over the age of ten (Miller 1982: 220). Junior officers obliged, though not without hesitation. Waller did stipulate that women and children should not be killed, only men (over 10!) capable of bearing arms

**Figure 3.1 "Kill Everyone Over Ten."—Gen. Jacob H. Smith.** Theodore Roosevelt Papers. Library of Congress Manuscript Division. https://www.theodorerooseveltcenter. org/Research/Digital-Library/Record/ImageViewer?libID=o274576 Theodore Roosevelt Digital Library. Dickinson State University.

(Maguire 2010). Then, rather than taking ten Filipino scouts as prisoners, he executed them for treachery upon their return from the field. News of this campaign outraged anti-imperialists across the United States, who believed this kind of violence had no place within their conceptions of civilization and civilized war. Smith's orders became an anti-imperialist rallying cry.

When news about Balangiga broke as a result of testimony before the SIAP, Waller was called before a military court in Manila. His defense centered on the chain of command—although Smith testified that Waller acted on his own with regard to the executions of the scouts--and General Rules 100, specifically Article 24, which in the interest of "total war" allowed reprisals to convince the enemy to end the war quickly. In the face of Smith's denial further witnesses were called on Waller's behalf to testify about Smith's orders. In the end, Waller was found guilty and sentenced to lost pay (Maguire 2010), but his testimony had implicated Smith.

Smith used the rules of war to defend his course of action in the Philippines, specifically pointing to the doctrine of reprisals as an acceptable tactic. Meanwhile, anti-imperialists focused on Smith, using these same rules to argue in the anti-imperialist press that the war in the Philippines went against both the moral principles of civilization and U.S. legal standards of civilized war. During the Indian Wars, Smith had won the nickname "Hell Roaring Jake," but now he was vilified as "Howling Jake" (Maguire 2010: 50). Roosevelt attempted to placate anti-imperialists by indicting Smith for "conduct to the prejudice of good order and military discipline" (as quoted in Maguire 2010:50). This only further enraged AIL leaders, who argued that his response missed the point entirely.

In 1900, President McKinley had appointed William Howard Taft, a former lawyer and chair of McKinley's first civilian Philippine Commission, as civilian Governor of the Philippines. Taft became the standard bearer for benevolent assimilation policies, focusing on implementing a tutelary colonial government (Go 2008). Taft spent two weeks testifying before the SIAP.

One topic of his testimony was, as planned, the character of warfare in the Philippines. When anti-imperialist Senator Patterson asked him the question "Is guerilla warfare ligitimate [*sic*] warfare?" Taft responded:

> I am not an expert on the laws of war, but I have always understood that it was hardly within the laws of war or legitimate warfare for men to wear the uniform at one time and then slip into a village and appear friendly and then go out again and ambush people.

Patterson then invoked an inter-imperial comparison to make his point:

> They have guerilla warfare in South Africa [referring to the Boer War], and yet when those who are conducting it are captured they are treated, as I understand, under the rules of warfare. They are not regarded as outlaws.

Taft responded:

> There certainly never was a case when an insurgent captured was, with the authority of the commanding officer, treated otherwise than according to the laws of war. But as to what the rules are with respect to guerilla warfare, you will have to ask an army officer, for I am not competent to tell you.[9]

Arguments that disclaimed and disavowed violent activities in the Philippines became routine for Taft. Taft's testimony instead aimed to establish the U.S. civil government in the Philippines as civilized in contrast to the Filipinos/as. For instance, he asserted that the uneducated native was:

> cruel to animals and has as little regard for human life [. . .]. Therefore, in many instances where soldiers were ambushed, where Signal Service men were ambushed, there were bodies mutilated and evidences of cruelty that were most likely to cause retaliatory measures.[10]

When Senator Culberson, another anti-imperialist, asked Taft if he had heard that American soldiers had "been guilty of what might be termed cruelty,"[11] Taft responded that he had never heard of soldiers mutilating bodies, but admitted he had heard charges that the water cure was rife in Manila.[12] Taft further stated that, in general, Filipinos/as did not treat human life with "sacredness." As a Neo-Lamarckian, he went a step further to racialize "uneducated" Filipinos as the most savage:

> The uneducated Filipino is a docile person, but left to the natural ferocity which war and hostility of that sort provoke he becomes very cruel. War of course, provokes some cruelty in everyone. Certainly the experience in China is evidence that *civilization* itself does not prevent it at times.[13]

Again referencing the inter-imperial field by invoking the Boxer Rebellion, Taft insinuated that having civilization, as he allowed that China did, did not mean that all of a country's peoples were civilized.[14]

Patterson pursued the question of civilization and race by asking: "When a war is conducted by a superior race against those whom they consider inferior in the scale of civilization, is it not the experience of the world that the superior race will almost involuntarily practice inhuman conduct?" Taft responded, "There is much greater danger in such a case than in dealing with whites. There is no doubt about that."[15] He went on to say that American forces in the Philippines treated the Filipino/a people with more "compassion [. . .] restraint [. . .] and [. . .] generosity" than their previous foes, presumably the Spanish.[16] The implication of the Taft-Patterson exchange was that "inhuman conduct" increases when whites fight nonwhites as compared to when whites fight whites, the assumption of the superior race of whites went without saying (Jung 2015); through this, they reaffirmed both white supremacy and racist exceptions.

Throughout the SIAP, military officers repeatedly invoked General Rules 100 as the standard of accountability for the military's actions in the Philippines. Secretary of War Elihu Root alleged, "the war on the part of the Filipinos has been conducted with the barbarous cruelty common among uncivilized races, and with general disregard of the rules of civilized warfare," in contrast to the U.S. military who had tried 44 officers, soldiers, and "camp followers" for not abiding by the General Rules 100 and convicting thirty-nine of them.[17] But, some of these claims were slippery at best. Colonel Wagner, the assistant to the Adjutant-General, testified that the indiscriminate burning of barrios, or villages, and towns was permissible under the General Orders No. 100, given that it was not always possible to distinguish between friendly and hostile Filipinos/as, which meant that it could be reasonable to level entire barrios believed to harbor insurgents or high levels of hostility.[18]

When Senator Culberson tried to force Wagner to draw an unambiguous line for when leveling a barrio would be against General Rules 100, Wagner said the line was up to the judgment of the officer in charge. At the apex of their exchange, Culberson asked:

> I am speaking with reference to the deliberate act of burning the houses of non-combatants, as seems to have been done in some cases in the Philippines, which have been testified to before this committee. That is the case I am trying to get your judgment upon.

Wagner disavowed the question, replying that he had no knowledge of such indiscriminate burning, but then also appealed to military necessity:

> The destruction of the property of noncombatants, when the property is known to belong to noncombatants and there is no military necessity for destroying it, is inexcusable. The destruction of property of noncombatants may be necessary, though, for two reasons. It may be impossible to separate the property of innocent people in their towns from property of the guilty. The whole community there must suffer, if the crimes of the community have been sufficient to warrant it. Again, as I stated before, I think, the property of a noncombatant must be destroyed if an enemy is making use of that to our prejudice and hurt in military operations.

Wagner both justified exceptions to the established rules of war and suggested that distinguishing between villagers was too much to expect. In other words, if imperialists had mixed opinions about the Filipino/a people, they were also, and perhaps more significantly, indifferent to them.

Legal states of exception did not originate with the SIAP. They are collective products of a history of struggle that arise out of a concept of political or military "necessity." Those with power, like military officers and imperialist senators, define "necessity" in order to override a rule for specific parties or a specific period of time while still maintaining the rule *in general*. That is, the definition of "necessity" creates the space for an exception. In this case, imperialists created new racist exceptions to defend their positions in debates with anti-imperialists, defining nonwhite bodies on the borders of law as outside of the civilized order, where rules of war ceased to apply, thus making them exceptional cases, where torture and reconcentration camps could occur legally.

## The Water Cure

The SIAP began to focus on the "water cure," as it was called, in the middle of April 1902. The U.S. military used the water cure to extract information from Filipinos, usually about the locations of caches of guns.[19] In descriptions of the torture, soldiers or their associates pinned the victim down on his back, forced his mouth open, poured water down his throat until his stomach swelled, and then pushed the water out. They repeated the process until the captive talked.

When soldiers testified before the committee about the water cure, they claimed that the U.S. military learned it from the Macabebe Scouts (aka Gordon Scouts) under Lieutenant Conger and Captain Glenn. They said that Filipinos had learned it from the Spanish and used it on the Macabebes, and that the practice spread as U.S. soldiers learned it from other companies.[20] Seiward J. Morton testified about his experience with the water cure:

I was on guard and acting corporal of the scouts. A man named Bender, who belonged to Company I, I think, of the Eighteenth Infantry came up and told me he wanted me to help "water cure" this native. I told him that I had no particular objection. [. . .] We were directed there to throw the native or take him down, and we picked the native up and laid him down. He was a small man, and he didn't make much resistance. One man had hold of his leg, and I had hold of his leg, and another man had hold of a leg, and we laid him on his back. Another man had hold of an arm, each arm. Then Bender took the water with a cup, dipped it out of a pail, and first they took a stick about 2 inches wide and placed it between the native's teeth like this [indicating]. The stick was probably about a quarter of an inch thick. When they did that they twisted the stick around so that it forced the native's mouth open the width of the stick. Then Bender dipped the water from the pail and poured it in the native's mouth, and finally the native stiffened; that is, he appeared—I thought he was going to die then. I had never seen it done before then. I refused to have anything more to do with it, and

Bender and I had a slight altercation there; I don't remember the exact nature of it, but I told him I would have nothing more to do with it. My connection with the affair ended there.[21]

As a result of the SIAP testimony, national newspapers finally began to cover the water cure. The first *New York Times* stories appeared in April 1902, reporting on the details of how it was performed and soldiers' claims that victims were fine by the following day. The water cure inspired Chicago anti-imperialist and poet Bertrand Shadwell to write "Death of a Filipino under Torture," which he gave to Welsh for publication in *City & State* "free of charge" to help publicize the issue.[22] Shadwell also wrote "Imperialism in the Philippines" about killing guides who refused to lead the U.S. military to "insurrectos."[23]

Before the soldiers testified, Senator Patterson had asked Governor Taft about the "so-called water cure," but Senator Beveridge interrupted and asked

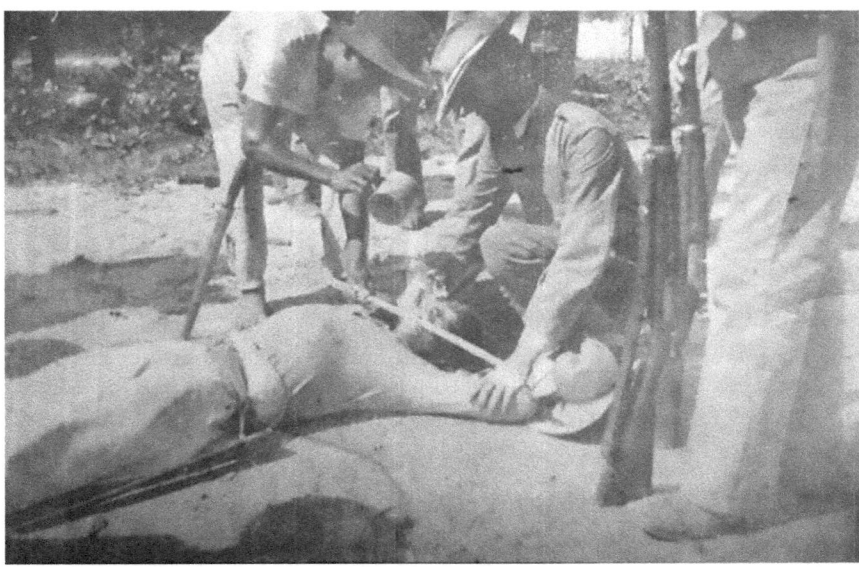

**Figure 3.2   This image depicts the "water cure" administered by "a Macabebe named Pedro," who was the cook, and "private Harry G. Ford (Co. A. 17th) [h]olding the bamboo stick in the Filipino's mouth."** The Filipino being tortured was reportedly named "Mary Anno." J. LeRoy Smith obtained the image during an interview with Michael J. Bergen, formerly Company A. 17th U.S. Infantry. Bergen stated that "it was taken in May, 1901, at Sual, Philippine Islands, by Corporal George J. Vennage (Co. A. 17th U.S. Infantry), now in the post office at Mani[l]a." Bergen reported that Vennage had a "small pocket k[o]dak with him on the 'hike'." Photo from the Herbert Welsh Collection, Historical Society of Pennsylvania. Image taken by author.

him to address the issue of "irreconcilables" sent to Guam (such as revolutionary and Filipino national hero Apolinario Mabini),[24] and the issue of the water cure was dropped. General Robert Hughes testified after Taft. When asked about the water cure, he flatly denied having ever heard of it, but he also danced around the subject cagily asserting that the water cure could mean many different things. After finally admitted to having heard of it used once by American police, he claimed they would not use it again,[25] another disavowal.

Once again, imperialists demonstrated that violence that would normally be seen as transgressing the boundaries of civilized behavior was acceptable to them when used against "savage"—that is, racially different and inferior—Filipinos. Incorporating these racist exceptions to the rules of war effectively expanded the United States institutionalized racism, especially once racist exceptions became procedurally inscribed into state institutions through new racist laws.

General Funston took another tack toward promoting white supremacy, flat out denying charges that white men used the water cure, and claiming that soldiers who reported such events were trying to get attention and exhibiting "braggadacio."[26] But even if some soldiers did flaunt their violence in letters home, this very flaunting raises the question of what they were trying to prove. Did they want their audience to think they were good white American soldiers, putting people of color in their place? Whatever conscious or unconscious ideas they had about their performance as U.S. soldiers, these letters conveyed how specific ideas about the inferiority of people of color serves to legitimate physical violence (Jung 2004).

Sgt. Charles Riley from Northampton, Massachusetts, was the first soldier to testify about the water cure. He said that he had seen the water cure performed twice on the mayor of Igbaras, facilitated and witnessed by officers in the regular army. Private William Lewis Smith testified about the same incident. He said that Macabebes were also there, aiding the U.S. forces against insurgent forces under the command of Lieutenant Conger, who was aided by Dr. Lyons, who was contracted by the military. Riley testified that about 80 soldiers witnessed the incident, and many of them stated that they had seen many more instances of the "treatment."[27] Senator Beveridge, who was unequivocally defensive of U.S. activities in the Philippines, disputed this point on the basis of hearsay.[28]

Officers repeatedly justified U.S. slips into what could be considered illegal warfare by arguing that Filipino insurgents did not adhere to the rules of war, for instance, by raising the white flag of surrender only to surprise attack U.S. troops. Senators Hoar and Turner suggested that Filipinos should be called to testify before the committee to respond to these charges, but none ever were.[29] Senators Culberson and Burrows continued to ask officers and soldiers whether the victims of the water cure were the same insurgents committing treacherous acts of war, but the repeated answer was that the water cure was not used to punish Filipinos for egregious acts of violence, but rather was a tool for extracting information. This information, in turn, justified the burning of villages.

SIAP testimony led to the court-martial trials of Lieutenant Arthur L. Conger, Major (then Captain) Edwin F. Glenn, and Captain and Assistant Surgeon Palmer Lyon (then a contract surgeon), all of whom were in charge of the Macabebe Scouts, who were officially deemed the main administrators of the water cure.[30] Courts-martial even re-established white supremacy by positioning whites at the highest level of "civilization." They asserted the separation between the Macabebes, who were considered uncivilized to begin with, and the U.S. military. They also implicated individual white military personnel, who descended into the uncivilized practices of nonwhites, rather than the institutions or policies from which these practices sprang. Like the other forms of violence in the Philippines, the debates on the water cure showed how U.S. imperialism was rooted in ideas of white moral superiority and racist violence and elaborated exceptionalist rationales.

Addressing the question of whether soldiers conducted the water cure of their own volition or at the request of their commanding officers, Seiward J. Morton, quoted earlier, stated:

> I do not know of any instance where a native was 'water cured,' under the orders of a soldier alone, and I do not think a soldier would assume that responsibility. Whenever an act is executed by a soldier and an officer is present the inference can safely be drawn that that officer gave the order and that the soldier was obeying it.

Senator Beveridge responded, "You should do as the Senator from Texas suggests, simply give the facts, and the committee is competent to draw inferences."[31] Captain Fred McDonald testified that he did not know of any officer who gave orders for the water cure; rather, he said, they simply acquiesced to it.[32] Nevertheless, the *New York Times* reported:

> Mr. Rawlins (Utah)] said outrages in the Philippines were due, not to the soldiers themselves, but to the highest military authorities in the islands, The responsibility for them indeed was to be placed properly at the door of the Administration officials here in Washington.

Rawlins added:

> Until recently, [. . .] I had thought that these things were sporadic and isolated, but I have been forced to the belief that they are but a part of the general plan of campaign.[33]

The SIAP forced imperialists to face some of the extraordinary routinization of the violence the U.S. military was carrying out. However, anti-imperialist leaders were disappointed with the limitations on their witnesses and the curtailing of testimonies of soldiers who were willing to discuss more of what they saw of the water cure, whether they were supporters or critical of its use.

## Reconcentration

The SIAP also took on the fraught topic of reconcentration (testifying before the SIAP, both soldiers and officers referred interchangeably to "concentration" and "reconcentration" camps). Once it was clear to U.S. military commanders that the war was not ending quickly or easily, they began looking at the local population's role in aiding the insurgents. Some came to see the local population as a fair military target, though others found this questionable. In a heated exchange in the Senate between Senators Tillman and Spooner in late January 1902, Tillman referred to them as reconcentration camps similar to "the horrors introduced into Cuba by Weyler." He stated:

> a private letter from an army officer in the Philippines had been received in Washington, and that the officer was quoted as saying with respect to the establishment of concentration camps: "If this thing is to continue, I will have to apologize to Weyler."

Another officer was quoted as adding: "The time has come when I'm ready to apologize to him now."[34] From the opposite corner, Commander General Bell announced,

> every barrio in Batangas and Laguna will be burned, if necessary, and all the people concentrated in the town... Henceforth no one will be permitted to be neutral... The towns of Tiaong, Delores and Candelaria will probably be destroyed unless the insurgents who take refuge in them are destroyed (as quoted in Ileto 2002: 11).

In fact, Morton and Mark H. Evans testified that when Filipinos fired on a contingent of marching soldiers, the United States responded by burning all the houses and buildings in the vicinity.[35]

To establish a historical precedent, Captain Fred McDonald testified that "Sherman's march to the sea" used exactly this sort of indiscriminate burning.[36] Some military officials held that these practices adhered to the interest of "total war," which, as described in General Rules 100, would end a war more quickly. Storey and Lichauco (1924) described the reconcentration policy as thus:

> General Smith had been in charge of subduing the island of Samar and his first step had been to install a system of reconcentration. For the benefit of those unfamiliar with this drastic term it should be explained that reconcentration (as

practised [*sic*] by Weyler in Cuba and the American commanders in the Philippines) means the establishment of a certain prescribed zone or place where the people of a district may be herded together. The establishment of this zone is announced by proclamation or otherwise some days in advance and all persons must leave their homes and come within this area, there to remain until further orders. All persons found outside that zone are then treated as public enemies. (pp. 138–139)

As noted earlier, anti-imperialists had a particular antipathy for Smith because of his orders to "kill and burn." *The New York Times* quoted Senator Turner describing Smith as " 'a monster in human form,' who had devoted an entire province to a merciless extermination."[37]

Reconcentration effectively created "protective zones" within "deadlines," as the military referred to them (Ileto 2002), while anti-imperialists called them "reconcentrations" or "concentration" camps.[38] Because this policy was so new, neither the military nor anti-imperialists had a consistent label for it, although Ileto (2002) suggests that "Bell seemed unaware that his actions were replicating what Spain and its missionaries had achieved two centuries

**Figure 3.3** **"Reconcentrado camp : Tanauan, Batangas; 1060; 1900/1930."** http://quod. lib.umich.edu/s/sclphilimg/x-1060/phlf031. Everett Thompson photograph collection [photographs]. University of Michigan Library Digital Collections. Accessed: August 15, 2019.

earlier. Through the policy of *reduccion*, scattered settlements were reconcentrated in Spanish-style pueblos dominated by a church-center" (p. 13). But, by any terms, the practices shared the concentration of civilians under military control within certain borders.

The assistant to the Adjutant-General, Arthur Wagner, testified about his report on the camps. He was careful to establish that inhabitants remained grouped with neighbors and that "sanitary conditions were carefully looked after,"[39] a claim made in response to accusations of "cholera camps," where disease ran rampant from filthy conditions and malnourishment. On May 21, 1902, *The New York Times* reported on a letter from an army officer read to the committee by Senator Bacon:

> The letter said the camp was located in a soggy place where rain fell continually and outside of which every living thing was shot. In that camp there were thirty cases of smallpox and five cases were added each day. Clouds of vampire bats circled softly over the place awaiting the dead coming to them every day. The camp was "like some suburb of hell."[40]

Senator Hoar compared the conditions in reconcentration camps to the conditions at Andersonville Prison during the Civil War, something to which most progressive Americans could reference as devastating conditions.[41]

Military apologists supported the use of the camps in several ways. Stuart Creighton Miller (1982) described General MacArthur's strategic military justifications:

> Everything outside of the camps was systematically destroyed—humans, crops, food stores, domestic animals, houses, and boats. Actually, a similar policy had been quietly initiated on the island of Marinduque some months before. When one editor got wind of it, the War Department anxiously inquired of MacArthur if Major Fred A. Smith had ordered the natives into the five principal towns on Marinduque. MacArthur wired back: His action effectively suppressing insurrection there which past three months presented obstinate resistance. Exclusively a military measure carried out without objectionable or offensive features and effected end in view (p. 208).

MacArthur considered military measures against civilians unproblematic, so long as they were implemented in the interest of total war and brought the desired outcome. When asked about the concentration camps, Colonel Wagner pointed to pigs scavenging in the camps as evidence of sanitation, not filth, since they ate waste throughout the camp.[42] He further testified that the camp inhabitants had absolute freedom, within the "dead lines," of course. He also noted:

> The orders to the troops were to shoot anybody beyond the dead line who went without a pass—or, rather, the natives [the Constabulary] were informed that

those were the orders; but orders were given under no circumstances to shoot any decrepit person, child, or woman and to avoid shooting a person under any circumstances if the necessary end could be obtained without it.[43]

Senators sometimes coached witnesses to use more sanitized language. For example, when Wagner referred to the use of "military force" for policing the "dead lines," Senator Dietrich suggested that perhaps he meant "protection" from insurgents and ladrones. Clearly, the meaning and interpretation of these military actions were key to imperialist justifications for such severe policies. Imperialists self-consciously rearticulated these interpretations with civilization to maintain at least legal, if not moral, legitimacy.[44]

Trying to defend the camps, Senator Beveridge asked Wagner whether there were clear differences between the Spanish Weyler camps in Cuba—widely disapproved of by the U.S. public—and U.S. reconcentrations in the Philippines. Although Wagner claimed that all he knew about the Spanish camps was the popular belief that starvation and unsanitary conditions were rampant, under further pressure from Beveridge, he resorted to the idea of superior morality, stating that "comparing these camps of ours with the Spanish camps would simply be comparing mercy with cruelty."[45] *The New York Times* underscored this tactic in its report on Wagner's testimony that the concentration camps were a means of protecting Filipinos/as from ladrones, which had been "admirably accomplished."[46]

Earlier in the SIAP, when Taft was questioned on General Bell's order on reconcentration in Batangas (one of the strongholds of the Filipino nationalists), he said that reconcentration would not be needed once an embargo was put on trade in areas where there was still fighting (specifically Batangas), which would financially stifle the wealthier insurgents and prevent them from obtaining more weapons. Taft in essence blamed the insurgents for subjecting their people to "the greatest privation and suffering,"[47] alleging that, by continuing to fight, they were committing a "crime against civilization" and "a crime against the Filipino people," a line of argument picked up by other imperialists defending U.S. military actions.[48]

Following Taft's lead, General Hughes described the escalation of violence against insurgents, especially civilians, in terms of civilization and the established rules of law. He said the policy against civilians, in particular, became

stiffer; and in this way: In the first campaign, or the first summer, you might say, we started out to contend with a united force, and we attacked it and pursued it in exactly the same way that you would do in any civilized country--no harm to noncombatants; everything we got paid for, if they could prove property, etc. They were notified, however, before that campaign was over, owing to a few shots that were fired at some people near camp, that if that sort of thing was practiced, that if they allowed the guerrillas to conceal themselves in their barrios and town inside our lines and fire on our detachments passing through, we would burn the place. In this course of time there were quite a number of fires as the result of that practice.[49]

These measures were still not enough, he said, and more "stringent" measures were later called for.

The committee questioned Hughes about how the decision was made to depart from "civilized warfare," for instance, whether the discretion for appropriate violence was put to the commander in charge without limits on severity. Hughes replied, "There is one rule that is generally pretty safe, and that is that the army officer is an educated man, *a man educated in civil society*,"[50] implying that the civilized nature of U.S. officers, at that time all white by decree, justified giving them discretion over the question of severity. Though the committee pressed further, the line of questioning broke down, escalating into an argument between committee members. Still, Hughes indicated that the Filipinos were ferocious not only in their treatment of American soldiers, but in their treatment of each other, which implied that their "capacity for civil government" was clearly questionable and the guidance of the United States was still imperative.[51]

Like Taft before him, Hughes disclaimed knowledge of any specific atrocities in question, and therefore did not feel competent to comment. He seemed unaware of anything that might have occurred under his command that did not come directly from his orders. Finally, when explicitly pressed on the issue of "concentration" policies, he stated in terms that echo the spirit of defenses for child detention facilities today:

It is a misnomer to call it a policy of concentration, because the world has learned to put a significant meaning to that word. The policy as practiced in the Philippines has no element of cruelty in it. It is simply an order to the inhabitants of a particular locality to move from one portion to another, and there they reside and carry on their operations and business. If the locality into which they have moved does not afford them ample support, the United States Government provides them with food and shelter. The people are pleased with it, because they are permitted to lead an easy life, much easier than at home. There is no element of punishment or deprivation. They are simply requested to come into a certain district.[52]

There was no testimony from Filipinos living in the concentration camps to counter his claims, although the Filipino newspaper *El Renacimiento* vociferously opposed the practice by 1902 and especially after the Reconcentration Act of 1903 (Kramer 2008).

General MacArthur testified that the U.S. military's standards of war, as established through general orders and courts-martial, were on a "high ideal plane." He further argued that "in conducting war all of humanity is brought to the surface, and in individual instances excesses have been committed," putting the onus for reports of cruelty in military conduct on individual soldiers. He reiterated this point:

> Individual men have committed individual outrages; but when we compare the conditions that exist in the Philippines to-day in that respect with what have existed in all modern wars between civilized states the comparison is absolutely in favor of the self-restraint and high discipline of the American soldier.[53]

MacArthur reported that he commanded an army "representing the highest stage of civilization."[54] Following up, Senator Beveridge asked, "The general conduct of our soldiers and officers there, irrespective of orders from headquarters, was in the direction of kindness, mercy, and humanity, was it?"[55] Beveridge again highlighted the agency of individual soldiers and officers, this time in carrying out the moral "civilization" he saw in imperialism. In contrast, anti-imperialists looked at the violence as a systemic institutional problem stemming from the corrupting influence of imperialism and racism. As Hoar put it, immorality, in the form of excessive violence, was the "fruit" of the tree planted when the U.S. ratified the Treaty of Paris.[56]

For obvious reasons, the SIAP did not solicit Filipino testimonies beyond that of Felipe Buencamino, who collaborated with the colonial and military government and was sympathetic to U.S. occupation. However, an emboldened Clemencia Lopez took it upon herself to submit her testimony in cooperation with anti-imperialists. After Sixto Lopez refused to pledge allegiance to the United States, the military responded by targeting his family. In early 1901, they seized his three brothers, Cipriano, Manuel, and Lorenzo. Manuel and Lorenzo were held without any charges, while Cipriano was held, with no evidence, for the alleged crime of hiding fifty guns. None of them had any promise of a trial, as Filipinos/as had no rights to the *writ of habeas corpus*. Clemencia believed that the U.S. military government had confiscated the Lopez family home, land in Batangas, and ship as a penalty for Cipriano's alleged involvement with insurgents. Cipriano had been part of Aguinaldo's army, but surrendered his regiment in 1900 under terms that he could not be charged with any actions against the U.S. military (Eyot 1904 [2001]).

Clemencia and her younger sister Maria were in Hong Kong visiting Sixto when their brothers were apprehended. There, Clemencia decided to go to the United States to appeal directly to the U.S. government on behalf of her family, rather than depend on the justice of the military government in the Philippines (Eyot 1904 [2001]). This was why she was able to testify before the SIAP as the only Filipina to testify as a critic of U.S. policy. She also sent a letter directly to President Roosevelt on March 15, 1902, arguing that her brothers were being held for political reasons and imploring him to release them.[57] Clemencia's attorney, anti-imperialist Louis Brandeis, and later the first Jewish Supreme Court Justice, was a mutual friend of the Warren family (Green 1989). He helped Clemencia submit her letter to the hearings and submitted his own letter to accompany hers in support. She offered the only firsthand account of U.S. practices of indiscriminate control of material goods and bodies in the Philippines: indeed, her brothers had no individual rights, and her family had no economic rights.

Clemencia's testimony and the letters she exchanged with her sisters throughout the saga became the basis for a new AIL publication, *The Story of the Lopez Family*, published in 1904. The letters, which discussed the retention of their brothers and conditions in Manila and Batangas, were interspersed with anti-imperialist commentary.[58] The publication emphatically restated the fundamental anti-imperialist position on the Philippines:

> All of the misunderstanding, all the injustice, all the evil, all the cruelty and horror are due to the violation of an eternal principle which affirms the right of every people to govern itself. And all the considerations about "philanthropic intention" and the "white man's burden" and the "elevation of alien races" and the "blessings of good government" and the "resplendent world-mission of America" cannot excuse the violation of that principle or obviate the evils and horrors that must follow its violation. (Eyot 1904 [2001]: 31)

"Eternal principle" was a reference to Hoar's widely regarded (by anti-imperialists) two-hour speech in Congress against the passage of the Philippine government bill spearheaded by Senator Lodge, which centered on the "eternal principle" of the consent of the governed.[59]

But, two years before this book appeared, anti-imperialists began to worry that the SIAP would be shut down prematurely. On June 21, Senator Patterson informed Sniffen, Welsh's assistant, that Lodge was delaying and evading the question of when the investigation would conclude.[60] By June 26, they were convinced Lodge would actually bar further testimonies. As they had anticipated, at the end of the month, when Congress recessed, Lodge stopped convening the committee for hearings, even though anti-imperialists continued to request further interviews.

The SIAP had no resolution. Lodge simply walked away from further inquiry. Anti-imperialists were distraught. They had prepared many more soldiers to testify. Rather than reverse the violence in the Philippines, the hearings reasserted and further substantiated imperialist structures of power, in particular by demonstrating the power to ignore and suppress information gathered by anti-imperialists. An internal anti-imperialist memo to the AIL Philippine Committee assessed the situation:

The policy the Administration now proposed to pursue is consequently apparent. Admitting that some things, inexcusable in character, did, not improbably, occur in the course of recent operations in the Malayan Archipelago, it will be claimed that no useful end is to be gained by a further probing therein. It will further be asserted as something not admitting of denial that, after all, the conduct of our officers and soldiers was on the whole humane and were considerate to an unprecedented degree, and that no more "severities" were practiced except in cases altogether exceptional, than, reasonably speaking, were unavoidable, if not necessarily incident, to the work of bringing about peace, and accomplishing the highly beneficent results always in view. [. . .] *It is to be a policy of oblivion and construction*; as such, it is plausible, and undeniably attractive.[61]

Anti-imperialists anticipated that the "domineering spirit" of indifference and aloofness would lead to a "policy of oblivion" in which allegations of abuse were "ignored" or "treated in a formal manner." Although anti-imperialists had used the SIAP to put imperialists on their heels by exposing the atrocities in the Philippines, imperialists used the law to legitimate their exceptionally violent practices and nothing was resolved.

## AFTERMATH OF THE SENATE INVESTIGATION

For a time, anti-imperialists believed the findings of the SIAP had finally brought popular opinion entirely to their side of the Philippine question. Although prematurely cut off, the information gathered by Herbert Welsh, Matthew Sniffen, James Smith, Mary Storer Cobb and A. L. Mumpers, had been influential:

It may not unfairly be said that they altered the whole attitude of the United States towards the Philippines; and, *by making military rule odious and suspect, greatly hastened the advent of civil government*. This, in justice to Mr. Welsh, should appear of record. It was the production of evidence which admittedly broke the silence of Mr. Lodge in the Senate, and caused him to make those reports to the President which led to the immediate issuance by Secretary Root, *under direct orders, of public and peremptory instruction that all acts of the kind disclosed should forthwith cease, and that those responsible for them in the past should be arraigned before the proper tribunals.*[62]

Indeed, Welsh and his team continued to interview soldiers across New England, the South, and the Midwest, meeting with over 20 by the end of the year. Sniffen, Smith, and Mumpers made painstakingly detailed reports, crosschecking facts and looking for additional information that testified to the honest character of the soldiers, just in case the SIAP continued.[63] Welsh also organized three memorials, statements of fact that not only remonstrated the military conduct in the Philippines but also petitioned for Philippine independence to be sent before the Senate, but to no avail. They were blocked.[64]

Still unable to give up, hoping that the hearings would be reopened, Welsh continued to send new evidence to Senator Lodge,[65] but his requests fell on deaf—or at least indifferent—ears. The AIL had spent much of its resources bringing soldiers to testify before the committee. Once it was clear the investigations would stay closed, the AIL held a public protest with a mock investigation in Senator Carmack's office, where they heard and notarized the testimony of the soldiers who had been waiting to testify.[66] While the investigations would never be reopened, there was a new urgency by Congress to pass the civil government act for the Philippines. They successfully passed the act in May. Then, almost two months after the SIAP recessed, on July 1, 1902, Congress enacted the Philippine Organic Act, which gave legal authority to create a civil, not military, government in the Philippines. Then, on July 4, 1902, Roosevelt declared the military operations in the Philippines over despite continued fighting. The AIL leaders realized now there were entirely new rules with which they would have to fight the occupation of the Philippines. The Constitution and U.S. law—the AIL's foundation—was no longer relevant. This was the proverbial "dark night of the soul" for anti-imperialists.

Nevertheless, the AIL investigative committee continued to move forward on principle, which at this point was all they had. Their next publication was *Secretary Root's Record: "Marked Severities" in Philippine Warfare: An Analysis of the Law and Facts Bearing the Action and Utterances of President Roosevelt and Secretary Root*, a volume intended to show that the government's rhetoric of civilization was just that.[67] The epigraph quoted Roosevelt's statement from his "4th of July Oration" where he declared the war in the Philippines was over: "Words are good if they are backed up by deeds, and only so." The volume quoted Root as suggesting the war had been fought with "scrupulous regard for the rules of civilized warfare," and Roosevelt as asserting that "Determined and unswerving effort must be made to find out every instance of barbarity on the part of our troops, to punish the guilty of it, and to take, if possible, even stronger measures than have already been taken to minimize or prevent the occurrence of all such instances in the future." *Marked Severities* explored whether this was the case, and concluded that it emphatically was not, putting the responsibility for the "barbarities" squarely on the shoulders of Root. Secretary of War under McKinley and Roosevelt and an attorney by training, he was the only individual with enough power and knowledge of the situation to have stopped the extraordinary brutality.

On March 19, 1903, anti-imperialists held two more mock hearings at Boston's Faneuil Hall, one in the afternoon and one in the evening, featuring testimony from witnesses who had been prohibited from testifying before the SIAP because they had already left the military. Another broadside, *Mass Meetings of Protest Against the Suppression of Truth About the Philippines,* came out of these mock hearings. It included the commentary of eleven speakers, including George Boutwell (still President of the AIL), Moorfield Storey, Herbert Welsh, and Thomas Patterson (Secretary to Sixto Lopez).

One of the stories Welsh told at the hearing was of the water cure being performed on Father Augustine, a Catholic priest. As the SIAP hearings were winding down interviews, Albert Cross, a U.S. soldier, had testified about the event to Welsh's investigators. Cross was stationed in Banate in the Philippines under the command of Captain Brownell and reported having seen the water cure administered too many times to count.[68] He said that Brownell ordered him to give Father Augustine the water cure because he sympathized with and aided insurgents. In private correspondence, he told Sniffen that he believed Augustine received the "water cure treatment" because U.S. officials thought he had "hidden insurgent funds."[69] Cross reported that the water cure was administered to the priest three times, and the last killed him. Cross was requested to assist in the third round, but he asked to be excused as he felt it was "not right." The soldiers who administered it said they attempted to revive the priest and sent for a doctor, but nothing could be done at that point.[70]

The case of Father Augustine angered U.S. Catholics,[71] who found the idea of civilizing a people who had a large Catholic population (after hundreds of years of Spanish colonization) insulting.[72] Norah Gleason of Germantown, Pennsylvania, started a personal letter-writing campaign to the president. After she received a report on the treatment of Father Augustine from Secretary Root, she responded to the president:

> If you would kindly consider the injustice done to this poor priest, and by so doing you will do much towards your Catholic subjects, both in the United States and the Philippines. For although Secretary Root says it does not seem a matter of action for you, he must be mistaken, for you as the present head of both countries have the authority to act in such a small matter, and would naturally be the right one.[73]

Given that Father Augustine was a priest, not just any "insurrecto," many witnesses had been willing to come forward and testify. Indeed, the commanding officer General Hughes was considered for further inquiry after the SIAP ended, and Welsh had been more than willing to provide information for his inquiry.[74]

Welsh closed his remarks at the mock trial by defending his motivations for interviewing and ascertaining facts on the violence in the Philippines:

I have been sometimes reproached for taking up these individual cases and clinging to them with such painful detail. I do it, not because I love these details or because, as a dear friend in New York wrote to me, I have any glee in finding out wickedness. Nay, it is not that. It is simply a knowledge which I have gained during a twenty years' experience in Indian affairs, that the way to arrive at the practical enforcement of a principle is to walk through all the tiresome and devious paths of concrete case.[75]

One more "concrete case" emerged powerfully from the anti-imperialist arguments reiterated by the other speakers, because it directly covered a topic anti-imperialists had only hinted at in their other publications. Thomas Patterson, a friend of the Lopez family, reported on a letter from Juliana Lopez, Sixto and Clemencia's younger sister, dated January 31, 1903, which described the rape of a Filipina woman by U.S. soldiers. The woman was the sister-in-law of one of the Lopez family's workers who had killed a U.S. soldier, and they believed the rape was a retaliation. Juliana reported that rapes commonly occurred when drunk soldiers walked the streets at night, so young women would not go walking at night for fear of these "thie[ves] of woman's honor."[76] Although it was not commonly discussed, rape clearly transgressed any notions of "civilized" behavior, let alone benevolence.

For all its disappointments, the investigations showed how imperialists repeatedly invoked and rearticulated civilization through the invention of racist exceptions deployed to maintain the supposed moral superiority of whites in the face of evidence of their indiscriminate—by their own standards—use of violence. The ritualized performances involved in the SIAP ostensibly enacted the democratic practice of hearing multiple points of view to gather pertinent information for the governing body to make recommendations for institutional change. But the conclusion was foregone at the outset, and the result, rather than committed democratic practice, was a placating ritual of civilization, which purged and cleansed the profane individuals (the proverbial bad apples) purportedly rotting the sacred democratic system. Although anti-imperialists were able to scratch the surface of affairs in the Philippines, their senators were in the minority and unable to sustain the investigations. Imperialist politicians had stifled the investigations before more damaging information, like the case of Father Augustine, came out and again roused the public's consternation.[77] Thus, although the SIAP challenged and nominally checked the claims of benevolent assimilation, U.S. imperialist practices continued, largely unchanged, but now institutionalized. When it became clear that there would be no public uprising, AIL secretary Erving Winslow wrote to Welsh, "What headlines, Oh, no. What interests them is the price of beef."[78]

On May 30, 1902, Memorial Day, at the opening of Arlington Cemetery, President Roosevelt spoke about the "atrocities" in the Philippines (quoted in *Marked Severities*). Invoking comparisons of racist violence in the intra-imperial field, he targeted Democrats and apologists for lynching:

> Is it only in the army in the Philippines that Americans sometimes commit deeds that cause all other Americans regret? No! From time to time there occur in our country, to the deep and lasting shame of our people, lynchings carried on under circumstances of inhuman cruelty and barbarity cruelty infinitely worse than any that has ever been committed by our troops in the Philippines; worse to the victims, and far more brutalizing to those guilty of it. The men who fail to condemn these lynchings, and yet clamor about what has been done in the Philippines, are indeed guilty of neglecting the beam in their own eye while taunting their brother about the mote in his.
>
> Understand me. These lynchings afford us no excuse for failure to stop cruelty in the Philippines. *But keep in mind that these cruelties in the Philippines have been wholly exceptional,* and have been shamelessly exaggerated. We deeply and bitterly regret that they should have been committed, no matter how rarely, no matter under what provocation, by American troops.[79]

Roosevelt pointed again to the "necessity" for brutality in war under the General Rules 100, and reiterated that the justification for exceptions to the rules of war lay in the actions of the other side: "Our enemies in the Philippines have not merely violated every rule of war, but have made these violations their only method of carrying on the war." Congress just had passed the Organic Act, enabling the transition from a military colonial government to a civil colonial government. Then, as planned, on July 4, 1902, Roosevelt declared the "insurrection" in the Philippines over and terminated the military government though fighting continued.

The Philippine Committee[80] wrote Roosevelt a thirteen-page letter in response to the failures of the SIAP and Roosevelt's interpretation of them in the Memorial Day speech. Specifically, they took issue with his characterization of the events described in the hearings as "exceptional," arguing that to prove this point "The testimony of representative Filipinos has been jealously and systematically suppressed." Describing how military personnel not only "indignantly denied" administering the water cure, but claimed to have administered it on themselves with "no injurious effects" and sometimes even found it "beneficial to the health," they asserted that "the impudence of the mockery is manifest." They also wrote at length on reconcentration:

> These, as a feature in recent Spanish and South African Operations, excited in us as a people the deepest indignation, combined with the most profound sympathy for those thus unmercifully dealt with. When resorted to by our officials in the Philippines, these camps are represented as a species of recreation grounds, into

which the inhabitants of large districts rejoiced to be drawn, and from which they departed with sorrow. [. . .] By one army officer they have been likened to "suburbs of Hell." *Meanwhile, the most persistent effort on our part has failed to obtain from the War Department or any other official source any statistics of disease or mortality in those camps. The published statistics relating to the British camps in South Africa of a similar nature were, on the contrary, precise and periodical.* Such being the case, the reports of our medical inspectors on the concentration camps in the Philippines are contrary to reason, and opposed to all human experience. (p. 8)

Given the lack of available information, it was even more egregious that their efforts to "supplement the evidence" had been "obstructed":

We presented a formal memorial to Congress, asking for a complete and impartial investigation to be made on the spot; no action was taken thereon. We sought to have witnesses called by the Senate Philippine Committee, and a more complete inquiry instituted, in which both sides should be heard; our efforts were unavailing. Finally, when evidence led up to the threshold of revelation, officers of the proper department of the Army appointed to make inquiry reported "that considerations of public policy, sufficiently grave to silence every other demand, require that no further action be taken." It was apprehended that "facts would develop implicating many others." Again, there was danger that "the honor of the Army" would be assailed. So further investigation was summarily stopped (p. 8).

The investigations stopped just when the atrocities that anti-imperialists had been decrying were coming to the fore. Rather than have a difficult reckoning, imperialists thought it more important to save the face of the military so as to not lose all reputation.

With the investigations shutdown, there was little hope to interest the public, even as Welsh continued to uncover information on incendiary cases, like Father Augustine, that he hoped would offer as a pathway to empathic engagement. Charles Francis Adams, a more conservative member of the AIL executive committee, sympathized with Welsh, but wondered whether further investigations were warranted, given the public's inattention. In a letter to Welsh, Adams conjectured:

For instance: if our friends who opposed the Boer war in Great Britain, who made such a loud and very proper protest against many of the severities of that war, including the concentration camps, the destruction of homesteads, etc, etc, were to now keep up that fusillade, I think you would agree with me that it was a useless expenditure of force. The thing is now over and done; and the evil deeds of the past, while possible to affect at the time, cannot be remedied after the event.

Our position is now much the same. I should be glad to see justice done in the case of Father Augustine, and am entirely willing to contribute whatever I can to that end. On the other hand, I have to recognize the fact that public interest on the subject has died out, and that it is difficult, if not impossible, to revive it. Under these circumstances, the only matter for consideration is, what practical course we should pursue.[81]

A practical way forward was on the minds of all committed anti-imperialists left. They had given their political reputation, their money, their time, and much of their identity to the cause. Now, without recourse to any hope of a government supported reckoning, it was difficult to see a next move. They were at a crossroads, experiencing a crisis of faith in the system of U.S. government carrying out its most sacred political ideals. As fully enfranchised, responsible citizens, futility was difficult, if not impossible, to accept.

Anti-imperialists felt the immobilizing chill of public indifference and its cooling effect on their effectiveness in lobbying government officials. Gilbert Bates, an anti-imperialist supporter, wrote to Welsh in August 1902, detailing the power of indifference:

> It is said that money is the root of all evil. Well, there is another 'Root' [a reference to Elihu Root] that closely approaches it in evil-production, indifference. Familiarity begets indifference, indifference begets and encourages hypocrisy, immorality and corruption, raises false standards and lowers true ones, while exchanging the best elements and principles for the worst.[82]

Never quitting, the AIL advocates forged on. Before the close of the SIAP, a committee with members from Chicago, Boston, Philadelphia, and New York met in New York to discuss their next move.[83] With the water cure explained away as exceptional and a few officers punished and examples of reconcentration justified as military necessity, racist states of exception became codified and procedural. Nevertheless, anti-imperialists' ethical witnessing would continue to focus on atrocities in the Philippines. Anti-imperialist leaders held tight to the principles of democratic governance, if they could enforce the actual letter of the U.S. Constitution, then they would push forth with the Constitution as a powerful symbol of fundamental, inalienable, perhaps, even universal human rights, as the following chapter describes.

## NOTES

1. "President Retires Gen. Jacob H. Smith." *New York Times,* July 17, 1902.
2. "Ask that Hostilities Cease and Filipinos Receive Peace." *The Washington Times,* February 5, 1902
3. "The Anti-Imperialist Petition." *The New York Times,* February 6, 1902.

4. Lanzar contacted living anti-imperialists as well as the family members of anti-imperialist leaders who had passed away, and collected and organized their vast materials. With an archivist's eye to preservation and a historian's eye for documentation and evidence, she saved many anti-imperialist documents, especially from Herbert Welsh and Erving Winslow. Most of those papers are now held at the University of Michigan, where she received her Doctorate in Political Science.

5. Likely, this focus is because the war in the Philippines and the extraordinary violence that accompanied it has been forgotten and ignored. One exception is Daniel B. Schirmer's (1972) brief chapter "Against Atrocities: The Last Campaign."

6. Two major publications on this were broadsides published in 1903, *To Lincoln's Plain People* and *Mass Meetings of Protest*.

7. Article 4. General Orders No. 100: the Lieber Code. http://avalon.law.yale.edu/19th_century/lieber.asp

8. Article 22. General Orders No. 100: the Lieber Code. http://avalon.law.yale.edu/19th_century/lieber.asp

9. "Affairs in the Philippine Islands: Hearings before the Committee on the Philippines of the United States Senate." April 10, 1902. Washington: Government Printing Office. Sen. Doc. 331 of the 57th Congress, p. 73 (here forward this document is referred to as SIAP).

10. SIAP, p. 74.

11. Ibid.

12. Ibid.

13. SIAP, p. 77, emphasis added.

14. For more on the Boxer Rebellion see Steinmetz (2007).

15. SIAP, p. 77.

16. Ibid., p. 78.

17. Ibid., p. 950.

18. Ibid., p. 2857.

19. One soldier, Sergt. Januarius Manning, also testified that his company employed the water cure to obtain confessions for the murder of a Private O'Hearn. SIAP, p. 2255.

20. Ibid., for example, testimony of Januarius Manning.

21. Ibid., pp. 2897–2898. Other soldiers testified that they saw the water cure administered, but often by the Macabebe mercenaries. Macabebes scouts were treated as a Filipino ethnic group with antagonism toward the Filipino's responsible for the revolution, mainly Tagalog and mestizo Filipinos.

22. "Death of a Filipino Under Torture," by Bertrand Shadwell, J.R. Hayden Papers, Bentley Historical Society, University of Michigan, Ann Arbor; Bertrand Shadwell also authored the poem "Aguinaldo," written after Emilio Aguinaldo surrendered to the U.S. forces in the Philippines.

23. "Imperialism in the Philippines," by Bertrand Shadwell, Herbert Welsh Papers, Hatcher Graduate Library, University of Michigan, Ann Arbor.

24. Mabini had been the first prime minister of the first Filipino government, while Emilio Aguinaldo had been the first President. He was sent to Guam in 1901, under the U.S. accusations that he was inciting insurgency. Mabini authored some of the

foundational texts of the Malalos government. During and after the Filipino revolution, he suffered from paraplegia having survived a disease with the lasting effects of paralysis. He posed a significant threat to the U.S. Empire from his pen, and, therefore, he was exiled.

Regarding "irreconcilables" like Mabini, Taft recalled 25 were sent to Guam to quiet the insurgency in the Philippines

25. SIAP, pp. 654–655.

26. Ibid., p. 951.

27. Ibid., pp. 1527–1531.

28. "The Philippine Question Up in the Senate." *The New York Times,* May 6, 1902.

29. Ibid.

30. General Smith was also tried for court-martial for his orders to "kill and burn," covered earlier.

31. SIAP, pp. 2898–2899.

32. Ibid., p. 2784.

33. "The Philippine Question Up in the Senate." *The New York Times,* May 6, 1902.

34. "Spooner and Tillman have a Spirited Tilt." *The New York Times,* January 29, 1902.

35. SIAP, pp. 2900–2901.

36. Ibid., p. 2786.

37. Ibid.

38. Letter from Winslow to Welsh, Bentley; F. Warren Diary, Nov. 11, 1901, J.R. Hayden Papers, Bentley Historical Library, University of Michigan, Ann Arbor.

39. SIAP, p. 2947.

40. "Philippine Bill Assailed." *The New York Times.* May 21, 1902.

41. "Hoar Denounces Philippine War." *The Carroll Harold.* May 28, 1902.

42. SIAP, p. 2849.

43. Ibid., p. 2849.

44. Outside of the investigation, some were trying to pass a Philippine Government Bill led by Lodge, Chairman of the SIAP, establishing through Congress, a colonial government in the Philippines. Therefore, the information coming out of the investigations had political implications beyond establishing facts.

45. Ibid., p. 2852.

46. "The Concentration Camps." *The New York Times,* May 29, 1902.

47. SIAP, p. 79.

48. Ibid., p. 78.

49. Ibid., p. 558.

50. Ibid., p. 560, emphasis added.

51. Paul Kramer (2006) outlines this argument on the part of the United States.

52. SIAP, p. 665.

53. Ibid., pp. 870–871.

54. Ibid., p. 871.

55. Ibid., p. 871.

56. "Philippine Bill Assailed." *The New York Times*, May 21, 1902.

57. SIAP, pp. 2607–2610.

58. For more information on the origination of this publication, see Jim Zwick's introduction to the 2001 republication.

59. "Mr. Hoar's Speech on the Philippines." *The New York Times*, May 23, 1902.

60. Box 84. Herbert Welsh Collection, Historical Society of Pennsylvania.

61. Box 84, The Philippines, Herbert Welsh Collection, Historical Society of Pennsylvania, although the Memo does not claim an author, it looks to be the words of Moorfield Storey. My emphasis.

62. Ibid., my emphasis.

63. Box 84. Herbert Welsh Collection. Historical Society of Pennsylvania.

64. Michael Cullinane, "The Anti-Imperialist League and the Senate Investigations." Liberty and Anti-Imperialism, July 14, 2007. Http://www.antiimperialist.com /webroot/AILdocuments/CarpioSenIn.

65. Joseph Ralston Hayden Papers, Bentley Historical Library, University of Michigan, Ann Arbor.

66. Box 84, Philippines. Herbert Welsh Collection, Historical Society of Pennsylvania.

67. *Secretary Root's Record: "Marked Severities" in Philippine Warfare: An Analysis of the Law and Facts bearing the Action and Utterances of President Roosevelt and Secretary Root.* Boston: Geo. W. Ellis Co, 1902.

68. Cross testimony, October 13, 1902. J.R. Hayden Papers, Bentley Historical Library, University of Michigan, Ann Arbor.

69. Letter from Cross to Sniffen, April 6, 1901. J.R. Hayden Papers, Bentley Historical Library, University of Michigan, Ann Arbor.

70. "Ex-Soldier's Tale of the 'water cure,' *The Philadelphia Inquirer*, April 24, 1902, J.R. Hayden Papers, Bentley Historical Society, University of Michigan, Ann Arbor.

71. Letter to President Roosevelt from Norah Gleason, March 26, 1903. J. R. Hayden Papers, Bentley Historical Society, University of Michigan, Ann Arbor.

72. Petition of the Catholic Central Union, San Antonio, 1903; St. Boniface, Benevolent Society, Burlington, Iowa, Committee on Insular Affairs, n.d. NARA, Washington, D.C.

73. Gleason to President, April 13, 1903, J.R. Hayden Papers, Bentley Historical Society, University of Michigan, Ann Arbor.

74. Letter from Welsh to Hon. Knox, December 12, 1902. J.R. Hayden Papers. Bentley Historical Library, University of Michigan, Ann Arbor.

75. *Mass Meetings of Protest Against the Suppression of Truth About the Philippines*, Boston, 1903. Philippine Box, Swarthmore Peace Collection, Swarthmore College.

76. Ibid.

77. Letter from W.J. Palmer to E. B. Smith March 18, 1903. American Anti-Imperialist Papers, Bentley Historical Library, University of Michigan, Ann Arbor.

78. Letter to Welsh from Winslow, May 7, 1902. American Anti-Imperialist Papers, Bentley Historical Library, University of Michigan, Ann Arbor.

79. President Roosevelt, "Memorial Day Address." May 30, 1902, emphasis added.

80. Members of the committee included Moorfield Storey, Charles Francis Adams, Jr., Herbert Welsh, Carl Schurz, and Edwin Burritt Smith.

81. Letter to Welsh from Adams, December 12, 1902. J.R. Hayden Papers, Bentley Historical Library, University of Michigan, Ann Arbor.

82. Letter to Welsh from Gilbert Bates, August 19, 1902. Box 85, Herbert Welsh Collection, Historical Society of Pennsylvania.

83. Members of the committee included Edwin Burritt Smith, Herbert Welsh, Charles Francis Adams, Carl Schurz, Andrew Carnegie, and Moorfield Storey as their attorney (Schirmer 1972).

## Chapter 4

# Tracking Benevolent Assimilation

The birth of the Philippine Organic Act on July 1, 1902, killed the anti-imperialists' hope for the U.S. Constitution and U.S. law having any enforceable authority in the Philippines. Lost and bewildered, they grasped to find a new map for an anti-imperialist path, one still based on the values set forth in the Constitution. Furthermore, anti-imperialist advocates were convinced that government officials went to great lengths to veil the theft and violence in the Philippines. They wanted to raise that veil. In a Senate speech on May 31, 1902, anti-imperialist Senator Carmack stated, "It is a cheering sign that the second sober thought has come, that the better nature of the American people is again in the ascendant, when the party responsible for a buccaneering war is compelled to *veil the grossness of its designs*" (as quoted in Storey and Lichauco 1926: 178, emphasis added). That imperialists could no longer uncritically celebrate the "buccaneering war" was progress, of a kind. Somehow, principles still mattered. Anti-imperialists interpreted this newly defensive position as a small achievement of their work in the SIAP. However, they also believed the SIAP could have, and would have, exposed more severities had it continued. Hiding the "grossness of its designs" did not eliminate the results. Instead, imperialists pivoted, changing imperialist state formations in the United States and the Philippines to accommodate their plans, codifying them in the face of anti-imperialist dissent.

Imperialists learned from the SIAP that they needed to justify violence through codification, that is, make it legal within given parameters. Of course, they decided the parameters. Keeping this lesson in mind, they began stripping Filipinos/as of their legal rights of defense against the colonial government. New racist exceptions assisted in veiling the violence by codifying it within an imperialist legal system. In fact, the new status of "unincorporated territories" created a legal space for a separate colonial regime.

Therefore, the U.S. colonial regime incrementally wrote the rights of the people inhabiting these territories out of colonial laws in order to effectuate their plans accordingly. This meant that new colonial legal procedures methodically bounded and implemented violence and further inscribed racist practices into the laws and institutions of the United States. Imperialist state formations affected the treatment of people of color both at home and abroad. This chapter shows how anti-imperialists tried to frustrate the "unremarkable" and "routine" nature of these new imperialist state formations by further monitoring and exposing the exceptional violence. Broadening their scope from the letter of the law to envisioning the Constitution as a symbol of fundamental human rights, anti-imperialist leaders appealed to U.S. citizens at home for empathic connections based on the rights of humanity for Filipinas/os.

Concentrating on exposing the violence in the Philippines, the AIL lobbied politicians, petitioned Congress and the President, and publicized the records of military officials. Having learned from experience, they did not stop there. They also went around the government in Washington to work directly with Filipinos/as, gathering information from soldiers, trading information with Filipino newspapers and ilustrados, and sending U.S. investigators to the Philippines.[1] Erving Winslow opened his "Report of the Secretary" at the annual AIL meeting on November 25, 1905, by quoting William Lloyd Garrison: "We will be heard."[2] He went on to report that the AIL was shifting its focus to

> devote a large proportion of [the AIL's] means and its energies henceforward [to] the circulation through the press of trustworthy Philippine intelligence. We hope that a visit to the Philippines of a member of the Committee will have created some new channels of communication, but we have already established many, while the Philippine native newspapers furnish much valuable and useful information.[3]

Because of the lingering disparities between the official government accounts of the war and their own sources, AIL leaders determined that gathering their own information in the Philippines was urgent for preventing the U.S. public from being misled. Highlighting the number of people involved in this effort, Winslow thanked the following men who investigated on behalf of the AIL or provided testimony on "conditions in the archipelago": "President Schurman, George Kennan, Professor Henry Loomis Nelson, Professor H. Parker Willis, Mr. W. J. Bryan, Dr. D. J. Doherty, Mr. Fiske Warren, Professor Frederick Starr, Senator Patterson, Representatives Shafroth, W. A. Jones, and many others" (1908: 13). They had no less than two women who also provided information among the "many others."

Immediately after preparing for the SIAP in 1902, the AIL formed their own Philippine Investigating Committee, sometimes referred to as the Adams-Schurz Committee, which was comprised of Moorfield Storey, Charles Francis Adams, Carl Schurz, Edwin Burritt Smith, and Herbert Welsh.[4] Charged with continuing his leadership on the intelligence campaign, Welsh asked his contacts for funds supporting the latest project. He asserted the importance of these efforts:

> The startling and terrible facts which have already been brought to the public attention through the trials of Major Waller and General Jacob Smith; the Cornelius Gardener report of conditions in Tayabas, Province of Luzon, the evidence of returned soldiers, particularly that of Sergeant Riley and Private Smith, which I personally secured, before the Senate Committee; these, and many other things are too numerous to mention, show beyond peradventure that the country is confronted to-day with a most serious situation. This situation is serious not only because it affects the rights and fortunes of ten million people in the archipelago, but because it affects no less powerfully the honor and discipline of the United States Army and the credit of the American nation in the eyes of the civilized world.[5]

Between May 1, 1902, and February 4, 1903, according to Welsh's treasurer's report, the Committee raised $6,835.34 and spent all but $519.51, with the bulk of its expenditures going to printing, travel expenses, and attorney fees to secure witnesses.[6] Funding investigators in the Philippines would be no small economic task.

At this point, the AIL branches in different cities had different localized priorities, so the separate branches in New York, Philadelphia, and Boston ended up funding their own investigators in the Philippines. This decentralization was accompanied by a move toward closer collaboration with Filipinos/as, both through AIL-sponsored American observers on the ground in the Philippines and with Filipinos in the United States. This interracial activism strengthened the anti-imperialist humanitarian position in public debates over the selective application of the established rules of war and the use of torture to extract information through the water cure, implementing reconcentration camps, and the suspension of the *writ of habeas corpus*, as well as the resounding manufactured indifference to and stonewalling of what would be called, the "Moro Massacre." While some degree of racist paternalism continued to shape U.S.-Filipino/a relationships, the continued emphasis on cross-national/racial collaboration signified the triumph of the progressive arm of the anti-imperialist movement's ethical witnessing through empathic connections. The transnational move was a harbinger of the AIL leaders' next steps as the Philippines continued to recede from the public interest while the problem of racism in the United States and its empire persisted.

## ANTI-IMPERIALIST CITIZENS IN THE PHILIPPINES

The AIL leadership disagreed over how closely to identify the AIL with the investigators they were sponsoring in a dispute that echoed the Atkinson Affair. They finally determined that investigators should be independent, at least nominally. Three new investigators were chosen to visit the Philippines by three different arms of the AIL after 1902. Each of these investigators was charged with sending home firsthand accounts about what was the truth on the ground in the Philippines.

### Helen C. Wilson

One of these unofficial investigators was Helen Calista Wilson, a woman educated at Radcliffe and affiliated with the Boston branch of the AIL (Balce 2016). Fluent in Spanish and connected with the Boston Brahmins, Wilson had access to U.S. officers and Filipino ilustrados in the Philippines and could converse directly with Spanish-speaking Filipinos/as. In the following decades, Wilson would travel to Russia after the Russian Revolution to live and work in a Utopian community. Upon leaving the community, she would then travel with her friend, physician Elsie Reed Mitchell, across Russia and Central Asia, publishing a travel book about their adventure, *Vagabonding at Fifty: from Siberia to Turkestan*, after returning to the United States.[7] Before all of that, however, she traveled alone to the Philippines.

In 1903, the Philippine Commission passed the Reconcentration Act (aka the Brigandage Act), which allowed the governor-general to grant provincial governors the *legal* authority to reconcentrate rural communities under the control of the Constabulary (Kramer 2006). This Act created a legalized state of exception in the form of an internment camp. That same year, on a trip sponsored by Fiske Warren (rather than directly by the AIL), Wilson anonymously published a timely firsthand account of the reconcentration policy, *A Massachusetts Woman in the Philippines* (1903), that gave the U.S. public its first glimpse of how the military operations in the Philippines were daily affecting the Filipina/o people, not just insurgents.[8]

Wilson discovered during this trip that it was difficult to gain the confidence of Filipinos/as without an introduction from a well-known Filipina/o, so she turned to the Lopez family with whom Warren was friends.[9] Warren and his siblings had hosted Clemencia during her stay in the Boston area and introduced her to Louis Brandeis, who became her attorney in the SIAP, in Washington D.C. (Green 1989). On her trip to Manila in 1903, Wilson stopped in Hong Kong and, armed with proper introductions, met with members of the Junta, including a brief meeting with Galicano Apacible and a longer one with Felipe Agoncillo. She felt that they were "discouraged" by the situation in the Philippines, and "a little bit embarrassed to know how to deal with a strong-minded woman travelling [*sic*] around the world alone."[10] It is worth noting, this is also what Clemencia Lopez had done in the few years prior.

Wilson also met General Artemio Ricarte, who had been one of Aguinaldo's chief officers in the revolution. He had been imprisoned and released in Guam with Apolinario Mabini. Whereas Mabini returned to Manila and took an oath of allegiance to the United States, Ricarte, like Sixto Lopez, chose to go to Hong Kong rather than take the oath. Although this separated him from his family, he refused to be made a "traitor"[11] to either the Philippines or the United States. According to Wilson, he asked her to express his deep gratitude to "those in America whose protest resulted in his freedom."[12]

Upon arrival in Manila, Manuel Lopez, one of Sixto and Clemencia's brothers who had also been imprisoned, met Wilson. He found her a room to rent with a Filipino family, an elderly couple caring for their grandson after their daughter had died. The daughter had married a white American soldier, who was the father of the child and visited periodically. Manuel also accompanied Wilson to Balayan, where she toured the towns and met military personnel, U.S. teachers, and Filipinos/as. Of one town, she wrote:

> Tuy was burned to the ground by the Spanish, and the stone foundations of the large houses and the church were destroyed by the dynamite. The people have built for themselves little nipa and bamboo houses amongst the ruins, but the only indications of their "astounding progress" is in the names of the streets which an enterprising presidente has changed with a due regard to the new future which lies before them. The desolate and dusty main road with its discouraged pigs and chickens is McKinley street, while to the right and left branch off Washington Ave., Michigan Ave., Roosevelt Ave., etc. Every one [*sic*] who could get a way [*sic*] has gone; there are almost no work animals, and the people are utterly discouraged and wretchedly poor. Yet only six years ago this was a vigorous and flourishing little town, and the ruins of the big church and the heaps of shattered stone about the town seem to indicate some little past prosperity. I asked the Justice of the Peace if they hoped for better times soon, and he turned his dark and melancholy face away and said No, he was afraid it would be a long time.[13]

The people she met in Tuy told her about the public torture of one man and the death by water cure of another.

Touring the country with Manuel Lopez, Wilson met former U.S. soldiers who had become colonial teachers, as had several women she knew from home whom she met again in Manila—the first ship of 600 American teachers had come to the Philippines from San Francisco in 1901. Other Americans advised her to get work with the colonial government for guaranteed steady pay, but she believed this would create tension, or at least distance, between her and Filipinos/as. Instead she started work as an independent stenographer. Wilson observed that Filipinos/as and U.S. civilians alike deemed the colonial administrators under the governorship of Luke Wright inept at best. Wright centralized the U.S. colonial government (Go 2008) and suspended the writ of *habeas corpus* in Batangas and Cavite, instituting another colonial state of exception that allowed Filipinos (like the Lopez brothers) to be imprisoned without being charged (see next).

Wilson also specifically investigated the effects of reconcentration. On June 30, 1905, *El Renacimiento*, a Filipino newspaper advocating for independence, published "Filipino Opinion of Reconcentration," expressing their continued contempt for the practice:

> It seems that the magnanimous spirit which in the American Congress cried out so indignantly against the Weylerian proceedings in Cuba is unconcerned about conditions in the Philippines. The ordinance of the civil commission has fallen like a pestilence on the unfortunate people of Cavite. It is only natural that the present state of affairs should fill us with the gravest apprehension. We say frankly and with deep sorrow that this measure which causes so much suffering is not justified by the good at which it claims to aim. There are created by it feelings of animosity and rancor that will not be forgotten for many years,--perhaps never.[14]

After reading this and other *El Renacimiento* reports on reconcentration, Wilson decided to visit the camps in person. She went to "camps at Talisay, Naic, Imus, San Francisco de Malabon and other places where the conditions were at least as bad."[15]

Although Wilson was an anti-imperialist, her reports demonstrate her commitment to fair and accurate investigation. With her Filipino interpreters, she determined that although the official rationale for reconcentration was to overcome "hostile" groups, two neighboring villages in Bacoor were reconcentrated to gain the surrender of one outlaw, Felizardo, whom Wilson likened to the "James boys" of the U.S. Civil War. Wilson also detailed the living conditions in the camps. "Reconcentrados," as their inhabitants were called, lived in overcrowded bamboo huts, were made to attend roll call every night, and were given no food rations but had to beg food from people in the town or live on the shellfish they could gather near the shore. There was widespread malnutrition in the camps, along with "exposure" to the elements, and attendant illnesses, including malaria and dysentery:

> There were several children with the thin little bodies and bloated abdomens which the pictures of reconcentration in Cuba and famine in India must have made familiar to every one; not such extreme cases, it is true, but none the less [*sic*] testifying to insufficient, improper or filthy food.[16]

In differentiating between U.S. reconcentration in the Philippines and Spanish reconcentrations in Cuba, Wilson again proffered a measured analysis:

> The reconcentrados were free of the town during the day time; in spite of a great deal of evident destitution, there was no one actually dying of starvation, and while there was much illness it is doubtful whether the death rate was increased to an extraordinary degree. What had been done, apparently, was to take these 500 souls, warn them to bring food and provisions with them, and then turn them loose in the corner of a ten-acre lot to do the best they could for themselves.

If the United States was supposed to be teaching Filipinas/os the practice of democracy, she asked, "What conceptions of citizenship, of sovereign law, of individual rights and liberties are these people learning from us?"[17]

Wilson sent her reports to the *Springfield Republican*, which published them in July 1905 (Kramer 2006), but by then the U.S. had finally discontinued its reconcentration policy (Zwick 2005). When Wilson returned to Boston in 1908, the AIL arranged for a luncheon in her honor as well as a meeting with a "Mr. Dimayuga and any other such Filipinos as the secretary may think proper to invite."[18] These Filipinos she was to meet in Boston were likely *pensionado* students as "the secretary," Erving Winslow, was involved with supporting the Filipino Student Organization in America and often contributed to their magazine to which Dimayuga also contributed (see next).

## H. Parker Willis

The New England AIL (Boston and Philadelphia) also sent Economist H. Parker Willis to the Philippines. Willis graduated with his PhD in economics from the University of Chicago and had studied under J. Laurence Laughlin, a Chicago AIL vice president. Subsequently, Willis had been the Washington correspondent for the *Springfield Republican*. In 1902, he was an economics professor at Washington and Lee University as well as a correspondent for the *Journal of Commerce* and lead writer for the *New York Evening Post*.[19] In the decades after his return from the Philippines, Willis would help write the Federal Reserve Act, found the U.S. Federal Reserve System and become its first Secretary and later the Chief Economist, though that actual title did not come until later in the Federal Reserve's history. He would also begin the Philippine National Bank for which he was the first President and the Philippine American Chamber of Commerce and continue with his academic career.[20]

In 1902, Willis corresponded with Herbert Welsh to prepare for the assignment in the Philippines.[21] Along with news updates, Willis planned to make an academic study, sending back periodic reports to the AIL. He sent Welsh a

"Plan for Organizing a Systematic Philippine Investigation" that outlined his assessment of the situation. Willis believed that the Philippine Civil Government bill of 1902 opened the door for "a gross misuse of the appointments in the islands," which would only continue the unfortunate practice of using the Philippines as "a dumping ground for refuse political material," that is, "worthless political workers who must be rewarded."[22]

One way to rectify the situation was to create "fear of scandals at home if the fundamental principles of decent government are too grossly violated."[23] "Reliable" and "steady" information was "absolutely essential" to this strategy. Believing the Associated Press to be subservient to the will of the government and hobbled by the cost of reporting from the Philippines and the claims of newspapers at home that the stories were too "old" to print, Willis argued that an AIL representative needed to be stationed in the Philippines for an "indefinite" amount of time. This person would staff what was essentially a "Philippines news service" that would give stories on the Philippines to one paper in each market to be published nationally on the same date. A "Philippine Information Association" would fund this news service. Willis' plan impressed Welsh and the committee enough that they sponsored him as their investigator in the Philippines. Willis also secured support as writer for the *Journal of Commerce* and the *Engineering and Mining Journal*.[24]

Initially, Willis corresponded with Welsh. But Welsh had a physical and mental breakdown in June 1903. This was more than activist burnout. He had literally experienced the dark night of the soul, refusing to accept U.S. imperialist operations in the Philippines but feeling he had little to no effect on changing it despite his devotion. He was overworked and overwrought, and his doctor ordered him to cut back his work on the Philippines.[25] At that point, Willis began corresponding primarily with Moorfield Storey, one of his main benefactors (along with Charles Francis Adams of Boston and William J. Palmer of Colorado). When Willis completed his investigations in 1904, Storey was instrumental in carrying through funding for the publication of his results, which appeared as *Our Philippine Problem: A Study of American Colonial Policy* (1905).

Willis made use of information gathered by the new colonial government from the Philippine Census, which was conducted in 1903. The Census determined that "the total population of the Philippine Islands is 7,635,425, of which number 6,987,686 are classed as 'civilized,' 647,740 as 'wild.' " The AIL in Boston published the Census to underscore both "the claim of the Anti-Imperialists that the Philippine people [were] capable of national evolution without foreign assistance" and the depredations caused by the U.S. war and colonial government: "A comparison with previous statements of the population show[ed] a large falling off in many cases from the computations made by Spanish authorities, which is to be attributable to the mortality caused by war, famine and disease incidental thereto, resulting from benevolent assimilation."[26] Willis elaborated on these conditions in a report published in the *New York Evening Post* on October 28, 1904, as an appendix to anti-imperialist Senator E.W. Carmack's speech before the Senate on "Conditions in the Philippines":

> As General Davis mildly states the situation (Report, 1903, p. 31): "Americans in the Philippines have not so far been an unmixed blessing to the native inhabitants." We have, in fact, destroyed the public buildings of the country, inflicted continuous crop losses, during a period of six years; ravaged and burned large sections of territory; produced conditions leading to the death of most of the farm animals and to serious human and animal epidemics; brought foreign trade to an unprofitable condition by our tariff legislation; inaugurated a tremendously expensive government for the benefit of foreign officeholders; established a partisan judiciary; crowded the prisons, and deported or sent to the gallows the best and most patriotic of the native leaders.

In his study, Willis estimated that 600,000 Filipinos/as had been killed, though he believed he was erring on the conservative side:

> Crops, houses, and villages were destroyed or burned for the purpose of depriving insurgents of means of support, and reconcentration was finally resorted to. General J.F. Bell estimated in 1902 that one-sixth of the natives in Luzon died as the direct or indirect result of the operations, a figure which would mean a total death-roll of at least 600,000 persons.[27] (Willis 1905: 23)

Since then, there has been significant debate on the number of Filipino casualties (Gates 1984).[28] While the high estimate of 3,000,000 deaths from fighting and U.S. reconcentration policies was based on a misprint quoted by Gore Vidal in the *New York Review of Books* in 1981, historians and critics of U.S. involvement in the Philippines place the number between 200,000 (Blount 1913; Wolff 1960) and 600,000 (Constantino 1975; Miller 1982; Willis 1905; Zinn in Schirmer 1972).[29] The point, however, is that whether the number of deaths was 100,000, it was still too many for anti-imperialists. But, their fears that half a million or more people had died were exacerbated by the difficulty of finding reliable information and the fact that they kept finding previously unrevealed information that had been intentionally obscured.

Concerns about secrecy were not ungrounded. A 1902 Senate Document quoted a telegraph sent to all commanders in Batangas in 1901, which articulated the U.S. total war approach and its concomitant obscurantism:

> To combat such a population, it is necessary to make the state of war as insupportable as possible, and there is no more efficacious way of accomplishing

this *than by keeping the minds of the people in such a state of anxiety and apprehension that living under such conditions will soon become unbearable. Little should be said. The less said the better.* Let acts, not words, convey the intention.[30]

Anti-imperialists took these statements at their word, firmly believing that acts had been committed without public statement or adequate reporting. The consequences of these acts were dire:

> Although no very careful estimate of the total casualties has been made, it is certain from the records, official and semi-official, that the Filipinos killed in battle far outnumbered the American losses. Judge Blount's examination of the available war records showed a ratio of sixteen Filipinos to every one American killed (20).[31] (Storey and Lichauco 1926: 122)

Indeed, as Storey and Lichauco went on to point out, the total war approach led to drastic results as officers "let acts, not words, convey the intention":

> Examination of the casualties in the fiercest struggles of the nineteenth century, for example, show always a striking similarity between the proportion of men killed and the men wounded on the field of battle. Generally this ratio is six to one, or at least five to one, that is to say for every one man killed in battle five or six victims are wounded. [. . .] Turn now to the Philippine campaign where the aim of the military administration was to be one which would 'win the confidence, respect and affection of the inhabitants of the Philippines (3). What do the official war records show? Almost the reverse, that is to say that *for every Filipino wounded in battle, five were killed.* (pp. 126–127, my emphasis)

Willis was the key figure in tracking and exposing these drastic results of benevolent assimilation policies. Though it couldn't change the past, having the records laid out in numbers with comparisons that put the violence in the Philippines in perspective was the point. Principles of progressive civilization still mattered.

## Dr. David J. Doherty

The New York AIL also seeking another investigator, contacted Fiske Warren to ask about the expertise of Dr. David J. Doherty.[32] Warren learned of Doherty, who was working as a medical doctor in the Philippines, on his visits there in 1901 and 1903. In 1904, the New York AIL officially split from the Boston and Philadelphia branches and renamed itself the Filipino Independence Association, then the Filipino Rights Association, and finally the Filipino Progress Association (a progression of name changes that reflect

**Figure 4.1** According to the description on the back of the photo: "Seated Row (Right to Left): Shuster—Gov. Smith—Luzuriaga—Doherty" "Standing Row Priv. Sec. Wright—Alb. Barretto (Immediatrista)—Raingel [?] (of Renacimiento)—Artizao [?] (of Democracia)—Capt. Rissner[?]—Albert Ferguson (Assoc. Press)—Rupert Ferguson (interpreter) & Jaun Armuling[?] (Federal). *Source*: Edward Ordway Papers, Manuscript and Archives Division, New York Public Library.

debates and resignations over strategic focus). Around the same time, the Chicago organization also split from the Boston group, making the AIL no longer a national organization. Josephine Shaw Lowell spearheaded the efforts in New York to secure Doherty.[33]

Doherty already had done research in the Philippines, including submitting a report on disease in the Philippines to Congress. He had an interest in linguistics as well, having already published a book on the Hawaiian language. In 1900, he translated a German report titled "The Philippines: A Summary Account of their Ethnographical, Historical and Political Conditions" (Blumentritt 1900), and he later published a book on Tagalog. In 1904, he wrote a report on conditions in the Philippines, about which Carl Schurz, a member of the New York group, wrote positively to Adams:

> The report on the Philippine affairs written by Mr. Doherty is the most instructive and important paper on that subject I have ever read. Mr. Doherty is evidently a keen observer and what he says bears the mark of candor and conscientiousness. The views he opens of the man in which the Filipinos are treated by the constabulary are startling in the highest degree. As you are aware, I am a Forty-eighter. When I look back upon the things which drove us into revolution in Germany at that period, I can only say that they were as nothing compared with the police-despotism to which the Filipinos are subjected under our flag.

The observations of Mr. Doherty on the administration of justice, on the character of the American population there and on the aspirations of the Filipinos as to their future are of the highest value. I think this paper ought by all means to be brought to the notice of President Roosevelt. He ought to be made to read the whole of it. (pp. 308–309)[34]

In 1906, Warren made another trip to Manila and the New York group finally enlisted Doherty as an investigator. In the first six months, he was associated with the New York group, Doherty wrote to newspapers at home, reporting on issues in the Philippines.[35] But the work was not always easy. In letters to Ordway, Doherty noted the difficulty of getting news from sources other than the government. Therefore, he had to speculate, for instance, that "in Samar the war against the Pulahanes (or 'bandits') is one of extermination, which will run along in guerilla fashion for along [*sic*] time."[36] In an official letter to the Filipino Independence Association, Doherty reported that he was working with editors of Filipino newspapers who were upset about the "race question," so he was trying to smooth things over with them and find a Filipino editor to work with.[37]

Doherty also continued to support the Filipino/a people. He helped establish the Filipina women's society "La Proteccion de la Infancia" or "Gota de Leche," which organized efforts to encourage and subsidize sterilized milk for feeding infants as part of a larger effort to promote the general health of infants and mothers.[38] He donated funds to purchase the organization's first building. The organization originally consisted mainly of elite Filipinas who worked with white colonial American women to raise funds. According to Ordway, the racial breakdown of attendance at their first major fundraiser, a garden party, was "65% pure Filipino, 20% mestizo and only 15% American" (presumably white).[39] Doherty passed away in 1908, one year after founding the organization. Before he passed, however, he provided the New York organization with his assessments of conditions in the Philippines, and his suggestions for addressing them.

Wilson, Willis, and Doherty were three examples of U.S. anti-imperialists who worked in the Philippines to support the Filipino/a people in their struggle against colonialism, while also sharing critical information from the ground with anti-imperialist organizations back home. One notable common element in their work was their commitment to working with Filipinos/as in their information-gathering and their professional and philanthropic efforts. Their ethical witnessing was practiced out of a concern for an accurate and empathic connection to the Philippine experience and motivated them to go directly to the source.

# FILIPINO VOICES

## Filipino Voices and the Writ of Habeas Corpus

On July 31, 1905, Governor Luke E. Wright again suspended the *writ of habeas corpus* in the provinces of Cavite and Batangas. Wright wanted the Philippines to be more conducive to business interests than it had been under the governorship of Taft, who worked with the existing patronage system of government (Go 2008: Kramer 2006). Despite President Roosevelt's declaration that the war was over, fighting had not stopped in these provinces. Suspending the *writ of habeas corpus* legally designated those still fighting against the United States as "insurrectos" or "ladrones" and took away their protections under military code. This enacted a new legal state of exception, where proof of a crime was unnecessary for imprisoning a Filipino/a. In the face of frequent attacks against the Filipino Constabulary, which was cooperating with the United States, Wright stated:

> Whereas, because of the foregoing conditions there exists a state of insecurity and terrorism among the people which makes it impossible in the ordinary way to conduct preliminary investigations before the justices of the peace and other judicial officers;
>
> In the interest of public safety, it is hereby ordered that the writ of habeas corpus is from this date suspended in the provinces of Cavite and Batangas. (as quoted in Dy Yap 1972: 54)

The Philippine Commission's Reconcentration Act of 1903, another legal state of exception creating legal framework for the colonial use of internment, had laid the groundwork. Suspending *habeas corpus* resulted in Filipinos being imprisoned for reasons from flying the Filipino flag to supporting the insurrectos. Looking back, Erving Winslow (1908) described the circumstances: "The vaunted liberty which has been given to the Filipinos has been circumscribed by unusual and severe sedition and libel laws. [. . .] Any public exposure, even in private premises, of insignia of the Philippine Republic has been legally made an act of sedition. In the archipelago truth of a libel constitutes no defence [*sic*] for it" (pp. 9–10). Given that Filipinas/os in these provinces could be imprisoned without evidence, it was a significant challenge for their lawyers to obtain their freedom.

One tactic for repealing the legal "state of emergency" and reinstating the *writ of habeas corpus* was to use anti-imperialist channels to inform the U.S. public.[40] Filipinos/as and Americans collaborated in these efforts. Fiske Warren worked with Filipino lawyer Alberto Barretto, a member of the Philippine Independence Party,[41] to alert anti-imperialists in the United States and create additional alliances.[42] Doherty also took up the issue, researching previous trials in the colony against Filipinos for use as precedent.[43]

In 1905, *Barcelon v. Baker* directly challenged the principle of exceptions to Filipino/a rights established by the colonial system[44] that codified reconcentration (Dy Yap 1972). Anti-imperialists in the United States publicized the case as it went before the Supreme Court. Erving Winslow wrote to Edward Ordway that the Supreme Court:

> decided that the suspension of the habeas corpus in case of disorder or insurrection is a matter entirely within the province of the executive and legislative department, that is, the Governor General and the Commission,--and that the Supreme Court has no right to make any inquiry on behalf of a petitioner as to whether the facts upon which the suspension of the habeas corpus were based existed [*sic*] or not.[45]

Therefore, the ruling established by the Supreme Court that U.S. colonial subjects had no recourse to legal protection in the United States from any colonial decrees. Filipinos/as were entirely subjects of the U.S. colonial administration and no branch of government would stand forth to defend them based on existing U.S. law.

In the summer of 1905, a contingent from Congress visited the Philippines to study the situation. Although some wanted to confine the trip to an economic study, anti-imperialist advocates prevailed and Filipinos/as were able to voice their complaints to the group:

> It was only through the efforts of a member of the League who then happened to be in the Philippine Islands, urged and enforced by Senator Patterson and Representative W.A. Jones, that two days' hearing was given to the pleas which the Filipinos wished to offer and which they did offer, individually and by representative delegations, in behalf of immediate independence. The record of this hearing, which took place in Marble Hall at Manila August 29 and 30, 1905, was published and widely distributed, constituting, as it did, a reasonable appeal for a national evolution under the controlling influence of the large class of intelligent and educated Filipinos competent to guide their countrymen towards a satisfactory and orderly government. (Winslow 1908: 10)

It was a move that demonstrated anti-imperialists evolution in ethical witnessing from pontificating on values of democracy to putting these values to practice by advocating for Filipinos/as to voice their views firsthand. Anti-imperialists referred to this meeting as "The Marble Hall Conference with Filipinos."[46] Anti-imperialists found the meeting heartening because it affirmed that Filipinos/as still wanted independence and were willing to express that desire to U.S. authorities, despite imperialist arguments that

Filipinos/as did not want independence, and that any who said they did were only incited by anti-imperialists.

In the interest of enlightening the U.S. public on the situation in the Philippines, providing access to Filipino/a views unfiltered by the U.S. press or government officials, and demonstrating Filipinos/as' capacity for self-government, the AIL began translating newspaper editorials from *El Renacimiento*, *La Vanguardia*, and *El Ideal*, publishing them "before the eyes of many hundreds of thousands of readers"[47] in the United States as "Voice of the Filipinos."[48] In this way, Filipinos expressed opposition to a replay of the 1904 World's Fair displays of Filipino tribes at the 1908 Fair.[49] The AIL executive committee also asked the Commissioner of Immigration whether it was illegal to find Igorots for exhibition.[50] Filipinos/as also expressed frustration and disillusionment with the "indefinite postponement of their aspirations" for independence.[51]

Anti-imperialists were figuring out a new path forward in the Philippines with the direct voices of Filipinos/as. When these collaborative efforts brought the Filipino/a voice to the United States, it further transformed anti-imperialists' ethical witnessing. They would have to expand their vision for Filipino rights beyond the delimited U.S. Constitution. They would have to dream a new way forward and begin advocating for a more expansive universal human rights that opposed all unjust, racist laws across the globe. It was an ethical evolution born out of a willingness to listen to Filipinas/os' views on their own experience.

## Filipino/a Voices and the Pensionado Act of 1903

Back in the United States, Filipino students, many of whom were government-funded *pensionados*, attempted to foster relationships with anti-imperialists. Although anti-imperialists were sympathetic to the students, they were careful about how they went forward in aiding them. This friendly, yet tentative, relationship between anti-imperialists and Filipino/a students has gone unnoted in previous histories of anti-imperialism. However, this relationship offers a fascinating addition to understanding the interconnections and collaborations between Americans and Filipinos/as and what this meant for Filipino/a resistance and anti-imperialist ethical witnessing.

The Education Act of 1901 was written in part by Bernard Moses, Philippine Commissioner and professor at the University of California, Berkeley, and laid the groundwork for the American colonial education system. When the *USS Thomas* left San Francisco in July 1901 loaded with 600 American teachers, men and women, seeking to educate and civilize the new colonial subjects, Fred Atkinson was at the helm. His characterization of the educational mission in the Philippines is telling in its paternalistic approach:

The Filipino people, taken as a body, are children and, childlike, do not know what is best for them. That they possess ideals and ideas creates a faith and a hope that ultimately they may be able to institute a republic modeled on the American lines. In the ideal spirit of preparing them for the work of governing themselves finally, their American guardianship has begun. Our political sway has not been imposed upon the people to any greater extent than was necessary; and by the very fact of our superiority of civilization and our grater[*sic*] capacity for industrial activity we are bound to exercise over them a profound social influence.[52]

Atkinson was among those David Haskins called "conscientious imperialists," who believed America had a duty to Filipinos/as and that, racially, Filipinos/as needed Americans to help them along the march of civilization. In fact, Atkinson characterized America's colonial rule in the Philippines as an advantageous "accident" for Filipinos/as who would benefit from a better system of education and government than under the Spanish. Meanwhile, General MacArthur characterized the colonial education enterprise as an extension of military operations to pacify and tranquilize the population.[53]

These projects extended from the Philippines to the United States. In 1903, the Philippines Commission passed the Pensionado Act, which allowed Filipino/a students to be sponsored and educated in U.S. colleges and universities. As part of plan to specifically educate Filipinos/as in ways of democratic governance, many *pensionados/as* majored in government, political science, or infrastructural studies like engineering and agriculture. The intention was for these students to return to the Philippines and participate in the colonial government. From early on, both Filipino/a men and a few women studied in the United States.

In 1905, just two years after the Pensionado Act, Filipino/a students started the *Filipino Students Magazine*. They based the magazine in Berkeley, California, although they were studying across the United States, with most in the Midwest (Murphy 2019). As an "English magazine controlled entirely by Filipinos," they requested submissions from anyone interested in the Philippines, but especially from Filipino/a students.[54] Conscious of their double role in representing Filipinos/as in the United States and serving as a bridge between the United States and the Philippines (Murphy 2019), they dedicated their first issue to President Roosevelt and the second to nationalist hero, Jose Rizal. In that first issue, they also noted that "though it is almost unavoidable to let race feeling enter when one's people are unjustly criticized [*sic*], still as far as possible we will confine our subjects to Literature, Science, and Arts, to cultivate which is our sole purpose.[55] The audience included Filipino/a students, Americans interested in the Philippines, and Filipinos interested in the students in the United States, so the magazine was written in both English and Spanish, with some articles in both languages, but most in one or the other. The English articles targeted English-speaking audiences, the Spanish articles targeted Spanish-speaking audiences, and the articles they deemed most important appeared in both languages.

Once the first issue honoring Roosevelt appeared, the students invited anti-imperialist leaders to contribute meditations on "The Philippine Question." The resulting articles made suggestions for how Filipinos/as could work to secure Philippine Independence, and gave advice for navigating the American public. Between 1905 and 1907, several AIL officers, including Secretary Erving Winslow, Treasurer David Haskins, Jr., President Moorfield Storey, and J. LeRoy Smith contributed articles.

Winslow was a steady supporter. For the second issue, dedicated to Filipino independence leader Jose Rizal, he contributed "To the Filipino Students," where he encouraged the students to press for independence and release any feelings of obligation to the United States for their education:

> The Filipino students who are pursuing their studies in various institutions of learning in the United States need not consider themselves hampered or bound by any debt of gratitude to the officials of an administration which is drawing large revenues by taxation without representation from the Philippines. It is their own countrymen who are really paying the expenses of these young men [and women], just as their own countrymen are paying the expenses of sanitation, education, and government in the archipelago, affairs over which they have no control. Thus there is no obligation to these students to deny the aspiration for independence which exists in every true Filipino heart, nor to slacken in the pursuit of all peaceable methods of promoting it. It is not morally competent to the United States to require any oath to obey its sovereignty unless that sovereignty is limited and defined by the Constitution of the United States. It is quite certain therefore that no oath can be binding which may have been exacted from them by compulsion of the Philippine authorities or any other sovereignty than that of the Constitution itself, which, in the opinion of four out of nine Justices of the Supreme Court [in *Downes v Bidwell* (1901)], and some of the best constitutional lawyers of the country, does not recognize colonial possessions and colonial administration.[56]

For Winslow, the Constitution was still the foundation with which Filipino students would need to build their rights.

Another article in the same issue, "The Purpose that Should Govern Us" by Gerónimo Huising, a student at the University of Illinois, discussed to what purpose Filipinos should study in the United States and learn U.S. customs. Huising declared his wish for independence.

No matter that certain nations refuse us now the acknowledgment of our more legitimate rights; very soon we shall convince them that *there is no human force capable to act against the irresistible impulse toward freedom which rules the Universe.*

Huising was beginning to make an argument based on universal human rights in the face of empire. He followed up with a gracious, if wishful, acknowledgment of his faith in the United States and its adherence to the Monroe Doctrine, exemplifying Filipino/a cultural emotives communicating respect, humility, and gratitude

besides this. Washington, Franklin and Lincoln's great nation, that sees and observes us in all our actions, appreciates our judiciousness, prudence, aptitude, and our energetic resolution; this nation will not delay us longer than is necessary, we believe. So we must work for our rights and keep our aspirations noble, thus showing them once more, like the immortal Monroe: "America is for the American people, and the Philippines is for the Filipinos."[57]

In the next issue, Moorfield Storey and David Haskins made contributions that echoed Winslow's earlier contribution. They gave their assessment for how to break through imperialists' stonewalling. Storey suggested that the way to independence was no longer through arms, but through appeals to the "uneasy conscience" of Americans that would provide proof of Filipino/a fitness for self-government, and through pressing every "just cause" for complaint. He declared, "The weapon of the Filipino patriot then is the truth."[58] Haskins identified the greatest opponent to Filipino/a freedom as those "conscientious imperialists" who saw it as the duty of the United States to give "good" government to the Philippines. The way to thwart their claims was to prove there was good government in the Philippines.

The English-language contributions of the Filipino/a students continued to carefully balance wishes for independence and rights with expressions of gratitude and generosity toward the American colonizers. Other articles described the geography and industry of the Philippines, using American comparisons to help their audience understand. One repeating column titled "United States Queries" listed common questions Americans asked Filipinos/as. It was at once humorous and derisive, holding a space for Filipinos/as feel a sense of solidarity in the face of stereotypical questions about their "civilization" and competence. The column also held up a mirror to interested Americans, so they could see themselves as they interacted with Filipinos. The questions had no commentary, for it was unnecessary:

Were you at the St. Louis exhibit, too?
I don't think you are a Filipino.
You don't look like Igorrot, igorote, igorrrottttteeee—whatever you call it.
How do you feel with that suit on? American made. eh?
Where did you get those American shoes?
When did you begin to wear shoes?
What church do you go to?
Do you know Bishop Aglipay?
I didn't know you didn't have bark-of-tree houses!
Do you like our houses?
What kind of homes do you live in?
You don't get much cold up there, do you?
You don't mind the warm weather, do you?[59]

Back in the Philippines, the insular government responded with acrimony to the calls for independence in articles by anti-imperialists and Filipinos alike. In fact, by November of the magazine's inaugural year, Winslow learned that a new Filipino student magazine had been started in Washington. It was to be "more or less" under "government supervision" and free from exposure to "nefarious" anti-imperialist influences.[60] Because imperialists were questioning whether Filipinos/as actually wanted independence or were just influenced by anti-imperialists, some anti-imperialists questioned whether their involvement might in fact be detrimental to the Filipino/a cause. Schurz exemplified this sentiment in a letter to Winslow dated February 20, 1906:

> I have been seriously considering what I, or any of us old anti-imperialists, might write for the Filipino [student's association] paper in California that would be of any real use to the Filipinos themselves or to anybody else. Might we tell them to hold fast to the idea of independence? It has always been our contention that the Filipinos were unanimously for independence, and would remain so, *without* being confirmed in their faith by us. This has been always, and is now, one of our principal points. Would it be wise now to do anything that might make it appear as if we had reason not to believe in our own contention? Will it not be much wiser to let those young men go on by themselves and to avoid the appearance as if they were in our leading-strings and as if they needed pushing from this quarter. (Bancroft 1913: 443, emphasis in original)

Schurz was responding to a request, authored by Felipe Buencamino, Jr., from students who sought to align themselves with the AIL and asked for financial and political support, both of which the AIL provided, the latter in personal correspondence and contributions to the magazine.

As this interaction demonstrates, anti-imperialists were ambivalent about their involvement with Filipino organizations, hesitating to become over-involved and undermine the larger goals. Yet, the experience of the students and history of the magazine also shows the interdependent relationship between anti-imperialists and the Filipino movement for independence in the Philippines. While this relationship was weak overall, it persisted with meaningful benefits for both sides: the U.S. anti-imperialists received information and materials for their campaign to change the minds of the U.S. public from first-hand experiences, while the Filipino/a students received support for their cause.

## U.S. INDIFFERENCE AND THE MORO MASSACRE

While Wilson, Doherty, and Warren were still in the Philippines and increasing numbers of Filipino students were attending U.S. universities, news broke in the United States about the "Moro Massacre" (also known as the Battle of Mt. Dajo and the Battle of Jolo) in 1906. This "battle" took place on the island of Jolo in a crater at the top of Mt. Dajo, where the U.S. military surrounded Filipino/a Muslims. Major-General Leonard Wood, who twenty years later became Governor of the Philippines, led the attack. At the end, 600 Filipinos/as and 18 U.S. soldiers lay dead. No prisoners were taken. The incident sparked a new spate of anti-imperialist cartoons and editorials criticizing the extreme violence.

**Figure 4.2   Moorfield Storey Papers, Library of Congress.** Image taken by the author.

The Boston AIL made a postcard of a photograph of the aftermath that showed U.S. soldiers standing over men, women, and children lying dead in the crater. Above the picture read the words of congratulations that President Theodore Roosevelt sent to Woods: "I congratulate you and the officers and men of your command upon the brave feat of arms wherein you and they so well upheld the honor of the American flag." The reference information beneath the photo echoed this tragic irony:

> From a negative made on the spot the day of the "brave feat of arms" when six hundred Moros, men, women and children were killed by the Army under Gen. Wood: "a logical incident in the sequence of events which will include the whole history of the Philippine possession."

Juxtaposing the picture with Roosevelt's words underlined the hypocrisy and contradictions of the situation, and served as a protest against the extraordinary—yet accepted and even lauded—violence against the Moros. This was ethical witnessing at its most basic, forcing the acknowledgement of the slaughter.

Frustrated by public indifference and the administration's stonewalling, anti-imperialists still wanted to raise the consciousness of U.S. citizens at home about the continued violence occurring in the Philippines. Although using a postcard with a picture that displayed the dead was a new tactic for the AIL, they deployed it in the historical context of trading postcards that recorded the lynching of black men. For some, lynching postcards served as dark proof of white barbarity, but others saw them as spectacular proof of white superiority. Either way, the pictures and news of the massacre elicited a new spike in the public debate on the Philippines.[61] It was a direct appeal to the empathic connections opened through witnessing suffering as political expression.

Moorfield Storey had become president of the AIL after the death of George Boutwell. He wrote about the massacre in the *Boston Daily Advertiser* on March 13, 1906, making comparisons of the U.S. record of violence across the inter-imperial and intra-imperial fields:

> Suppose we had heard that the British had dealt thus with a Boer force, that the Turks had so attacked and slaughtered Armenians, that colored men had so massacred white men, or even that 600 song birds had been slaughtered for their plumage, would not our papers have been filled with protests and expressions of horror? [. . .] This outrage unhappily is only one in a series. The bloody record of the Philippine conquest tells of many battles where Filipinos were killed, but none were wounded and no prisoners taken; of systematic torture, of villages destroyed by wholesale, of cruel reconcentrations, of brutality in every form... The spirit which slaughters brown men in Jolo is the spirit which lynches black

men in the South. When such crimes go unpunished, far more when the men who commit them are praised and rewarded the youth of the country is taught an evil lesson. Race prejudice is strengthened and the love of justice, the cornerstone of free institutions, is weakened. When a man is lynched the community which tolerates the offence [*sic*] suffers more than the victim. When we honor brutality in our army we brutalize ourselves. Our colleges have failed if they have not taught a better civilization than this, our churches have failed if this is their Christianity.[62]

Storey's comparison of violence in the Philippines and violence against blacks at home centered on the effects of racist state formations that inscribed an underlying and unquestioned white superiority. When such violent crimes went not only without punishment, but even came with praise, imperialists thoroughly discredited their own claims to civilization. Having established a foundation for his ethical witnessing with the AIL, three years after writing these words Storey became the first president of the National Association for the Advancement of Colored People. After years of working in this vein, it was time to push the boundaries of existing race relations to imagine new organizations and new ways of fighting for U.S. democracy.

**Figure 4.3 "Covering It Up."** Moorfield Storey Scrapbook. This image depicts Secretary of War, William H. Taft and President Theodore Roosevelt using the flag to cover up the incident on Jolo, Philippines. Library of Congress. Picture taken by author.

**Figure 4.4 "Peace in Jolo."** *The World,* March 11, 1906. This image shows President Theodore Roosevelt holding his sword, "Wood," in the aftermath of "Peace in Jolo." Moorfield Storey Scrapbook, Library of Congress. Picture taken by author.

The article "Sharp Clash on the Moro Massacre" in the *Boston Herald* took a different stance: "we are carrying the white man's burden. We are the greatest race on earth, but we must remember its superiority, its nobility and its responsibility. And as the other side is barbarous, ignorant, savage, so much more deeply must we recognize our responsibility."[63] By the logic of racist exceptions, for some whites even the most extraordinary white violence would not prove that whites could be savage or ignoble.

Another article in the *Washington Post,* by AIL Vice President Charles Parkhurst, responded to this type of "conscientious" imperialism:

Consider the easy and self-satisfied way in which we regard the mowing down of the savage and semi-savage in the Philippine Islands, when they stand in the way of the national purpose, of which, after eight years of 'benevolent assimilation' we have just had a most startling and heart-rending example in the bombarding to death of 600 men, women, and children, collected in a crater in the Moro Islands.[64]

**Figure 4.5 "Upholding the Honor of the American Flag."** Moorfield Storey Scrapbook, Library of Congress. Picture taken by author.

For imperialists and some former anti-imperialists, the Filipinos/as killed were unquestionably "savage," a term that described their lifestyles and indicted their stunted development. Although anti-imperialists protested and imperialists proffered some justificatory explanations, the public responded largely with an indifference that Storey believed would not have been equated had it happened to "600 songbirds." Meanwhile the administration continued to laud the military's effectiveness in the Philippines, covering up the massacre with praise and patriotism.

## BENEVOLENT ASSIMILATION AS A WHITE VEIL: U.S. INDIFFERENCE AND FORGETTING

Self-satisfied indifference regarding colonial subjects and nationals is a collective phenomenon of empire's citizens. It is also an indication of a system of privilege, which structures feelings, even of indifference and complacency, so that they require little effort to maintain. We are left to worry only about ourselves or those in our in-groups. Empathic connections to the suffering of those outside our in-groups are meant to be beyond our purview, too different, too difficult to imagine their feelings. These regulations of feeling pave the way for the legalization of violent racist exceptions and the reproduction of racial inequalities. For instance, in his preface to *Our Philippine Problem,* H. Parker Willis (1905) wrote:

> It is high time that citizens of the United States, interested in the conduct of our government in harmony with its fundamental principles, should abandon the attitude of indifference or obstinacy which many of them have hitherto adopted. Whatever be our ultimate policy with reference to the islands, it can be properly and honourably worked out only through the same direct interest and hearty co-operation on the part of Americans which is the moving spirit in our management of home affairs. (pp. v–vi)[65]

It was clear to Willis that anti-imperialists were no longer struggling only to convince government officials of the dire consequences of imperialism for the United States and the Philippines; they were also struggling to convince the U.S. public that the Philippines and Filipinos/as still mattered. Given that the United States had already achieved its major goal, emotional maintenance for a posture of domination (or the "domineering spirit," as Swift put it in 1899) required only the minimal effort of stonewalling, which meant remaining indifferent, aloof, or comfortably oblivious to the legal and violent exceptions in the Philippines.

Erving Winslow also lamented this lethargic emotional expression in his 1905 Secretary's Report: "Our cause must gain by every shock to that self-satisfied complacency with which the guardianship of the weaker by the stronger nations, especially when the guardian is Anglo-Saxon, has been accepted of late as a heaven-born institution."[66] The disposition of indifference fostered a complacency that only increased after the Senate hearings ended and President Roosevelt declared the war over. The administration also became more effective at reducing the "shocks" anti-imperialists tried to administer to revive the public debate.

When anti-imperialist critiques of U.S. actions in the Philippines arose. defenders of imperialism invoked what were considered widely laudable aspects of benevolent assimilation policies, like the education system. In fact. colonial education in the Philippines made significant institutional inroads and some elections were held, allowing defenders to argue that the U.S. involvement in the Philippines could not only be reduced to violent practices. The experiment in exporting democracy and education interested U.S. Americans much more than the continued violence to make it happen or whether Filipino/as had rights that were observed.

The anti-imperialist activists who remained active after 1902 were the white men who focused their ethical witnessing on practices that strove to foster empathic connections with Filipinos/as and challenged white supremacy, though they were not altogether without elitist, sexist, and racist prejudices. Before he became an anti-imperialist leader, Herbert Welsh was a founder of the Indian Rights Association, which advocated for American Indians, and Moorfield Storey, always critical of lynching, was simultaneously the first president of the National Association for the Advancement of Colored People in 1910 and president of the AIL. These two organizers held great influence over the AIL's strategy after 1901, the third campaign, and they were the most likely to listen to the anti-imperialist views of people of color, advocating empathic connections with their ethical witnessing.

The extent to which their racial paternalism informed their goals for Filipinos/as is unclear. Given the time period, it is hardly surprising that the articles they published in the *Filipino Students Magazine* offered paternalistic advice for navigating toward Filipino/a independence.[67] What is clear is that their activism transformed them. Welsh suffered a nervous breakdown after the SIAP was shut down, but once recovered he later went on to work on more international conflicts and began taking annual summer treks to his lake home from Philadelphia to New Hampshire. Storey became even more involved in advocating for racial justice for blacks at home as a successful activist lawyer and President of the NAACP. Fiske Warren resigned as a member of the AIL's executive committee so that he could work more directly with Filipinos/as without tarnishing the reputation of the AIL. Helen Wilson stayed in the Philippines for five more years and helped to found a Philippine Feminist organization (Balce 2016) before she moved to Russia to live and work on a utopian community after the revolution. H. Parker Wilson went on to help found the U.S. Federal Reserve and the Philippine National Bank. Fiske Warren used his financial resources, social networks, and influence to make firsthand Filipino/a voices heard in the United States, and to help U.S. investigators speak truth to power from the Philippines. These roles aligned with their expertise and resources.

They each leveraged their personal resources to maximize their influence in thwarting benevolent assimilation, which they saw as a set of policies and an ideology that functioned as a veil to shield the U.S. public from questions of U.S. culpability in the racist—though legalized as exceptional—violence in the Philippines. It is also clear that without their interracial connections with Filipinos/as, they would have accomplished far less in their quest to protect the Constitution and the Filipino/a people. I argue, however, their defeats forced them to strengthen their ethical witnessing by dreaming up organizations with principals of a more universal human rights.

## NOTES

1. Jim Zwick, "Petition for Senate Hearings." http://www.boondocksnet.com/ai /people/for_senate_inv.html; Jim Zwick, ed., *Anti-Imperialism in the United States, 1898–1935.* http://www.boondocksnet.com/ai/ (September 8, 2005). This petition was signed by an incomplete list of 140 names.

2. *Record Books of the Anti-Imperialist League*, Vol. 3 (March 23, 1905–March 11, 1909), Maria Lanzar-Carpio Papers, Hatcher Graduate Library, University of Michigan, Ann Arbor.

3. *Record Books of the Anti-Imperialist League*, Vol. 3.

4. Report of the Sixth Annual Anti-Imperialist League Meeting, *Record Books of the Anti-Imperialist League*, Vol. 2 (December 6, 1901–March 9, 1905), Maria Lanzar-Carpio Papers, Hatcher Graduate Library, University of Michigan, Ann Arbor.

5. Letter to E. Lewis from H. Welsh May 16, 1902. Herbert Welsh Papers, Special Collections, University of Michigan, Ann Arbor.

6. List of receipts and expenditures, May 1, 1902. Herbert Welsh Papers, Special Collections, University of Michigan, Ann Arbor.

7. Helen Calista Wilson and Elsie Reed Mitchell, *Vagabonding at fifty: from Siberia to Turkestan* (Coward and McCann, 1929).

8. Unfortunately, I was not able to locate an image for Helen C. Wilson.

9. Helen C. Wilson, *A Massachusetts Woman in the Philippines* (Boston: Fiske Warren, 1903).

10. Wilson, *A Massachusetts Woman in the Philippines.* She also inquired about the health and status of Apolinario Mabini, finding that upon his release from prison in Guam he was incredibly weak. On arriving at Manila in February 1903 he took the oath of allegiance to the United States. Mabini died from cholera only a few months later.

11. Ibid.

12. Ibid.

13. Ibid.

14. "Filipino Opinion of Reconcentration." *El Renacimiento*, June 6, 1905.

15. Helen C. Wilson, *Reconcentration in the Philippines* (Boston: Anti-Imperialist League, 1906).

16. Wilson, *Reconcentration in the Philippines.*

17. Ibid.

18. *Record Books of the Anti-Imperialist League*, Vol. 3.

19. Fraser. Federal Reserve. Register of Papers. H. Parker Willis. Box 7, Folder 4, Item 33. https://fraser.stlouisfed.org/archival/1342/item/458464.

20. Willis would later maintain his academic career at Columbia University and George Washington University. He would also take editorship of the *Journal of Commerce* in 1919,.https://www.joc.com/sites/default/files/joc_inc/history/p11.html.

21. Welsh also had connections to Washington and Lee University.

22. Welsh Papers, Bentley Historical Library, University of Michigan, Ann Arbor.

23. Ibid.

24. https://www.joc.com/sites/default/files/joc_inc/history/p11.html

25. Box 61 and Box 55. Herbert Welsh Collection. Historical Society of Pennsylvania.

26. 1904. "The Philippine Census." Boston: New England Anti-Imperialist League.

27. Gates (1984) points out that Willis attributes this figure to the wrong Bell, but General Bell was more influential and would have carried more weight as a source.

28. I thank Karen Hogenboom, assistant government information librarian at University of Illinois, for pointing me to this article in my search for reliable figures that would compare the number of Filipino deaths over the course of the war.

29. In an attempt to shed light on this discrepancy, Gates (1984) undertook an investigation of the literature. He noted that Glenn May's study found the 1903 census "grossly inaccurate" and that parish documents in the Philippines were "highly unreliable" (p. 373). Acknowledging the unreliability of the available figures, Gates made population projections, comparing them to the 1903 census, and determined the number of war-related deaths in the Philippines to be between 127,593 and 362,659 (Gates 1984:374–375). Gates concludes, "This paper provides neither a reliable method for estimating war-related deaths in the Philippine-American War nor an exact estimate of their number. It does, however, indicate a few of the approaches that should not be used. [. . .] one should not trust the undocumented figures of authors who have an ulterior motive, such as proving that the American campaign in the Philippines was 'genocidal' or benevolent" (pp. 377–378). Of course, the original actors framed the Philippine-American War as either "genocide" or "benevolence," and subsequent students of this history have simply carried this framing forward.

30. SIAP, p. 1628. Telegraphic circular No. 22. To all station commanders, Batangas, December 24, 1901. (emphasis added).

31. Gates (1984) lists Blount's (1912) estimates among the more conservative reports of Filipino casualties.

32. Edward Ordway Papers, Manuscript and Archives Division, New York Public Library.

33. Ibid.

34. Letter from Carl Schurz to Charles Francis Adams, Jr. November 15, 1903 in Bancroft, Frederic. 1913. "Speeches, Correspondence and Political Papers of Carl Schurz." vol. VI. January 1, 1899–April 8, 1906. New York and London: The Knickerbocker Press.

35. Edward Ordway Papers, Manuscript and Archives Division, New York Public Library.

36. Letter from Doherty to Ordway, May 11, 1906, Edward Ordway Papers, Manuscript and Archives Division, New York Public Library.

37. Letter from Doherty to Ordway, June 10, 1906, Edward Ordway Papers, Manuscript and Archives Division, New York Public Library.

38. Ibid. This was also corroborated in a December 7, 1910 article, "The Mission of La Gota de Leche" published in *Renacimiento Filipino*.

39. Letter from Ordway, February 1, 1907, Edward Ordway Papers, Manuscript and Archives Division, New York Public Library.

40. Alberto Barretto, "Brigandage in Batangas and the Habeas Corpus Writ." *Springfield Republican*, June 18, 1905; rpt. *Truth Coming to Light Concerning the Philippines: Letter from Fiske Warren* (Boston: Anti-Imperialist League, 1906).

41. A. Barretto to J.G. Schurman, March 28, 1906. Edward Ordway Papers, Manuscript and Archives Division, New York Public Library.

42. Many of his contemporaries considered Warren a radical. Although he was not a Marxist, he did come to support single-tax issues in the vein of Henry George. Warren was also a nudist and started a commune in Harvard, Massachusetts. However, he came from a well-known, moneyed Boston family, so he had financial resources and connections even if he was still considered fringe (for more on Warren and his family, see Green 1989).

43. Doherty to Ordway, 1906, Edward Ordway Papers, Manuscript and Archives Division, New York Public Library.

44. Go notes that after 1903, the number of cases against Filipinos rose rapidly, due mainly to Filipino domestication of the colonial legal system, which meant that Filipinos began using the legal system for their interests and making their own cases (e.g., Go, Julian, *American Empire and the Politics of Meaning: Elite Political Cultures in the Philippines and Puerto Rico during U.S. Colonialism* (Durham and London: Duke University Press 2008)).

45. Winslow to Ordway, Nov. 14, 1905, Edward Ordway Papers, Manuscript and Archives Division, New York Public Library.

46. *Record Books of the Anti-Imperialist League*, Vol. 3.

47. *Record Books of the Anti-Imperialist League*, Vol. 4 (March 25, 1909–September 11, 1914), Maria Lanzar-Carpio Papers, Hatcher Graduate Library, University of Michigan, Ann Arbor.

48. Jim Zwick, "Filipinos in the Debate About Imperialism." http://www.boondocksnet.com/ai/vof/In; Jim Zwick, ed., *Anti-Imperialism in the United States, 1898–1935*. http://www.boondocksnet.com/ai/ (September 20, 2005).

49. El Renacimiento, "The Filipinos Do Not Want the 'Wild Tribes' Exhibited." *The Public* 9, March 9, 1907.

50. *Record Book of the Anti-Imperialist League*, Volume 3. Maria Lanzar-Carpio Papers. Hatcher Graduate Library, Special Collections Library.

51. El Renacimiento, "How the Filipinos Feel." *The Public* 12, July 2, 1909. El Renacimiento, "Occupation Day." *Report of the Eleventh Annual Meeting of the Anti-Imperialist League* (Boston: Anti-Imperialist League, 1909); El Renacimiento, "Buried Hopes." (Boston: Anti-Imperialist League, n.d.)

52. Fred W. Atkinson, *The Philippine Islands* (Boston: Ginn & Company, 1905 ), 6.

53. Atkinson, *The Philippine Islands*.

54. *The Filipino Students Magazine,* Vol. 1, No. 1, Bancroft Library, University of California Berkeley.

55. *The Filipino Students Magazine,* Vol. 1, No. 1.

56. *The Filipino Students Magazine*. Vol. 1, No. 2, Bancroft Library, the University of California at Berkeley.

57. *The Filipino Students Magazine.* Vol. 1, No. 2.

58. *The Filipino Students Magazine.* Vol. 1, No. 3, Bancroft Library, University of California Berkeley.

59. *The Filipino Students Magazine.* Vol. 1, No. 3.

60. Letter to Sniffen from Winslow, November 18, 1905. Herbert Welsh Collection, Historical Society of Pennsylvania.

61. Moorfield Storey collected many of these article clippings and cartoons, saving them in his scrapbook, including: "Letters to the Editor: The Battle in the Crater," "Parkhurst on Jolo Battle," "Sharp Clash on Moro Massacre," "Unavoidably Killed," "Moro Massacre Great Blot on American Name," "What Passeth in Moro Land," "Peace in Jolo," "Massacre of Moros," "A Moro Slaughter," "Soldiers View of 3 Days' Jolo Slaughter," "900 Killed?" "Jolo and the Moros," "Comment on Jolo Outbreak," "Moros a Fanatical People," "Six Hundred Moros Have Sworn Allegiance," "Lest We Forget," "The Latest Moro Slaughter," "Maj-Gen Woods Explains."

62. Moorfield Storey, "The Moro Massacre." (Boston: Anti-Imperialist League, n.d. [1906]). http://www.boondocksnet.com/ai/ailtexts/mm_moromass.html; Jim Zwick, ed., *Anti-Imperialism in the United States, 1898–1935.* http://www.boondocksnet.com/ai/ (September 27, 2005).

63. Emphasis added, Moorfield Storey Papers, Manuscript and Archives Division, Library of Congress.

64. Charles H. Parkhurst. "Slaughter Perpetrated 'In Honor of the American Flag.'" *Washington Post*, March 19, 1906. http://www.boondocksnet.com/ai/ailt exts/mm_woodbrig.html; Jim Zwick, ed., *Anti-Imperialism in the United States, 1898–1935.* http://www.boondocksnet.com/ai/ (September 27, 2005).

65. H. P. Willis, *Our Philippine Problem* (Holt & Company, 1905).

66. *Record Books of the Anti-Imperialist League*, Vol. 3.

67. Storey was unabashedly prejudiced against Irish workers in Boston and Welsh's work for Indians on reservations was paternalist framed in racialized "civilization."

# Conclusion

## *Ethical Witnessing in the U.S. Empire and the Dream of Inalienable Rights*

Over the course of the Philippine War, anti-imperialists changed their focus from protesting against imperialism to exposing its violence. In their first campaign, they opposed the Treaty of Paris and the Benevolent Assimilation Proclamation. In their second campaign, they looked to defeat President McKinley by supporting an anti-imperialist candidate for president, William Jennings Bryan. Finally, in the third campaign, they turned to exposing the racist violence perpetrated by the U.S. military in the Philippines. I have argued that even as this third campaign has been the least attended to by social histories, it was also the most historically consequential. During this third campaign, imperialists learned to codify U.S. racist exceptions in the face of anti-imperialist protests, which have contributed to imperialist practices that continue to be implemented in the United States today, such as the detention camps for migrants and refugees on the border of the United States. It was also in this third campaign that anti-imperialists developed ethical witnessing toward a more universal human rights based on the principles and symbol of the U.S. Constitution, after failing to enforce it as law.

Regarding the experience of colonial relations from those doing the colonizing Albert Memmi stated in the, *The Colonizer and the Colonized*,

> It is not easy to escape mentally from a concrete situation, to refuse its ideology while continuing to live with its actual relationships. From now on, ["the colonizer who refuses"] lives his life under the sign of a contradiction which looms at every step, depriving him of all coherence and all tranquility. (1991 [1965]: 20)

Indeed, anti-imperialist advocates lived within the contradictions unique to citizens of a democracy that also held an empire. In order to address this incoherence, they enacted ethical witnessing where they used their resources to bear witness to the agonizing experiences of Filipinas/os as part of their political expression. They also used their resources to fight the legality of the empire, until the empire itself was declared a legal exception. For instance, the last anti-imperialist campaign started out strong but was difficult to sustain in the face of new laws codifying imperialist exceptions to previous U.S. rules of law. From 1902 to 1906, anti-imperialists sustained their focus on violence in the Philippines, shifting from imperialist laws to the underlying values of rights beyond national boundaries. There was a lull in organized activism in 1907 and 1908 as they regrouped.

Indeed, the tone and form of this ethical witnessing changed over time as they faced defeat after defeat. It was in facing these defeats time after time that they came to a more expansive ethical witnessing beyond arguing for national rights to a more fundamental conviction of inalienable rights. These were convictions that they would have to bring to bear back home, for people of color as well as white women. By 1909, anti-imperialists had clearly learned from their experiences of ethical witnessing with Filipinos/as, as they implemented another shift, focusing on organizations that fought to *expand* rights and legal protections. In other words, the anti-imperialist advocates left standing started focusing on dreaming new organizations into reality—organizations that worked to expand rights and protections.

By 1909, anti-imperialist advocates actually began *cocreating* other organizations focused on rights. One of these organizations included the National Association for the Advancement of Colored People (NAACP), one of the most historically influential civil rights organizations in the United States. In 1915, anti-imperialists cocreated the Women's International League for Peace and Freedom (WILPF). Other organizations, such as the National Consumer's League (NCL), also had overlapping leadership with the AIL. Individually, other anti-imperialists also continued to work toward a more idealist and fair future for all. For instance, Helen Wilson went on to live and work in a Utopian community in Russia, while H. Parker Willis helped create the U.S. Federal Reserve to protect the economy from banks so big that they could take down the entire economy.

This final shift in anti-imperialist ethical witnessing paralleled a shift toward more proactively defining civilization by co-creating organizations that would exemplify it. They would not be found in dereliction of duty or allow themselves to remain victims of a lost cause– rather they would find purpose and passion in taking responsibility for creating a world that honored inalienable rights. They would remain on watch even as anti-imperialism as a cause for the Philippines waned. The ethical witnessing of the organizations to which they turned their attention operated with a vision for a more just and equitable society, instead of an oppositional agenda (as exemplified in the term *anti*-imperialism). The national organizations focused on reducing violence and inequality against people of color and workers within the metropole, while WILPF focused on reducing violence across borders. These organizations were part of a larger progressive project that attacked the limitations put in place by racist exceptions in favor of advocating for the expansion of civil rights and protections for people of color, workers, and women under national and international law.

## THE ANTI-IMPERIALIST LEAGUE COMES TO AN END

Perhaps the most difficult lesson learned by anti-imperialists was that facts alone were not enough to convince the American public of the contradictions between imperialism and democracy (for more on this lesson see Paula Ioanide's *The Emotional Politics of Racism: How Feelings Trump Facts in an Era of Colorblindness*). Given their patrician backgrounds, it makes sense that anti-imperialist activists were so idealistically devoted to the idea of American democracy. It was part and parcel of their privileged life experience. In 1908, the Boston AIL published *The Anti-Imperialist League: Apologia Pro Vita Sua* ("in defense of one's life"), in which Erving Winslow reflected on what the anti-imperialists had tried to accomplish through their ethical witnessing over a decade of opposition to imperialism. Although the AIL emerged as activists organized to oppose the ratification of the Treaty of Paris in 1898, Winslow noted, "the motto of the League during the whole of the last ten years has been 'Fiat Lux' [Let there be light], in the belief that the light of knowledge must finally bring the Republic back to its true mind and its righteous attitude" (p. 5). As Memmi wrote, these "colonizers who refused" to support the depredations of their nation were "deprived" of all "coherence and tranquility." Certainly, an important part of the anti-imperialists' ethical witnessing was to prevent tranquility and complacency by keeping the public engaged in the Philippines, which led to their efforts to expose the facts about imperialist violence to foster outrage and moral shock that even the most hardened imperialist would find difficult to stonewall.

Unlike the majority of the American public, the anti-imperialists understood the larger issues at stake beyond individual instances of violence. Winslow observed that

the painful duty of the League to expose the 'marked severities' inflicted by the United States troops upon the Filipinos during the progress of the war of subjugation [. . .], which is very thoroughly substantiated, was made very difficult by the efforts of the Secretary of War to whitewash the proceedings in the army. *The blame for the individual exercise of brutal conduct was not attributed so much to the persons perpetrating it as to the conditions in which they had been placed by their superiors.* (p. 8, my emphasis)

Although anti-imperialists did not refer to these "conditions" as racist exceptions, their focus on the policies under which soldiers operated (like reconcentration and taking no prisoners) showed their grasp of the systemic nature of imperialist violence. Despite the challenges the anti-imperialists faced, the three-way contrast between the government's rhetorical focus on the benevolence of the U.S. occupation, soldiers' stories of egregious violence, and the silence of the press served as an incessant and powerful call to duty (Storey and Lichauco 1926).

If the *Apologia Pro Vita Sua* served as a reminder that Filipinos/as continued to suffer under the rule of U.S. legal exceptions, it also reminded its readers of the past and present efforts of the AIL:

The horrible methods of "reconcentration" which continued up to a period so late as the summer of 1906, the expulsion of men, women and children from their homes, herded together under rigid surveillance, exposed to all weathers and without proper food, have been described. These Weyler methods, which contributed so largely to arouse the fiery indignation felt against the Spanish rule in Cuba, are enumerated in great detail in the League's publications. (pp. 8–9)

True to the AIL's initial reliance on reputation and influence to which Winslow shared as a Boston Brahmin, he once again listed the prominent anti-imperialists who participated in the cause, including government officials, academics, clergy, "judges, and lawyers," "citizens," and luminaries, tallying up total numbers and providing prominent names (pp. 4–5). Winslow also noted the credit bestowed upon the AIL's efforts by imperialists, including William Taft and President Roosevelt who

while encouraging the hope of Philippine independence within one generation instead of the two or three which was the former minimum limit, has exalted the Anti-Imperialists from the classification of "traitors," to which they were inured, to that of "doctrinaires"—or idealists—which, despite its intent, is the best possible tribute from one who reckons himself among the "practical men" whose scorn is so often the highest praise. (p. 5)

If anti-imperialists initially defended themselves against the label of traitor and took great pains to prove their patriotism, once deprived of coherence by being forced into the social position of colonizer, some of them began taking comfort in the term.

More importantly, and regardless of name-calling, Winslow wanted to make it clear that the anti-imperialists were not finished. He knew well that

Filipinos/as still sought independence, and he hoped new legislation might take them one step closer to their goal:

> The League is now making an earnest demand for the passage of a resolution by Congress similar to the "Teller amendment" in the Cuban settlement, promising independence to the Filipinos, so that content and good order may be established in the Philippines and hopeful and legitimate progress be made toward the goal which is pointed out to them; the only real security for the fulfillment of the pledge "the Philippines for the Filipinos." (p. 13)

Although it did not pass, the effort was not as futile as it may have seemed. By 1907, anti-imperialists began to notice mainstream newspapers portraying them differently. It seemed that the public was "surcharged with weariness and disgust toward the whole Philippine experiment," leaving anti-imperialists "more respected" and their proposals, which they continued to proffer, more persuasive.[1] In 1910, the AIL again petitioned the Senate and House of Representatives to declare "unequivocal" terms of independence for the Philippines, including treaties to protect the Philippines such as those enjoyed by Switzerland and Norway, protection from capitalists hoping to "exploit the islands for their own pecuniary benefit," and immediate adoption of measures that would "enable the Filipino people to develop their country for themselves and with their own capital."[2] At the close of the petition, they stated:

> With race problems, labor problems, taxation problems at home, let us not remain supine while we are being committed to the creation of like problems in distant colonies, problems which will remain to be a constant source of trouble and expense until the country does what we surge it to do now; that is, leave every people free to govern themselves.[3]

The freedom of self-government, the crux of their argument, had remained constant over the years.

Although the nationalist leader Manuel Quezon addressed the annual anti-imperialist meeting in 1919,[4] the messages from Filipinos/as became less clear over time, leaving the AIL unconvinced that the Filipino leadership elected under U.S. colonial rule had a genuine interest in independence (Zwick 2005). Uncomfortable appealing for Filipino independence without an accompanying Filipino campaign, the AIL finally disbanded in 1920. Throughout its history, as in its demise, the AIL was careful not to appear as if it was leading the campaign for Filipino independence. This stance was key to their position that they were not traitors, but rather moral patriots defending the sacred Declaration of Independence and the U.S. Constitution.

Creating the coalition that opposed U.S. policies in the Philippines transformed anti-imperialism, but the debates over imperialism—and specifically the constant pressure from the AIL and its allies—also transformed the United States. Outraged anti-imperialists argued simultaneously for Filipino/a rights and for the integrity of the democratic process of the United States. Anti-imperialists' ethical witnessing opened new avenues for Americans to advocate for political, civil, and economic rights. They preached a distinctly American democratic civil religion that harkened back to the Founding Fathers and the abolitionist movement.

By initially looking to the past to address the new problem of imperialism, they aimed for what Beisner (1968) called the *status quo ante bellum* (p. 120), making their creativity and inclusiveness conservative and limited. While most anti-imperialist leaders were socially liberal, they could not resolve their ambivalence about fully including white women (Murphy 2009), blacks (Gatewood 1984), or Filipinos/as. Their ambivalence reflected various conflicts over racial, gender, and class equality and justice at the turn of the twentieth century, when ideas of progress were steeped in racist ideologies of social Darwinism and Neo-Lamarckianism. While most of the anti-imperialist base had formal citizenship, the more marginalized anti-imperialists had fewer rights and were looking toward a more inclusive future. When anti-imperialist leaders limited their vision of the future to reiterating past conceptions of citizenship, they hindered the movement's initial appeal for its logical allies. Although from the outset many white women and black anti-imperialists, both women and men, tied anti-imperialism to stopping violence and the racialization of subject peoples through empathic connections to violence, the AIL leadership embraced this stance, but, too late to keep their momentum.

## ADVOCATING FOR RIGHTS

Racist nationalism that reified white supremacy feminized and dismissed the opposition to imperialist violence. As white men became less involved in U.S. organizing against imperialist violence, white women became more active and organized, not only nationally, but internationally, in what they saw as a more cosmopolitan mode than the patriotic—and masculinist—provincialism of earlier anti-imperialists.[5] This led to the historical shift where white women began to take over the vanguard of white anti-violence activism as they organized against political violence.[6] True to the predictable blind spots of white women, the International Council of Women of the Darker Races had to lobby WILPF to address U.S. involvement in Haiti, and in 1919, Mary Church Terrell noted that she was the only nonwhite person attending the WILPF meeting, which made her feel she was "representing women of all non-white countries in the world" (Winkler-Morey 2001).[7] There was still much work to do.

Meanwhile, white men's ethical witnessing became centered on racist political violence in the metropole, which they addressed through activist organizations like the biracial NAACP, which also included some highly regarded black and white women. Activist networks of anti-imperialists had significant overlap with ethical reformers and civil rights organizations, including not only the NAACP and WILPF, but the Women's Trade Union League (WTUL), the Society for Ethical Culture, and the Civil Liberties Bureau, a precursor of the American Civil Liberties Union (ACLU). When the NAACP was founded in 1909, Moorfield Storey served as president of both the AIL and the NAACP. Jane Addams, a cofounder of the NAACP and the National Consumer League (NCL), and vice president of the AIL, served as the first president of WILPF (Bussey and Tims 1980). Elizabeth Glendower Evans worked with Boston anti-imperialists, especially the Warren family and Louis Brandeis, as well as the WTUL, after she met Florence Kelley of the NCL in Chicago. She was also a delegate for WILPF at the Hague in 1915 and became National Director of the ACLU in 1920. Felix Adler, an anti-imperialist in New York, founded the Ethical Culture Society and the National Child Labor Committee, and was involved in the Civil Liberties Bureau. Time and again, anti-imperialist advocates began expanding their ethical witnessing to cocreate organizations that expanded rights for others.

Each of these organizations became an important force for progressive social change, with their work revolving around the expansion of rights and protections. They focused their energies on lobbying rather than electoral politics, taking a strategy from other women-led organizations (Clemens 1993). The anti-imperialist movement during the Philippine-American War may have declined with the rise of racist exceptions, but the ethical witnessing of these rights-advocating organizations emerged in the wake of that decline. Therefore, this history shows how the development of legal imperialist racist exceptions simultaneously led to the seeding of new rights organizations, which arose out of the contradictions between imperialism and democracy that anti-imperialists noted from the beginning.

## ACKNOWLEDGING RACIST EXCEPTIONS TODAY

Along with new rights organizations, anti-imperialist activities also inadvertently contributed to the emergence of racist exceptions that continue to be perpetuated, as evidenced by the similarities between the "water cure" and waterboarding, as well as reconcentrations and Japanese internment camps,

and black sites (secret prisons) and Guantánamo Bay and now, at last, detention camps for migrants and refugees that even tear apart families. Ann Laura
Stoler (2006) asserts that investigating these repeating historical legacies is

> neither to claim the conceit of prediction, nor to reduce what is specific to the
> violences of this contemporary moment as history replayed as farce. Rather, it
> is to suggest that *the conditions of possibility* for what U.S[.] empire looks like
> today may be deeply embedded in the blunt and elusive nature of a broader
> range of historical imperial formations. (p. 93, my emphasis)

Analyzing the history of anti-imperialist activities provides a deeper understanding of imperialist racist exceptions, which may seem like the lingering
hiccups of imperialist violence but are actually ongoing systemic problems that
still require a reckoning, where we are forced to face head on and reconcile with
these exceptional practices of violence. Today, exceptionalist discourses continue to legitimate or confuse the logic for legalizing violence against nonwhite
subjects by obfuscating their protected rights or simply stripping those rights
away through legal maneuvering, for instance of criminal law.

At the turn of the twentieth century, anti-imperialists had to contend
with space-time limitations (Sewell 2005), such as the distance between the
metropole and colony, that made it difficult to protest new imperialist racist
exceptions. Physical distance created a lag in obtaining information about the
Philippines and obstructed the timeliness of informing the U.S. public. This
time lapse also allowed imperialists to argue, once the flagrant violence was
unveiled, that the perpetrators had already left the military and were no longer
a threat to Filipinos/as or to U.S. "civilization" in the colony. Furthermore,
the distance between the metropole and colony allowed U.S. citizens the comfort of their indifference because what happened in the Philippines had little
effect on their daily lives. This same public indifference allowed imperialists
to frame the urgency of anti-imperialists as needlessly overwrought, which
helped them dismiss the SIAP before it did any real damage to the administration or its policies in the Philippines by encouraging more public empathic
connections with the experiences of Filipinas/os. Mining the resources of this
indifference to stonewall anti-imperialist positions, Roosevelt declared that
the war in the Philippines was over immediately on the heels of the dismissed
investigations, on July 4, 1902, further fostering American indifference, and
cultivated forgetting.

Nevertheless, believing the violence was both immoral and illegal, anti-
imperialists continued their struggle to establish racist violence as outside
the rules of war. The SIAP hearings did enable anti-imperialists to force
the military rule of law to be delineated, but in this process of delineation,
imperialists bracketed particular scenarios of violence against certain people,

and codified exceptions to the rules that they justified through the ambiguity of racist civilization. According to Sewell (2005), "The structural rearticulation could only be definitive when it had been sanctioned at the pinnacle of state authority" (p. 258), and racist exceptions indeed went from amorphous practices to structural rearticulation when the Supreme Court, Congress, and the Executive Office sanctioned ambiguous rationales for violent practices (like reconcentration) and the suspension of the *writ of habeas corpus*, and blamed individual U.S. soldiers and Macabebes for torture. This scenario is, not unsurprisingly, highly reminiscent of the garbled legal rationales for similar violence under the Bush administration's War on Terror, which was also accompanied by a startling, and calamitous public indifference—an indifference echoed recently in First Lady Melania Trump's wardrobe choice of a jacket stating "I really don't care. Do u?" on a trip visiting children on the U.S.-Mexico border held in facilities after being taken away from their families as part of Trump's zero-tolerance immigration policy.

Histories of the anti-imperialists have overlooked the results of their work and its impact on state formations today, likely because those results came later in their activities and were not part of their stated goals. While they did not win the policy battles, they soured the glory for white supremacists so that keeping the Philippines was only a short-lived imperialist point of pride. Discourses of American exceptionalism helped to obfuscate the violence and even justify it, further fostering contemporary public indifference to the consequences. This pattern of racist exceptions persists today, in U.S. wars against terror abroad, mass incarceration and police brutality, despotism against people of color at home, and in inhumane immigration policies.

Over the past forty years, especially after the Reagan-era "War on Drugs," there have been an increasing number of critiques of the U.S. prison system and police brutality. In *The New Jim Crow: Mass Incarceration in the Age of Colorblindness* (2012), Michelle Alexander detailed current practices of legalized racist exceptions in the United States by showing the disparities in how whites and people of color are treated under the law. Newer laws, such as "Stand Your Ground" and "zero tolerance" policies, further disadvantaged people of color, especially youth, by racializing the legal designation of felon. Little has been done institutionally to check this systemic racism or the widely divergent application of citizens' rights across race. Furthermore, the taken-for-granted nature of racist and ethnic violence actively maintains the repression and denial of history. As anti-imperialists learned, historical facts exist, but under the influence of white supremacy, they are still not enough. It took more than facts of violence to upend the hopeful racism of Neo-Lamarckianism, and in the face of today's hopeful colorblind racism, accompanied by a resurgence of neo-fascism, we will again need more than facts to convince the American public that racism and racist inequalities still exist or that they should be changed, depending on the audience. Facts are essential but so are institutional changes (Ioanide 2015), and I argue so are self-conscious strategies for empathic connections that shape and evolve ethical witnessing.

As Americans and as scholars, we have too often ignored the myriad ways in which racism birthed legal exceptions that helped establish and elaborate U.S. imperialism, leaving intact a continued legacy where codified practices grant racist exceptions. Mapping the practices of racist exceptions may help us to recognize them and make it harder to (dis)miss them when we advocate for the substantive, inalienable rights and freedom from violence for people of color—for which, there is no middle ground. In this spirit, the narrative of this book is a form of ethical witnessing. Bearing witness to anti-imperialists' story and clarifying how imperialist racist exceptions came into existence, I offer a map with which to identify and name analogous processes. Ethical witnessing draws a map of our interconnections, which we can flesh out together through empathic connections of listening how to better pursue democratic ideals.

Fully facing this history would require creating a new narrative of the development of the United States as a racist state predicated on racist exceptions with a dream of a democratic state predicated on ideals of democracy. If we are to become the latter, we will cocreate a fully realized multiracial democracy. Getting there would require acknowledging that the United States has aspired to and implemented elements of both empire and democracy, each fortifying the other. It would also require acknowledging that hopeful racism is still racism and legalized state violence against people of color is still a violation of inalienable rights. It would also require an awakening to the *militancy* of public indifference to racist violence, as an active stance of stonewalling. Once awakened to this fact, the compassionate act of bearing witness to the suffering of others would lead to the ability to take on other lenses, utilizing multiple vantage points in the creation of democracy.

At a time when the United States is increasingly polarized because of the greatest economic inequalities in a century, and the fastest changes to racial demographics ever, it can become a challenge for those with relative privileges, like fully recognized citizenship, to figure out how to effectively work for social justice. Ethical witnessing is one answer to this dilemma because it fosters active, responsible citizenship where one is empowered to use her privileged position (e.g., access to government recognition and social connections) to bear witness to the grievances of those who are exploited or oppressed, rather than shrink into indifference or into some other role as victim. It also requires engaged listening to those with whom we bear witness and reflexive organizing so that we do not make the politics narrowly about ourselves, but rather, centered on empathic connections.

The case of the anti-imperialists at the turn of the twentieth century offers one compelling example with which to think through what makes ethical witnessing effective, ineffective, and important even in its imperfections. In the instances where anti-imperialists had the political courage to struggle for democracy and racial justice, they provide an example of ethical witnessing with deep roots in the foundational dreams of American history of U.S. citizens from all strata of society facing the dilemma of how to oppose racist imperialist policies together. The deep roots of the anti-imperialists' convictions helped weather many storms. Through an example of empathically responsive, creative citizenship, the history of anti-imperialists gift us roots and provide us branches to reach higher in our quest to practice an empathically emboldened and consciously creative democratic citizenship.

## NOTES

1. *Report of the Ninth Annual Meeting.* Record Books of the Anti-Imperialist League, Vol. 3 (March 23, 1905–March 11, 1909), Maria Lanzar-Carpio Papers, Hatcher Graduate Library, University of Michigan, Ann Arbor.

2. These were some of the goals H. Parker Willis took up in creating the Philippine National Back and the Philippine American Chamber of Commerce.

3. Anti-Imperialist League, "To the Senate and House of Representatives." *A Petition of Sundry Citizens of the United States for Philippine Independence* (N.p., 1910).

4. *Report of the Twentieth Annual Meeting.* Box 1, Anti-Imperialist League Papers, Swarthmore Peace Collection, Swarthmore College.

5. "International" (actually white European and American alliances) woman's suffrage alliances incited this development, as they were organized politically for the vote.

6. I share Vron Ware's (1992) approach to white women's activism and issues of race and gender, which she states in her introduction to *Beyond the Pale*: "The purpose of exploring the histories of slavery and imperialism is not to bring white women to account for past misdeeds, nor to search for heroines whose reputations can help to absolve the rest from guilt, but to find out how white women negotiated questions of race and racism—as well as class and gender. In other words what we need to do is to trace ideas that have historically constructed definitions of white womanhood and to ask how these ideas have been formed either in conjunction with or in opposition to feminist ideology" (p. 43).

7. Winkler-Morey (2001) argues that it was only after women from Latin America and Afro-American women sought alliances with WILPF that "lessons about the realities of unequal exchange and the racism under-girding government justifications for U.S. hegemony" convinced WILPF to critique economic imperialism and forge transnational networks beyond Europe (p. 188).

# Epilogue

Herbert Welsh and Maria Lanzar played prominent roles in creating and saving many of the anti-imperialist documents. Lanzar, a Filipina student, met Welsh when she began work on her doctoral dissertation on the anti-imperialist movement at the University of Michigan. Although information on Welsh can be found in print and online, Lanzar's story and her role in saving many of the papers have thus far been unwritten. Because of their integral roles in saving these documents and much of the history of the AIL, I include their backstory.

## HERBERT WELSH

Anti-imperialist and editor of *City & State* Herbert Welsh left Philadelphia in the spring of 1903 for a restorative holiday in the south with his family. His first stop was Lexington, Virginia, but he never made it to his second stop at Camp Hill, Alabama. He collapsed on the way from a nervous breakdown brought on by his obsessive activism (Hagan 1985). In the years prior to the collapse, he fervently believes that his responsibilities as a Christian and a citizen charged him with trying to stop the United States from forcibly taking the Philippines from Filipino/a nationalists inspired that activism, ultimately to his personal detriment.

Beginning in 1899, he doggedly monitored the violence committed by the U.S. military in the Philippines. The efforts of his team of researchers helped spur the special investigation convened by the Senate in 1902 to review the affairs in the Philippines. The team spent months gathering and preparing witnesses for the investigation. But imperialist senators abruptly shut down the investigation once they finished calling their witnesses, ensuring that the Welsh team's witnesses never had an opportunity to testify. Incensed and desperate, Welsh and other anti-imperialists tried to get the investigations reopened, but by early 1903, it became clear that the leadership of the special committee had moved on. The investigation would not be reopened. With months and even years of his labor tossed aside by imperialist senators, Welsh collapsed once he stepped away for a holiday. On the advice of his physician, he dramatically scaled back his work on behalf of Philippine independence from that point on.

Welsh was born to a wealthy Philadelphia family, which afforded him time to devote his energies almost exclusively to his reform and humanitarian interests. He was a religious Episcopalian (Hagan 1985). After graduating from the University of Pennsylvania, he studied art in Paris and for a short while lived as an artist in Philadelphia. Though he developed a strained relationship with his wife, he was devoted to his children.

In 1882, at thirty-one, Welsh helped found what would become the most influential organization working on behalf of American Indians, the Indian Rights Association. The organization lobbied Congressmen and monitored government officials on Indian reservations. Welsh became good friends with Theodore Roosevelt, then Civil Service Commissioner, through their shared interest in American Indians and the West. This relationship reverberated ironically twenty years later, when Roosevelt ignored Welsh's letters, as president during the cessation of the special investigation that led to Welsh's collapse.

In 1895, Welsh founded *City and State* as part of the new media explosion of weekly journals in the late nineteenth century. As editor, Welsh focused on the issues he believed were most important for Philadelphia, Pennsylvania, and the country. From this platform, he targeted political corruption and later voiced the positions of the AIL that opposed the annexation of the Philippines. The year after his breakdown, he shut down the paper citing prohibitive financial issues with keeping it running.

It took several years for Welsh to recover physically, after which he took up other humanitarian interests and causes (though he still gave talks on behalf of Philippine Independence on Rizal Day, celebrated by Filipinos/as in honor of the national hero José Rizal). He worked on behalf of injustices in Armenia, Turkey, and Syria, and later in support of the League of Nations. At one point, he hosted a Reconstruction Tea at his apartment in Germantown, where illustrious guests, including the famed Black contralto Marian Anderson, gathered to discuss the unfinished work of Reconstruction policies. He continued ethical witnessing throughout his life.

## MARIA C. LANZAR

Two decades after Welsh and the special investigation collapsed, Maria C. Lanzar, a young Filipina doctoral student from the University of Michigan contacted Welsh to request his permission to look at the papers on the Philippines that he and his team had generated. The documents were voluminous, with multiple copies of papers, and in vast disarray. He was by then in his early seventies and an avid walker, walking from Germantown to Lake Sunapee, New Hampshire, every summer in daily 25-mile stints, in many ways still the tireless man he had been two decades prior.[1]

Lanzar matched Welsh in her determination and focus. Once she received her Master's degree from the University of the Philippines, she took the courageous step of becoming the first woman doctoral candidate in the Department of Political Science at the University of Michigan. Only a year later, Congress passed its massive Immigration Reform Act, which prohibited most Asians from immigrating to the United States. Ironically, U.S. benevolent assimilation policies of the time charged the colonial government of the Philippines with sponsoring talented Filipino/a students for higher education in the United States. Although Lanzar had a scholarship rather than a government sponsorship, she received special permission to attend the University of Michigan where she was the first Filipina to receive the prestigious Barbour scholarship for Asian women (McFerson 2002).

At Michigan, Lanzar focused her research on the U.S. opposition to Philippine annexation and the AIL, in which Welsh had played a major role. She was the first scholar to focus on the activism. Lanzar's dissertation advisor, political science professor Joseph Ralston Hayden, had advised her Master's thesis while taking part in an academic exchange program with the University of the Philippines. Having had some earlier contact with anti-imperialist activists, he likely put her in touch with them once they were in Ann Arbor.

Lanzar's timing was impeccable. The AIL had officially disbanded only two years before she began contacting its former leaders. Many of them were generous in sharing their documents with her. Welsh gave her his extra papers. Charles Winslow, the son of Erving Winslow, who was the secretary of the New England AIL, gave her many of his father's AIL papers. During trips from Ann Arbor to Washington, D.C., to gather information on the AIL, Lanzar conducted research and met others involved in the Philippine cause for independence. She also attended parties and met other Filipino/a students, as well as influential Filipinos/as.

Using the papers of former anti-imperialists, interviewing those still living, and combing through AIL annual reports, she began piecing together the history of the organization and its various chapters, which became her dissertation. With an archivist's eye and ethic, she also set out to save and organize the documents she received. The result of her efforts reside in the holdings of the Hatcher Graduate Library and the Bentley Historical Library at the University of Michigan, which contain the papers she donated and which many contemporary studies of anti-imperialism have largely relied on.

When Lanzar completed her dissertation in 1928, she went back to the Philippines to hold an academic appointment at the University of Philippines. She published her dissertation research in a series of articles in the *Philippine Social Science Review* in the 1930s, which were the first published academic studies of this history. She married Victorio Carpio, a fellow Michigan alumnus and lawyer, and went on to publish articles on the Philippine people under her married name, Lanzar-Carpio.[2]

Most Filipino/a students, including *pensionados/as*, studied governance and politics so they could take on positions within the colonial government. However, Lanzar-Carpio and her husband became representatives of the Philippine Republic in more international settings. In the 1950s and 1960s, they became UN representatives for the Philippines, and Carpio also became the Ambassador to Egypt. The Department of Political Science at the University of the Philippines named an endowed chair in Lanzar-Carpio's honor.

While many studies have cited Lanzar's early work, none have investigated her life or her role in making possible the historical analysis of these anti-imperialist activities. Lanzar's key role in saving many of the most important anti-imperialist documents allowed scholars to put the AIL on the agenda of social historians. In January 1924, discussing the possibility of Philippine independence and the prohibition against Philippine publishers publishing work on Philippine Independence, Lanzar wrote to Welsh:

> Well, I suppose, there is nothing else to do but force one's self to be patient—the weak individual or nation as against a powerful master. History will repeat itself, and it is my humble belief that however kindly, and well-meaning a master can be, a forced philanthropy will not always be received with lasting gratitude-for a nation's life, its separate existence, with all the uncertainties and danger of that life will always be clearer to its citizens than even a luxurious existence of a "slave"—the slavery of our present age. The sword plus the mighty gold still rules the world, Mr. Welsh.[3]

## NOTES

1. Herbert Welsh Papers, Historical Society of Pennsylvania.

2. Maria Lanzar Carpio, "Training for Practical Citizenship." *Woman's Home Journal* XIII(12) (1939).

3. Maria C. Lanzar to Herbert Welsh. Letter dated January 12, 1924. Box 87, Herbert Welsh Papers, Historical Library of Pennsylvania.

# Appendix

## APPENDIX A

### Sociohistorical Methods

I use a sociohistorical application of Michael Burawoy's (1998) "*extended case method* [which] applies reflexive science to ethnography in order to extract the general from the unique, [and] to move from the 'micro' to the 'macro' " (p. 5). Applying this method with archival documents, I chronologically follow the activities of anti-imperialists as they endeavored to obtain independence for the Philippines. As is common with marginalized actors in sociohistorical research, the evidence of black and white women, and all working-class anti-imperialisms is uneven, buried in the asides of personal correspondence and tempered in their publications (Jung 2003). However, as Taylor (1999) states, "The goal of feminist research is to make women's experiences visible, render them important, and use them to correct distortions from previous empirical research and theoretical assumptions that fail to recognize the centrality of gender to social life" (p. 11). Social history has a parallel goal for working-class histories and people of color. Beginning with an intersectionality framework led me to research whether women, working classes, blacks, and Filipinas/os were significantly involved in the anti-imperialist activities in the metropole. I drew on all available primary documents to describe the activities in which they were involved and the implications of their activism on the relations of anti-imperialists and anti-imperialist effects on imperialist state structures.

Therefore, I base this study on individual- and organizational-level data collected from archival and secondary sources. Individual-level data includes articles and poems by anti-imperialists published in newspapers and magazines that other anti-imperialists read as well as personal letters in individual archival collections. For imperialists, I look at political speeches and articles published in newspapers and magazines. Organizational-level data includes ledger books for the Boston AIL that anti-imperialists wrote and circulated, record books of the organization that included officer reports, member votes, and official policy, as well as correspondence of AIL officers acting in an official capacity to raise awareness on violence in the Philippines. I collected these documents mainly from the personal papers of AIL officers, although some works were available as independent publications, such as *Liberty Poems* (1900). I examined the archives of *The Woman's Journal* and various labor, socialist, and black newspapers, such as *American Freeman*, *Journal of the Knights of Labor*, *National Labor Tribune*, *Social Democratic Herald*, *The Colored American*, and the *Workers' Call*, as well as edited volumes of primary documents in Foner's (1984) *Anti-Imperialist Reader* and (Foner 1993) *Racism, Dissent, and Asian Americans from 1850 to the Present*, between 1898 and 1910 for evidence of working-class, black, Filipina/o, and women's anti-imperialist activity in particular and gendered anti-imperialist politics in general that may not have appeared in the collections of AIL leaders. I also analyze government documents, such as bills, congressional memos, and notes from the hearings of the Senate Investigation on Affairs in the Philippines.

I analyzed these documents for evidence of observable conflict between anti-imperialists and imperialists in their public activities and their personal correspondence. This led me to analyze anti-imperialists' agenda-setting practices, such as how anti-imperialisms were framed and what possibilities for organizing were on and off the table. Finally, I analyze these documents for cultural patterns of domination stitched into the fabric of anti-imperialist activism (Murphy 2009).

This project contributes to what Adams, Clemens, and Orloff (2005) identify as the "third wave of historical sociology," *which theoretically incorporates and empirically demonstrates the utility of race, gender, and class for understanding structural changes and reproductions as outcomes of struggles between opposition movements and state actors.* Specifically, I add to the record evidence of black and white women's anti-imperialism and their contributions to the anti-imperialist movement, which previous studies have overlooked and underestimated (Murphy 2009). I also add to the record evidence of Filipina/o students' correspondence and collaboration with anti-imperialists after 1902.

Finally, this study contributes to the sociology of empire and the sociology of democracy. Showing the struggle over the path to colonial development in the metropole, rather than the struggle over colonial management in the colony, enables me to explore the enduring importance of schemas and practices of race and gender in the development and limitations of imperialist institutional orders, such as racist states of exception. Therefore, this project elaborates on the processual development of empire's exceptions that yielded practices that produced, rationalized, and formalized racial inequalities that have undermined state democracy. Specifically, I analyze anti-imperialists' focus on violence, which was central to their attempts to expose U.S. subterfuge but more effectively negotiated limits to imperialist institutional legitimacy. Still, social histories such as Schirmer (1972) make important contributions to understanding the implications of the U.S. war in the Philippines that are worth reminding today's reader. For example, he noted, "Modern foreign policy is associated with the rise of the large-scale corporation, industrial and financial, as the dominant economic force in the country, exerting a most powerful influence upon the government of the United States. The Spanish-American War and the war to subdue Aguinaldo and the Philippine insurgents were the first foreign wars conducted as a consequence of this influence, the first wars of modern corporate America" (p. 3). Schirmer wrote these words during the Vietnam War, but the relevance continued in the era of wars in Iraq and Afghanistan and the historical rise of companies like Blackwater, Dynacorp, and Halliburton that became embedded with military institutions, for example.

In a project of imperialist racial reformation, the United States was reimagined and remade in conflicts over whether and how to colonize the Philippines. This was an ongoing process of U.S. Pacific expansion in taking Hawai'i, Guam, and Samoa. This imperialist project informed the expansive *remaking* of an imperialist racial state (both through transformative egalitarian racial institutions and white supremacist institutions, and most often through tensions between the two) at a point when Pacific politics threatened to unravel the work of previous racial formations of the United States. Filipinos fighting for independence against the United States propped open the door for anti-imperialists at home to enter the struggle.

I aim to underline the "changing same" (Bonilla-Silva 2006) characteristic of racialized imperialist violence by describing the process through which it happened during the Philippine-American War in order to theorize how to identify racialized states of exception and think through how they might be disrupted and transformed today. In the process, I also challenged the complacency of modern racial ideology based on the legacies of a white supremacist system that continues to deny the human rights of those considered not "civilized" and racialized as nonwhites, by showing how anti-imperialists ethical witnessing evolved to focus on expanding universal rights.

Imperialists argued the United States would bring "civilization," protection, and implement "benevolent assimilation" to the "little brown brothers"

(Wolff 1961) in the Philippines. They argued the anti-imperialists were weak and scared, feminizing them as the "aunties" (Hoganson 1998). Anti-imperialists argued taking the Philippines as a colony was poor business, fueled by race prejudice, and anti-democratic. Anti-imperialists argued imperialists were, therefore, poorly guided, greedy, and racist. What neither group questioned was the value of democracy, the desirability of "civilization" or the exceptional character of the United States.

## APPENDIX B

### Primary Sources

Archival Collections

Anti-Imperialist League 1899–1919 Papers
Jane Addams Papers
Philippine Box
Swarthmore Peace Collection, Swarthmore College

University of Michigan, Ann Arbor
Bentley Historical Library
        Anti-Imperialist League Papers
        Charles Carpenter, soldier 1900–1902
        Dean C. Worcester, An Open letter to the officers and members of the
        Anti-Imperialist League from Dean C. Worcester
        Earl D. Babst Papers
        Frank T. Corriston, soldier with pictures Philippine American War
        Herbert Welsh Papers, Anti-imperialist
        Jabez Thomas Sunderland Papers, Anti-imperialist
        Joseph Ralston Hayden Papers: Box 21, Fiske Warren Diary
Hatcher Graduate Library
        Herbert Welsh Papers
        Maria Carpio-Lanzar Papers

Jim Zwick Site (http://www.boondocksnet.com/ai/index.html) accessed in 2005

Massachusetts Historical Society
        Alonzo Woodside Papers
        Edward Atkinson Papers
        George Frisbie Hoar Papers

George S. Boutwell Papers
Mary S. Cobb Papers
Moorfield Storey Papers
National Party Records (Anti-Imperialist ticket) Papers

New York Public Library
Manuscript and Archives Division, Edward Ordway Papers

Library Company of Philadelphia
Historical Society of Pennsylvania
*City and State*
Herbert Welsh Collection

Library of Congress
Moorfield Storey Papers
W.A. Croffut Papers

National Archives and Record Administration
Senate Investigation on Affairs in the Philippines

Newspapers
African-American Newspapers
*Bee*
*Colored American*
*Freeman*
*Planet*

Labor Newspapers
*American Freeman/Appeal to Reason*
*Journal of Knights of Labor*
*National Labor Tribune*
*Social Democratic Herald*
*Workers' Call*

Progressive White Papers
*Boston Transcript*
*Christian Recorder*
*Springfield Republican*

Filipino/a Newspapers
*El Renacimiento*
*Filipino Students Magazine*

General Newspapers
*The New York Times*

## Documentary Volumes

Bancroft, Frederic. 1913. "Speeches, Correspondence and Political Papers of Carl Schurz." Vol. VI. January 1, 1899–April 8, 1906. New York and London: The Knickerbocker Press.

Foner, Philip S. and Winchester Richard. 1984. *The Anti-Imperialist Reader: A Documentary History of Anti-Imperialism in the United States.* Volume I, From the Mexican War to the Election of 1900. New York: Holms & Meier Publishers.

Keller, Albert Galloway and Maurice Rea Davie. 1924. *Selected Essays of William Graham Sumner.* New Haven, CT: Yale University Press.

Markowitz, Gerald E. 1976. *American Anti-Imperialism 1895–1901.* New York: Garland Publishing, Inc.

Schirmer, Daniel B. and Stephen R. Shalom. 1987. *The Philippines Reader: A History of Colonialism, Neocolonialism, Dictatorship, and Resistance.* Boston, MA: South End Press.

Smith, Edwin Burritt. 1909. *Essays and Addresses.* Chicago: A.C. McClurg & Co.

## Primary Volumes

Blount, James Henderson. 1912. *The American Occupation of the Philippines, 1898–1912.* New York: The Knickerbocker Press.

Blumentritt, Ferdinand. 1900. *The Philippines: A Summary Account of their Ethnographical, Historical and Political Conditions.* Translated by A. M. David J. Doherty, M.D. Chicago: Donohue Brothers.

Bridgman, Raymond L. 1903. *Loyal Traitors: A Story of Friendship for the Filipinos.* Boston, MA: James H. West Company.

Bryan, William S. 1899. *Our Islands and Their People As Seen With Camera and Pencil.* Vol. I. St. Louis, New York, Chicago, Atlanta: N.D. Thompson Publishing Co.

Dunne, Finley Peter. 1899. *Mr. Dooley: in Peace and War.* Chicago: Small Maynard and Company.

Elliott, Charles B. 1916. *The Philippines to the End of the Military Regime: America Overseas.* Indianapolis: The Bobbs-Merrill Company.

Lanzar, Maria. 1928. "The Anti-Imperialist League." Dissertation Thesis, Political Science, University of Michigan, Ann Arbor.

Storey, Moorfield and Marcial P. Lichauco. 1926. *The Conquest of the Philippines by the United States 1898–1925.* New York and London: The Knickerbocker Press.

Swift, Morrison I. 1899. *Anti-Imperialism.* Los Angeles: Public Ownership Review.

Williams, Ora. 1899. *Oriental America: Official and Authentic Records of the Dealings of the United States with the Natives of Luzon and their Former Rulers.* Chicago: Oriental America Pub. Co.

Willis, H. Parker. 1904. "Conditions in the Philippines." in *New York Evening Post.* Lexington, VA: Washington and Lee University.

Willis, Henry Parker. 1905. *Our Philippine Problem: A Study of American Colonial Policy.* New York: Henry Holt and Company.'

# APPENDIX C

## Incomplete List of Anti-Imperialist Broadsides by Date

1899. "Soldiers' Letters: Being Materials for the History of a War of Criminal Aggression."

1899. *The Chicago Liberty Meeting Held at Central Music Hall April 30, 1899*. Chicago: Central Anti-Imperialist League.

Gookin, Frederick. 1899. *A Liberty Catechism*, vol. Three. Liberty Tracts. Chicago: American Anti-Imperialist League.

Jordan, David Starr. 1899. *The Question of the Philippines*. Palo Alto, CA: Printed for the Graduate Club by the Courtesy of John J. Valentine, Esq.

Laughlin, J. Laurence. 1899. *Patriotism and Imperialism*, Vol. 2. Liberty Tracts. Chicago: Central Anti-Imperialist League.

MacCauley, Clay. 1899. *A Straightforward Tale*.

Schurz, Hon. Carl. 1899. *The Policy of Imperialism*. Chicago: American Anti-Imperialist League.

Valentine, John J. 1899. *Imperial Democracy*. San Francisco, CA: The Hicks-Judd Company.

Apacible, Galicano. 1900. *To the American People*.

Boutwell, George. 1900. *The President's Policy: War and Conquest Abroad, Degradation of Labor at Home*, Vol. Seven. Liberty Tracts. Chicago: American Anti-Imperialist League.

Cockran, W. Bourke. 1900. *Address*: New England Anti-Imperialist League.

Crooker, Joseph Henry. 1900. *The Menace to America*. Chicago: American Anti-Imperialist League.

Foreman, John. 1900. *Will the United States Withdraw from the Philippines?*, Vol. Fourteen. Liberty Tracts. Chicago American Anti-Imperialist League.

Pierce, Edward C. 1900. *The "Single Tribe" Fiction*, Vol. Fourteen. Liberty Tracts. Chicago: American Anti-Imperialist League.

Smith, Edwin Burritt. 1900. *Republic or Empire with Glimpses of "Criminal Aggression,"* Vol. Nine. Chicago: American Anti-Imperialist League.

Storey, Moorfield. 1900. *Is It Right?*, vol. Number Eight. Chicago: American Anti-Imperialist League.

Welsh, Herbert. 1900. *The Other Man's Country*. Philadelphia: J.B. Lippincott Company.

1900. *Liberty Poems: Inspired by the Crisis of 1898–1900*. Boston: The James H. West Co.

Smith, Edwin Burritt. 1901. *The Constitution and Inequality of Rights*. Chicago: American Anti-Imperialist League.

Storey, Moorfield. 1901. *Our New Departure: 1. Letter to a Friend, October 21, 1899 2. Speech at Brookline, October 26, 1900*. Boston, MA: George H. Ellis, Printer.

Brooks, Francis A. 1901. *The Unlawful and Unjustifiable Conquest of the Filipinos*. Boston, MA: Press of George H. Ellis.

Welsh, Herbert. 1903. *To Lincoln's Plain People: Facts Regarding 'Benevolent Assimilation' in the Philippine Islands*. Philadelphia, PA: "City and State."

1903. "Report of the Fifth Annual Meeting of the New England Anti-Imperialist League."

1903. *Mass Meetings of Protest Against the Suppression of Truth About the Philippines.* Boston.

O'Reilly, Jas. T. 1903. *The Civilizers of the Philippines.*

Bullock, Charles J. 1904. *The Cost of War.*

Codman, Charles and Henry Hardon. 1904. *Anti-Imperialism the Great Issue: Addresses by the Hon. Charles R. Codman and Mr. Henry W. Hardon Reply by the Hon. Alton B. Parker.* Boston: N.E. Anti-Imperialist League.

Willis, H. Parker. 1905. *The Economic Situation in the Philippines.*

Blount, James H. 1907. *Philippine Independence: Why?*

Unzon, Felix, Vicente Paz Rillo, Vivencio Ramos, Vicente Almanzor. 1907. *The Calamities of Balayan, P.I. Reply To a Criticism of a Petition Made to the Taft Expedition of 1905 by the Petitioners.*

Winslow, Erving. 1908. *The Anti-Imperialist League: Apologia Pro Vita Sua.* Boston, MA: Anti-Imperialist League.

1909. *Report of the Eleventh Annual Meeting of the Anti-Imperialist League.*

1917. *Report of the Nineteenth Annual Meeting of the Anti-Imperialist League.*

## APPENDIX D

### Benevolent Assimilation Proclamation as Publicized to the Filipino People, January 4, 1899

The destruction of the Spanish fleet in the harbor of Manila by the United States naval squadron commanded by Rear-Admiral Dewey, followed by the reduction of the city and the surrender of the Spanish forces, practically affected the conquest of the Philippine Islands and the suspension of the Spanish sovereignty therein. With the signature of the treaty of peace between the United States and Spain by their respective plenipotentiaries at Paris on the tenth instant, and as a result of the victories of American arms, *the future control, disposition, and government of the Philippine Islands are ceded to the United States. In the fulfillment of the rights of sovereignty* thus acquired and the responsible obligations of government thus assumed, the actual occupation and administration of the entire group of the Philippine Islands becomes immediately necessary, and the *military government* heretofore maintained by the United States in the city, harbor, and bay of Manila *is to be extended* with all possible despatch [*sic*] *to the whole of the ceded territory.* In performing this duty the military commander of the United States is enjoined to make known to the inhabitants of the Philippine Islands that in *succeeding to the sovereignty of Spain*, in severing the former political relations, and in establishing a new political power, the authority of the United States is to be exerted for the securing of the persons and property of the people of the islands and for the confirmation of all their private rights and relations. It will be the duty of the commander of the forces of occupation to announce and proclaim in the most public manner that *we come*, not as invaders or conquerors, but as friends, *to protect* the natives in their homes, in their employments, and in their personal and religious rights. All persons who, either by active aid or by honest submission, cooperate with the Government of the United States to give effect to these beneficent purposes will receive the reward of its support and *protection*. All others will be brought within the lawful rule we have assumed, with firmness if need be, but without severity, so far as possible. Within the absolute domain of *military authority*, which necessarily is and *must remain supreme* in the ceded territory until the legislation of the United States shall otherwise provide, the municipal laws of the territory in respect to private rights and property and the repression of crime are to be considered as continuing in force, and to be administered by the ordinary tribunals, so far as practicable. The operations of civil and municipal government are to be performed by such officers as may accept *the supremacy of the United States* by taking the oath of allegiance, or by officers chosen, as far as practicable, from the inhabitants of the islands. While the control of all the public property and the revenues of the state passes with the cession, and while the use and management of all public means of transportation are necessarily reserved to the authority of the United States, private property, whether belonging to individuals or corporations, is to be respected except for cause duly established. The taxes and duties heretofore payable by the inhabitants to the late government become payable to the authorities of the United States unless it be seen fit to substitute for them other reasonable rates or modes of contribution to the expenses of government, whether general or local. If private property be taken for military use, it shall be paid for when possible in cash, at a fair valuation, and when payment in cash is not practicable, receipts are to be given. All ports and places in the Philippine Islands in the actual possession of the land and naval forces of the United States will be opened to the commerce of all friendly nations. All goods and wares not prohibited for military reasons by due announcement of the military authority will be admitted upon payment of such duties and other charges as shall be in force at the time of their importation. Finally, it should be the earnest wish and paramount aim of the military administration to win the confidence, respect, and affection of the inhabitants of the Philippines by assuring them in every possible way that full measure of individual rights and liberties, which is the heritage of free peoples, and by proving to them that the mission of the United States is one of

## BENEVOLENT ASSIMILATION

substituting the mild sway of justice and right for arbitrary rule. In the fulfill-ment of this high mission, supporting the temperate administration of affairs for the greatest good of the governed, there must be sedulously maintained the strong arm of authority, to repress disturbance and to overcome all obsta-cles to the bestowal of the blessings of good and stable government upon the people of the Philippine Islands under the free flag of the United States.

WILLIAM McKINLEY.

## APPENDIX E

### Timeline

| | |
|---|---|
| 1823 | Monroe Doctrine: European powers should no longer colo-nize territories in the western hemisphere or interfere in the affairs of nations in the western hemisphere |
| 1848 | Mexican-American War |
| 1893 | first attempt to take Hawaii as colony |
| 1896 | Filipinos begin fighting for independence from Spain |
| 1898 | Spanish-American War begins and Hawaii is taken as U.S. territory |
| June 15 | First Anti-Imperialist meeting |
| December 10 | Treaty of Paris signed, ceding Guam, Puerto Rico, and the Philippines (for $20 million) to the United States |
| December 16 | McKinley sends Benevolent Assimilation Proclamation by mail |
| December 21 | McKinley wires proclamation to General Otis |
| 1899 | Philippine-American War begins (as well as Boer War in South Africa) |
| January 4 | Benevolent Assimilation Proclamation publicized to Filipinos |
| January 23 | Establishment of First Filipino Republic with Emilio Agui-naldo as President and Apolinario Mabini as Prime Minister |
| February 4 | Fighting begins between United States and Philippines |
| February 6 | Treaty of Paris passes in Senate by one vote |

Anti-imperialist meeting at Faneuil Hall

| | |
|---|---|
| April 30 | Chicago Liberty Meetings |
| October 17 | Chicago Anti-Imperialist Conference |

1900          water cure begins in the debate over war (Boxer Rebellion in China, United States sends troops from Philippines)

August 15      Liberty Congress of Anti-imperialist Convention endorses W. J. Bryan

November      W. J. Bryan defeated in Presidential bid

1901          reconcentration policy uncovered

July 4        Civil Government established under William H. Taft

1902          Senate Investigation on Affairs in the Philippines

July 4        End of Philippine-American War declared by President Roosevelt

1903          "A Massachusetts Woman" published by Wilson

Women's Trade Union League established

1905          habeas corpus rescinded in provinces of Philippines by Lucas Wright
Moorfield Storey president of AIL
H. P. Willis to Philippines
Fiske Warren to Philippines

1906          Moro massacre

Dr. D.J. Doherty in Philippines as representative of NYAIL

1907          Philippine Assembly Established (renewed call for Independence)

AIL begins to rely more heavily on Filipino publications, especially from *El Renacimiento*

| 1909 | investigation as to whether women should be considered full members of AIL |

National Association for the Advancement of Colored People established

| 1910 | women voted not to become full members of AIL |
| 1911 | Women's International League for Peace and Freedom established |
| 1912 | Guerilla fighting in Philippines ceases |
| 1914 | Jones Bill passed stating Philippines should have independent government |
| 1916 | Philippine Legislature organized |
| 1917 | United States enters World War I |
| 1920 | 19th Amendment passes granting women the right to vote |
| 1922 | AIL disbanded |

## APPENDIX F

### List of Acronyms

| AIL | Anti-Imperialist League |
| DAR | Daughters of the American Revolution |
| NAACP | National Association for the Advancement of Colored People |
| SIAP | Senate Investigation on Affairs in the Philippines |
| WCTU | Women's Christian Temperance Union |
| WILPF | Women's International League for Peace and Freedom |
| WTUL | Women's Trade Union League |

# References

1900. *Liberty Poems: Inspired by the Crisis of 1898–1900*. Boston: The James H. West Co.

1902. *Secretary Root's Record: "Marked Severities" in Philippine Warfare: An Analysis of the Law and Facts bearing the Action and Utterances of President Roosevelt and Secretary Root*. Boston: Geo. W. Ellis Co.

1903. *Mass Meetings of Protest Against the Suppression of Truth About the Philippines*, Boston, 1903. Philippine Box, Swarthmore Peace Collection, Swarthmore College.

Adams, Julia, Elisabeth S. Clemens, and Ann Shola Orloff. 2005. "Introduction: Social Theory, Modernity, and the Three Waves of Historical Sociology." In *Remaking Modernities: Politics, History, and Sociology*, edited by Julia Adams, Elisabeth S. Clemens, and Ann Shola Orloff. Durham and London: Duke University Press.

Addams, Jane. 1899. "Democracy or Militarism." *The Chicago Liberty Meeting: Liberty Tracts, Vol I*. April 30, 1899.

Agamben, Giorgio. 1998. *Homo Sacer: Sovereign Power and Bare Life*. Edited by Werner Hatcher and David E. Wellbery. Translated by D. Heller-Roazen. Stanford, CA: Stanford University Press.

———. 2005. *State of Exception*. Translated by Kevin Attell. Chicago: University of Chicago Press.

Alexander, Jeffrey C. 1995. *Fin de Siecle Social Theory: Relativism, Reduction, and the Problem of Reason*. London and New York: Verso.

Alexander, Jeffrey C. and Philip Smith. 1993. "The Discourse of American Civil Society: A New Proposal for Cultural Studies." *Theory and Society* 22:151–207.

Alexander, Michelle. 2012. *The New Jim Crow: Mass Incarceration in the Age of Colorblindness*. New York City: The New Press.

Atkinson, Fred W. 1905. *The Philippine Islands*. Boston: Ginn & Company.

Balce, Nerissa S. 2016. *Body Parts of Empire: Visual Abjection, Filipino Images, and the American Archive*. Ann Arbour: University of Michigan Press.

Bancroft, Frederic. 1913. "Speeches, Correspondence and Political Papers of Carl Schurz." Vol. VI. January 1, 1899–April 8, 1906. New York and London: The Knickerbocker Press.

Bannister, Robert C. 1979. *Social Darwinism: Science and Myth in Anglo-American Social Thought*. Philadelphia, PA: Temple University Press.

Barbalet, Jack. 2002. "Introduction: Why Emotions Are Crucial." Pp. 1–9 in *Emotions and Sociology*, edited by Jack Barbalet. Oxford, UK: Blackwell Publishing/ The Sociological Review.

Barrett, James. 2002. "Revolution and Personal Crisis: William Z. Foster, Personal Narrative, and the Subjective in the History of Communism." *Labor History* 43:465–482.

Barretto, Alberto. 1906. "Brigandage in Batangas and the Habeas Corpus Writ." *Springfield Republican* (June 18, 1905); rpt. *Truth Coming to Light Concerning the Philippines: Letter from Fiske Warren*. Boston: Anti-Imperialist League.

Bederman, Gail. 1995. *Manliness & Civilization: A Cultural History of Gender and Race in the United States, 1880–1917*. Chicago: The University of Chicago Press.

Beisel, Nicola and Tamara Kay. 2004. "Abortion, Race, and Gender in Nineteenth-Century America." *American Sociological Review* 69:498–518.

Beisner, Robert L. 1968. *Twelve Against Empire: The Anti-Imperialists, 1898–1900*. New York: McGraw-Hill Book Company.

———. 1970. "1898 and 1968: The Anti-Imperialists and the Doves." *Politica Science Quarterly* 85:187–216.

———. 1973. "The Anti-Imperialist as Mugwump: Successes and Failures." Pp. 95–109 in *American Imperialism and Anti-Imperialism*, edited by Thomas G. Paterson. New York: Thomas & Crowell Company.

Bellah, Robert. 1992. *The Broken Covenant: American Civil Religion in Time of Trial*. Chicago: The University of Chicago Press.

Berezin, Mabel. 2002. "Secure States: Towards a Political Sociology of Emotion." Pp. 33–52 in *Emotions and Sociology*, edited by Jack Barbalet. Blackwell Publishing/The Sociological Review: Oxford.

Beveridge, Albert. 1900. "Our Philippine Policy." *Congressional Record,* January 9, 1900.

Blount, James Henderson. 1912. *The American Occupation of the Philippines, 1898–1912*. New York: The Knickerbocker Press.

Bonilla-Silva, Eduardo. 2006. *Racism without Racists: Color-Blind Racism and the Persistence of Racial Inequality in the United States*. Lanham, MD: Rowman & Littlefield Publishers.

Bourdieu, Pierre. 1993. *Outline of a Theory of Praxis*. Cambridge: University of Cambridge Press.

Bourdieu, Pierre and Loic J.D. Wacquant. 1992. *An Invitation to Reflexive Sociology*. Chicago: The University of Chicago Press.

Boutwell, George S. 1900. *Address to the Laboring and Producing Classes of the United States*. Chicago: American Anti-Imperialist League.

———. 1900. "The President's Policy-War and Conquest Abroad, Degradation of Labor at Home." *Liberty Tracts*, No. 7. Chicago: American Anti-Imperialist League.

Burawoy, Michael. 1998. "The Extended Case Method." *Sociological Theory* 16(1):4–33.

Bryan, William Jennings. 1898. "Who Saves His Country Saves Himself." *Republic or Empire,* December 31, 1898.

———. 1899. "Liberty, Not Conquest." *Republic or Empire,* February 14, 1899.

Bussey, Gertrude and Margaret Tims. 1980. *Pioneers for Peace: Women's International League for Peace and Freedom 1915–1965.* London: Alden Press.

Clemens, Elisabeth S. 1993. "Organizational Repertoires and Institutional Change: Women's Groups and Transformation of U.S. Politics, 1890–1920." *The American Journal of Sociology* 98:755–798.

Collins, Randall. 2004. *Interaction Ritual Chains.* Princeton and Oxford: Princeton University Press.

Comfort, Anna Manning. 1899. "Home Burdens of Uncle Sam." *The Public 2,* May 13, 1899.

Crowder, Ralph. 1994. *John Edward Bruce & The Value of Knowing the Past: Politician, Journalist, and Self-Trained Historian of the African Diaspora, 1856–1924.* Doctoral Dissertation, Department of History, University of Kansas.

Cullinane, Michael Patrick. 2012. *Liberty and American Anti-Imperialism 1898–1909.* Palgrave Macmillan.

Davis, Jefferson. 1900. *The Arena.* Jan–Jun 1900.New York.

De Ocampo, Esteban A. 1977. *First Filipino Diplomat: Felipe Agoncillo (1859–1941).* Manila: National Historical Institute.

Denzin, Norman K. 1984. *On Understanding Emotion.* San Francisco: Jossey-Bass Publishers.

Diner, Hasia R. 1998. "Ethnicity and Emotions in America: Dimentions of hte Unexplored." In *An Emotional History of the United States,* edited by Peter Stearns and. Jan Lewis. New York: New York University Press.

Drinnon, Richard. 1980. *Facing West: The Metaphysics of Indian-hating and Empire-Building.* Norman and London: The University of Oklahoma Press.

Dunne, Finley Peter. 1899. *Mr. Dooley: In Peace and War.* Chicago: Small Maynard and Company.

Dy Yap, Francisco. 1972. "A Comparative Study of the Philippine and American Law on the Suspension of the Privilege of the Writ of Habeas Corpus." Master of Laws Thesis, Law, University of Illinois at Urbana-Champaign, Urbana, IL.

Dyer, Thomas. 1980. *Theodore Roosevelt and the Idea of Race.* Baton Rouge and London: Louisiana State University Press.

Elliott, Charles B. 1916. *The Philippines to the End of the Military Regime: America Overseas.* Indianapolis: The Bobbs-Merrill Company.

Ellul, Jacques. 1975. *The New Demons.* Translated by C. E. Hopkin. New York: The Seabury Press.

Eyot, Canning. 1904 [2001]. *The Story of the Lopez Family: A Page from the History of the War in the Philippines.* Edited by Jim Zwick. Manila: Platypus Publishing.

Ferree, Myra Max and David A. Merrill. 2000. "Hot Movements, Cold Cognition: Thinking about Social Movements in Gendered Frames." *Contemporary Sociology* 29:454–462.

Fine, Gary Alan. 2002. "Thinking about Evil: Adolf Hitler and the Dilemma of the Social Contsruction of Reputation." In *Culture in Mind: Toward a Sociology of Culture and Cognition.* New York: Routledge.

Foner, Philip S. 1958. *Mark Twain Social Critic.* New York: International Publishers.

Foner, Philip S. and Daniel Rosenberg. 1993. *Racism, Dissent, and Asian Americans from 1850 to the Present: A Documentary History.* Westport, CT: Greenwood Press.

Foner, Philip S. and Richard C. Winchester. 1984. "The Anti-Imperialist Reader: A Documentary History of Anti-Imperialism in the United States." In *Vol. I: From the Mexican War to the Election of 1900.* New York: Holmes and Meier Publishers, Inc.

Gates, John M. 1984. "War-Related Deaths in the Philippines, 1898–1902." *Pacific Historical Review* 53:367–378.

Gatewood Jr., Willard B. 1975. *Black Americans and the White Man's Burden.* Urbana: University of Illinois Press.

Go, Julian. 2003. "Introduction: Global Perspectives on the U.S. Colonial State in the Philippines." Pp. 1–42 in *The American Colonial State in the Philippines: Global Perspectives*, edited by Julian Go and Ann L. Foster. Durham and London: Duke University Press.

———. 2004. "'Racism' and Colonialism: Meanings of Difference and Ruling Practices in America's Pacific Empire." *Qualitative Sociology* 27:35–58.

———. 2007. "The Provinciality of American Empire: 'Liberal Exceptionalism' and U.S. Colonial Rule, 1898–1912." *Comparative Studies in Society and History* 49:74–108.

———. 2008. *American Empire and the Politics of Meaning: Elite Political Cultures in the Philippines and Puerto Rico during U.S. Colonialism.* Durham and London: Duke University Press.

Goodwin, Jeff, James Jasper, and Francesca Polletta. 2001. *Passionate Politics.* Chicago: University of Chicago Press.

Green, Martin. 1989. *The Mount Vernon Street Warrens.* New York: Charles Scribner's Sons.

Grimsley, Mark. 1995. *The Hard Hand of War: Union Military Policy toward Southern Civilians, 1861–1865.* Cambridge: Cambridge University Press.

Hagan, William T. 1985. *The Indian Rights Association: The Herbert Welsh Years 1882–1904.* Tucson, AZ: The University of Arizona Press.

Harrington, Joseph. 2002. *Poetry and the Public: The Social Form of Modern U.S. Poetics.* Middletown, CT: Wesleyan University Press.

Hobsbawm, E.J. 1987. *The Age of Empire 1875–1914.* New York: Pantheon Books.

Hochschild, Arlie Russell. 1983. *The Managed Heart: Commercialization of Human Feeling.* Berkeley, CA: The University of California Press.

Hoganson, Kristin L. 1998. *Fighting for American Manhood: How Gender Politics Provoked the Spanish-American and Philippine-American Wars.* New Haven, CT: Yale University Press.

Hoganson, Kristin L. 2001. "'As Badly Off As the Filipinos': U.S. Women's Suffragists and the Imperial Issue at the Turn of the Twentieth Century." *Journal of Women's History* 13:9–33.

Jacobson, Matthew Frye. 1995. *Special Sorrows: The Diasporic Imagination of Irish, Polish, and Jewish Immigrants in the United States.* Cambridge, MA: Harvard University Press.

———. 2000. *Barbarian Virtues: The United States Encounters Foreign Peoples at Home and Abroad, 1876–1917.* New York: Hill and Wang.

Ileto, Reynaldo C. 2002. "The Philippine-American War: Friendship and Forgetting." Pp. 3–21 in *Vestiges of War: The Philippine-American War and the Aftermath of an Imperial Dream, 1899–1999,* edited by Angel Velasco Shaw and Luis H. Fracia. New York: New York University Press.

Ioanide, Paula. 2015. *The Emotional Politics of Racism: How Feelings Trump Facts in an Era of Colorblindness.* Stanford: Stanford University Press.

Janiewski, Dolores E. 1998. "The Reign of Passion: White Supremacy and the Clash between Passionate and Progressive Emotional Styles in the New South." In *An Emotional History of the United States,* edited by Peter Stearn and Jan Lewis. New York: New York University Press.

Jasper, James. 1998. "The Emotions of Social Protest: Affective and Reactive Emotion in and around Social Movements." *Sociological Forum* 13:397–426.

Jordan, David Starr. 1899. *The Question of the Philippines.* Palo Alto, CA: Printed for the Graduate Club by the Courtesy of John J. Valentine, Esq.

Jung, Moon-Kie. 2003. "Interracialism: The Ideological Transformation of Hawaii's Working Class." *American Sociological Review* 63:373–400.

———. 2004. "Symbolic and Physical Violence: Legitimate State Coercion of Filipino Workers in PreWar Hawai'i." *American Studies* 45:5–36.

———. 2006. *Reworking Race: The Making of Hawaii's Interracial Labor Movement.* New York: Columbia University Press.

———. 2015. *Beneath the Surface of White Supremacy: Denaturalizing U.S. Racisms Past and Present.* Stanford: Stanford University Press.

Kaplan, Amy. 2002. *The Anarchy of Empire in the Making of U.S. Culture.* Cambridge, MA and London: Harvard University Press.

Kramer, Paul. 2002. "Empires, Exceptions, and Anglo-Saxons: Race and Rule between the British and United States Empires, 1880–1910." *The Journal of American History* 88:1315–1353.

———. 2006. *The Blood of Government: Race, Empire, the United States, & the Philippines.* Chapel Hill, NC: The University of North Carolina Press.

———. 2008. "The Water Cure. An American Debate on Torture and Counterinsurgency in the Philippines – A Century Ago": *The Asia-Pacific Journal: Japan Focus.* Accessed 2009, http://www.japanfocus.org/-Paul-Kramer/2685.

Lanzar, Maria. 1928. "The Anti-Imperialist League." Dissertation, University of Michigan.

Lasch, Christopher. 1958. "The Anti-Imperialists, the Philippines, and the Inequality of Man." *The Journal of Southern History* 24:319–331.

———. 1973. "The Anti-Imperialist as Racist." Pp. 110–117 in *American Imperialism and Anti-Imperialism,* edited by Thomas G. Paterson. New York: Thomas Y. Crowell Company.

Levy, Pema. 2015. "An Federal Appeals Court Just Denied Birthright Citizenship to American Samoans Using Racist Case Law." *Mother Jones.* June 5, 2015. http:

//www.motherjones.com/mojo/2015/06/appeals-court-denies-birthright-citizens hip-american-samoans.

Luzviminda, Francisco. 1987. "The Philippine-American War." In *The Philippines Reader,* edited by Daniel B. Schirmer and Stephen Shalom. Boston: South End Press.

Maguire, Peter. 2010. *Law and War: International Law and American History.* New York: Columbia University Press.

Markowitz, Gerald E. 1976. *American Anti-Imperialism 1895–1901.* New York: Garland Publishing, Inc.

McFerson, Hazel. M. 2002. *Mixed Blessing:The Impact of the American Colonial Experience on Politics and Society in the Philippines.* Westport, CT: Greenwood Press.

McPherson, James. 1975. *The Abolitionist Legacy: From Reconstruction to the NAACP.* Princeton, NJ: Princeton University Press.

Memmi, Albert. 1991[1965]. *The Colonizer and the Colonized.* Boston, MA: Beacon Press.

Miller, Stuart Creighton. 1982. *"Benevolent Assimilation": The American Conquest of the Philippines, 1899–1903.* New Haven, CT and London: Yale University Press.

Mukerji, Chandra. 2006. "Beauty in Paris: The Emotional Excitement of Memory." Pp. 1–6 in *A Message from the Chair*, vol. 21. Culture: Newsletter of the Sociology of Culture Section of the American Sociological Association.

Murphy, Erin L. 2009. "Women's Anti-Imperialism, 'The White Man's Burden,' and the Philippine-American War: Theorizing Masculinist Ambivalence in Protest." *Gender & Society* 23:244–270.

———. 2014. "In a Few Generations: Debating Race, Philippine Independence, and Colonial Development in the U.S. Colonial Field." *Critical Sociology* 41(2):219–235.

———. 2019. "'American Boys': *Pensionados* and Double Consciousness in the U.S. Colonial Field." Unpublished Paper (1–28).

Nichols, Christopher McKnight. 2011. *Promise and Peril: America at the Dawn of a Global Age.* Cambridge: Harvard University Press.

Ninkovich, Frank. 2001. *The United States and Imperialism.* Malden, MA: Blackwell Publishers.

Pandey, Gyanendra. 2006. *Routine Violence: Nations, Fragments, Histories.* Edited by M. B. a. H. d. Vries. Stanford, CA: Stanford University Press.

Papachristou, Judith. 1990. "American Women and Foreign Policy, 1898–1905: Exploring Gender in Diplomatic History." *Diplomatic History* 14:493–509.

Pease, Donald. E. 2009. *The New American Exceptionalism.* Minneapolis: The University of Minnesota Press.

Pettet, Robert Stevens. 1899. *Columbia's Apostasy: And other Poems and Essays.* Philadelphia. R.S. Pettet.

Reddy, William M. 2001. *The Navigation of Feeling: A Framework for the History of Emotions.* Cambridge: Cambridge University Press.

Reyes, Jose B. L. 1971. *Galicano Apacible: Profile of a Filipino Patriot.* Heirs of Galicano Apacible: Philippines.

Roediger, David. 1994. *Towards the Abolition of Whiteness*. Haymarket Series. Verso.

———. 2005. *Working Toward Whiteness: How America's Immigrants Became White*. Cambridge, MA: Basic Books.

Rosenberg, Emily. 1982. *Spreading the American Dream: American Economic and Cultural Expansion, 1890–1945*. New York: Hill and Wang.

Rydell, Robert. 1984. *All the World's a Fair: Visions of Empire at American International Expositions, 1876–1916*. Chicago: The University of Chicago Press.

San Juan, Jr., E. 2000. *After Postcolonialism: Remapping Philippines – United States Confrontations*. Lanham: Rowman & Littlefield Publishers, Inc.

Scheer, Monique. 2012. "Are Emotions a Kind of Practice (and Is that What Makes Them Have a History)? A Bourdieuian Approach to Understanding Emotion." *History and Theory*. 51:193–220.

Scheingold, S. A. (2004 [1974]). *The Politics of Rights: Lawyers, Public Policy, and Political Change*. Ann Arbor: The University of Michigan.

Schirmer, Daniel B. 1972. *Republic or Empire: American Resistance to the Philippine War*. Cambridge, MA: Schenkman Publishing Company, Inc.

Schirmer, Daniel B. and Stephen R. Shalom, ed. 1987. *The Philippines Reader: A History of Colonialism, Neocolonialism, Dictatorship, and Resistance*. Boston, MA: South End Press.

Sewell, William H. Jr. 2005. *Logics of History: Social Theory and Social Transformation*. Chicago: The University of Chicago Press.

Silbey, David. 2007. *A War of Frontier and Empire: The Philippine-American War, 1899–1902*. New York: Hill and Wang.

Singh, Nikhil Pal. 2004. *Black Is a Country: Race and the Unfinished Struggle for Democracy*. Cambridge, MA and London: Harvard University Press.

Slotkin, Richard. 1992. *Gunfighter Nation: The Myth of the Frontier in Twentieth-Century America*. New York: Atheneum.

Smith, Edwin Burritt. 1900. "Republic or Empire with Glimpses of 'Criminal Aggression'" *Liberty Tracts*, Vol. 9, Chicago: American Anti-Imperialist League.

Sommers, Shula. 1988. "Understanding Emotions: Some Interdisciplinary Considerations." Pp. 23–38 in *Emotion and Social Change*, edited by Carol Stearns and Peter N. Stearns. New York: Holmes and Meier.

Stearns, Carol Z. and Peter N. Stearns. 1988. *Emotion and Social Change: Toward a New Psychohistory*. New York: Holmes and Meier.

Stearns, Peter N. and Jan Lewis. 1998. *An Emotional History of the United States*. New York: New York University Press.

Steinmetz, George. 2005. *The Politics of Method in the Human Sciences: Postivism and Its Epistemological Others*. Duke University Press.

———. 2007. *The Devil's Handwriting: Precoloniality, and the German Colonial State in Qingdao, Samoa, and Southwest Africa*. Chicago: The University of Chicago Press.

Stoler, Ann Laura. 2006. *Haunted By Empire: Geographies of Intimacy in North American History*. Durham, NC and London: Duke University Press.

Storey, Moorfield and Marcial P. Lichauco. 1926. *The Conquest of the Philippines by the United States 1898–1925*. New York and London: The Knickerbocker Press.

Swift, Morrison I. 1899. *Anti-Imperialism*. Los Angeles: Public Ownership Review.

Taylor, Verta. 1999. "Gender and Social Movements: Gender Processes in Women's Self-Help Movements." *Gender & Society* 13(1):8–33.

Thoits, Peggy A. 1989. "The Sociology of Emotions." *Annual Review of Sociology* 15:317–342.

Tompkins, E. Berkeley. 1970. *Anti-Imperialism in the United States: The Great Debate, 1890–1920*. Philadelphia, PA: University of Pennsylvania Press.

Torruella, Juan R. 2007. "The Insular Cases: The Establishment of a Regime of Political Apartheid." *University of Pennsylvania Journal of International Law* 29(2):284–320.

Twain, Mark. 1901. "To the Person Sitting in Darkness." *The North American Review* 172(531):161–176.

Valentine, John J. 1899. *Forcible Annexation: Criminal Aggression: Benevolent Assimilation A Question of National Honor-Official Documents for Future Historians*. San Francisco, CA.

Ware, Vron. 1992. *Beyond the Pale: White Women, Racism, and History*. London: Verso.

Welch, Jr., Richard E. 1973. "Anti-Impeiralists and Imperialists Compared: Racism and Economic Expansion." Pp. 118–1125 in *American Imperialism and Anti-Imperialism* edited by Thomas G. Paterson: Thomas Y. Crowell Company.

Welch Jr., Richard E. 1979. *Response to Imperialism: The United States and the Philippine-American War, 1899–1902*. Chapel Hill, NC: University of North Carolina Press.

Wells, Ida B. 1997. *Southern Horrors and Other Writings: The Anti-Lynching Campaign of Ida B. Wells, 1892–1900*. Boston, MA: Bedford.

Welsh, Herbert. 1900. *The Other Man's Country*. Philadelphia: J.B. Lippincott Company.

Wexler, Laura. 2000. *Tender Violence: Domestic Visions in an Age of U.S. Imperialism*. Chapel Hill, NC: The University of North Carolina Press.

Williams, Simon. 2001. *Emotion and Social Theory*. London: Sage Publications.

Williams, William Appleman. 1972. *The Tragedy of American Diplomacy*. New York: Delta Book.

Williamson, Harold Francis. 1934. *Edward Atkinson: The Biography of an American Liberal*. Boston: Old Corner Book Store, Inc.

Willis, Henry Parker. 1905. *Our Philippine Problem: A Study of American Colonial Policy*. New York: Henry Holt and Company.

Wilson, Helen C. 1903. *A Massachusetts Woman in the Philippines*. Boston: [Fiske Warren].

———. 1906. *Reconcentration in the Philippines*. Boston: Anti-Imperialist League.

Wilson, Helen Calista and Elsie Reed Mitchell. 1929. *Vagabonding at fifty: from Siberia to Turkestan*. Coward and McCann.

Winkler-Morey, Anne Regis. 2001. "Good Neighbors: Popular Internationalists and United States' Relations with Mexico and the Caribbean Region (1918–1929)." Dissertation Thesis, Department of History, University of Minnesota, Minneapolis, MN.

Winslow, Erving. 1908. *The Anti-Imperialist League: Apologia Pro Vita Sua*. Boston, MA: Anti-Imperialist League.

Wolff, Leon. 1961. *Little Brown Brother: How the United States Purchased and Pacified the Philippine Islands at the Century's Turn*. Garden City, NY: Doubleday & Company.

Zwick, Jim. 1998. "The Anti-Imperialist League and the Origins of Filipino-American Oppositional Solidarity." *Amerasia Journal* 24:65–86.

———. 2001. "Foreward." In *The Story of the Lopez Family: A Page from the History of the War in the Philippines*, edited by C. Eyot. Manila: Platypus Publishing.

———. 2007. *Confronting Imperialism: Essays on Mark Twain and the Anti-Imperialist League*. West Conshohocken, PA: Infinity Publishing.

# Index

Page numbers in *italics* refers to Figures

205

# About the Author

**Erin L. Murphy** is an independent scholar with a doctorate in sociology from the University of Illinois at Urbana-Champaign. She is the cofounder and executive director of Sistering CU, a nonprofit organization, which focuses on postpartum education and postpartum support services.